I0809984

POSTCARD HISTORY SERIES

# South Carolina Postcards

## Volume II

### Southern Carolina: Beaufort to Barnwell

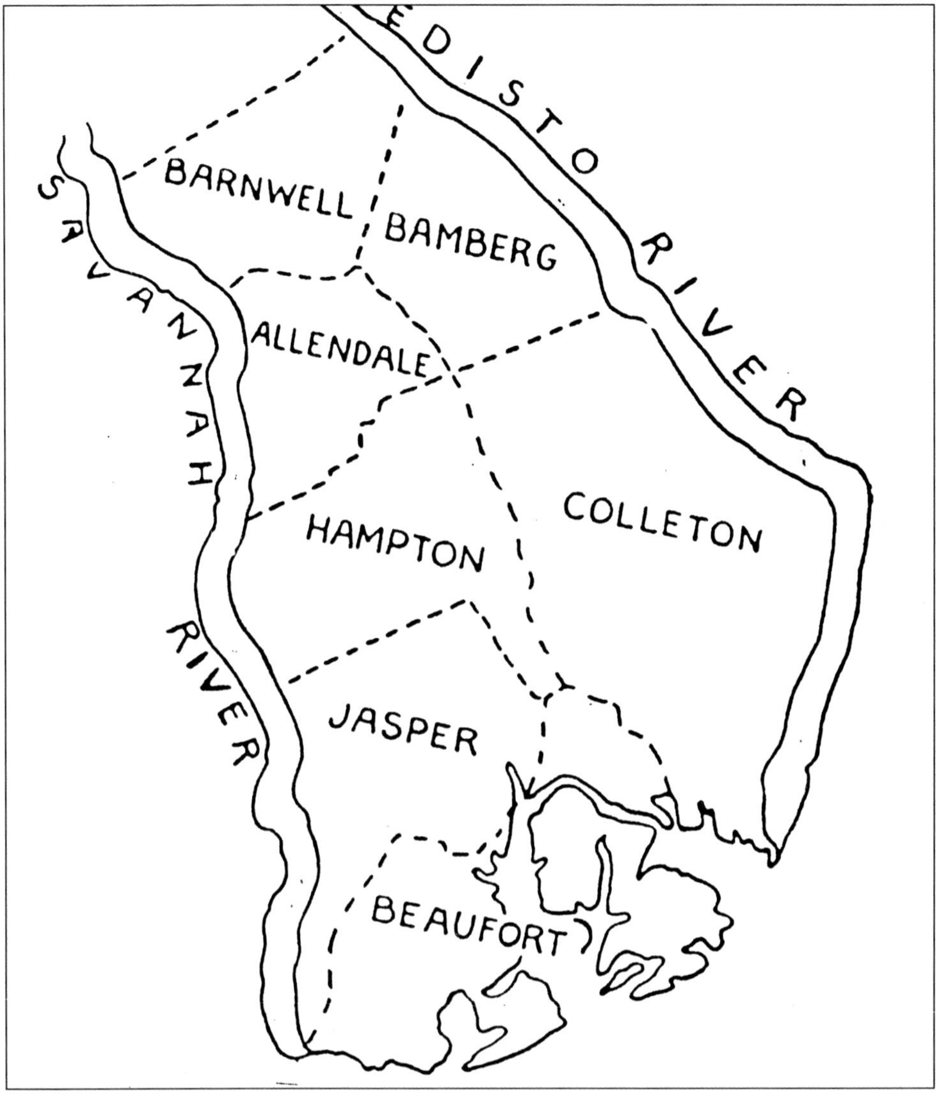


**REGIONAL OUTLINE MAP.** This map appears on the cover of *Opportunities in Edisto-Savannah Territory* (Denmark, SC: Edisto Public Service Company, 1927), in which Walterboro writer E.T.H. Shaffer defines "Southern Carolina" as that region comprised of the "Seven Sister Counties" lying between the Edisto and Savannah Rivers in the Coastal Plains of South Carolina: Allendale, Bamberg, Barnwell, Beaufort, Colleton, Hampton, and Jasper.

**AN ANTE-BELLUM RESIDENCE, BEAUFORT, S.C.** (Hand-Colored Collotype, 3 1/2" x 5 1/2", Albertype Co., Brooklyn, NY; C.G. Luther's Drugstore, Beaufort, sponsor; *c.* 1915.) Considered one of the great houses of the South Carolina coast, this Greek Revival-style residence stands on 2 acres overlooking the river in the eastern section of Beaufort called "The Point." It was built *c.* 1850 by Dr. Joseph F. Johnson, who was a planter as well as a physician. During the Civil War the house was used as a hospital, and the small detached laundry as a morgue. Often referred to as "The Castle" because of its medieval aura, it displays Spanish as well as English architectural influences. It is also known as the Porter Danner House.

POSTCARD HISTORY SERIES

# South Carolina Postcards

## Volume II

## Southern Carolina: Beaufort to Barnwell

Howard Woody and Thomas L. Johnson

ARCADIA PUBLISHING

ISBN 978-0-7385-6884-3

Published by Arcadia Publishing
Charleston, South Carolina

Printed in the United States of America

Library of Congress Catalog Card Number: 98-87877

For all general information contact Arcadia Publishing at:
Telephone 843-853-2070
Fax 843-853-0044
E-mail sales@arcadiapublishing.com
For customer service and orders:
Toll-Free 1-888-313-2665

Visit us on the Internet at www.arcadiapublishing.com

*For Arlene, my patient, ever-loving wife. H.W.*
*For my father and in memory of my mother. T.L.J.*

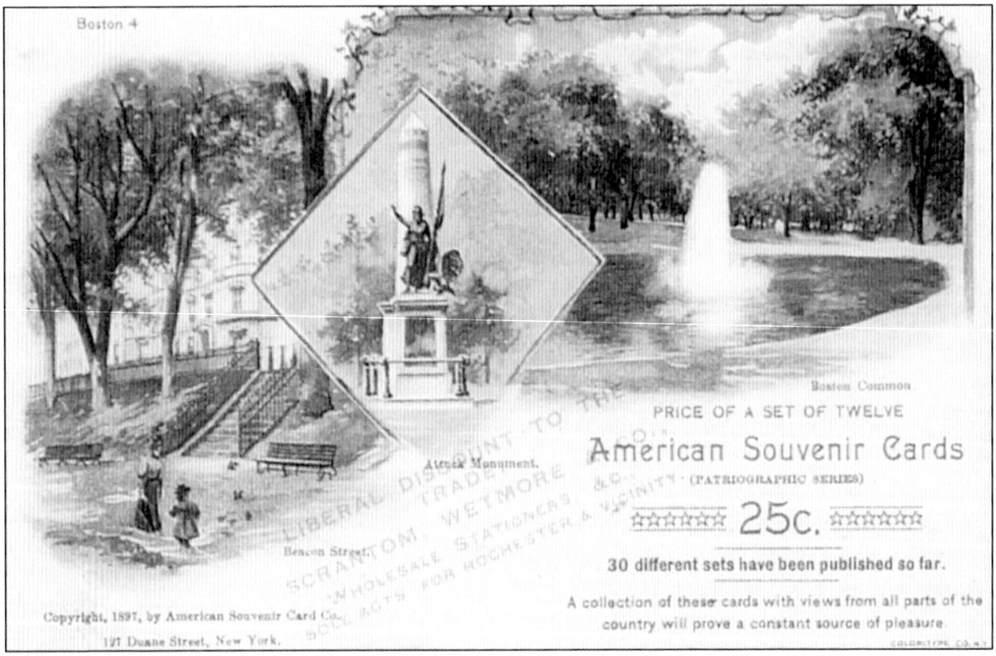


**PIONEER SAMPLE CARD.** (Color Lithography, 3 1/2" x 5 1/2", Colortype Co., NY; the American Souvenir Card Company, NY, publisher; 1897.) The most ambitious pre-1898 Pioneer publisher was the American Souvenir Card Company, New York. In 1897, it published 11 "Patriographic" sets for various sites, including Alaska, Chicago, and Washington, D.C. These collector sets were sold in souvenir shops in New York and other cities. Because this company, following the lead of the major German firms, published these sets before a local postcard-collecting community could be developed, it went bankrupt in early 1898.

# Contents


| | |
|---|---|
| Regional Outline Map | 2 |
| Introduction | 6 |
| Acknowledgments | 9 |
| Regional Map Showing Towns | 10 |
| 1. Beaufort County | 11 |
| 2. Jasper County | 57 |
| 3. Hampton County | 69 |
| 4. Colleton County | 87 |
| 5. Bamberg County | 95 |
| 6. Allendale County | 105 |
| 7. Barnwell County | 113 |
| Appendix: Data on Postcard Publishers | 126 |
| Index | 127 |

# Introduction

This volume of South Carolina postcards, the second in the series which aims to cover every county in the state eventually, furthers the goals set forth in the initial book, *South Carolina Postcards: Charleston, Berkeley, and Dorchester Counties* (1997).

The main purpose of the series is to show the essential role the lowly postcard plays in piecing together the history of South Carolina in the first third of the twentieth century. Interested viewers can see here how the public buildings, private dwellings, businesses, and institutions actually looked. They can study the faces, forms, and fashions of the persons portrayed individually or together, formally or informally. They can observe the scenes of work and play, can study the various events and occasions, and can witness the achievements and disasters.

Another goal is to provide the story of the postcard itself in its local manifestation. This prompts the discovery of who the photographers were, and which companies were publishing regional postcards, especially during their "Golden Era." This was generally considered to be the period from 1905 to 1912, when the genre's standards were at their peak, both in terms of excellent photography and fine printing.

Furthermore, this book, like the first, is a deliberate commemoration of the centennial of the Postal Service Act of May 19, 1898, which authorized and thus legalized the production of the Private Mailing Card and led to the opening of the floodgates of commercial and private postcard publication.

The geographical direction of this second book was a logical one that completed the presentation of the Lowcountry by swinging southwest to Beaufort and then proceeding northward. But how many counties, and which ones, should be included? Major factors to be considered were geographical cohesiveness, page limitations, and availability of relevant postcards. The decision was finally made to cover Beaufort, Jasper, Hampton, Colleton, Bamberg, Allendale, and Barnwell. The book would then wind its way up from Beaufort to Williston, the region's northernmost town with postcard documentation.

Then, as the serious work of research and compilation began, we discovered a small book called *Opportunities in Edisto-Savannah Territory*, published in 1927 by the Edisto Public Service Company as a promotional tract for its new hydro-electric power industry. In his foreword to this book, Walterboro writer and businessman E.T.H. Shaffer refers to the "Seven Sister Counties"—precisely the ones we had chosen for this volume—and indicates that the section was also sometimes called "Southern Carolina" or "Edisto-Savannah Territory" because the counties comprised the Coastal Plains, which lay between the two rivers and the Atlantic Ocean (*i.e.* the lower corner of the irregular triangle which defines the shape of South Carolina on the map).

Shaffer goes on to define the Seven Sister Counties, or Southern Carolina, as having an area of 4,269 square miles, with an average of 30 persons to the square mile for a total population at that time of 141,000. In addition to the mild climate produced by the lower latitude of the area combined with the presence of water (rivers, sounds, and the Gulf Stream), these counties shared the region's rich soil, longer growing seasons conducive to crop diversification, and huge timber reserves.

The images in the pages ahead will show that they also shared in honoring the institutions which characterized their traditionally agrarian society: the home, the church, the school, and the courthouse. The region was further defined during this period by the presence of the railroad—the relatively new lifeline of the farmer, the small-town merchant, and householder. In fact, it had been responsible for the very existence of many of the towns in Southern Carolina.

These seven counties held in common two other principal characteristics. One was the continuing reality of their past, with its glorious and conflicted history. Who could deny the splendor that survived, even if somewhat faded, in the residences along The Bluff or on The Point in Beaufort? And why forget that a good number of the postcards on these pages were produced within less than half a century after the end of the Civil War? That experience was often a definitive one with regard to the former use or present condition of many a structure pictured on postcards during the first two decades of the twentieth century.

The other of these main characteristics of Southern Carolina was its bi-racial makeup. And if the paucity of African-American images here is pronounced and disappointing, especially in the failure to turn up many in the counties beyond Beaufort, nevertheless among the most arresting and unusual view-cards in the book are the few which feature African-American subjects: the various school pictures taken in Beaufort and those of the Penn community on St. Helena Island, the stunning miniature of the quilting bee at Good Hope Camp near Ridgeland, and the "Colored Public School" at Barnwell.

For all of the similarities in pictorial matter which the seven counties exhibit here, each one also offers some distinct and extraordinary images of its own. Among these, in addition to those mentioned above, is the unforgettable array of Beaufort portraits: of Samuel Washington, Charles Chin Sang with his Chero-Cola truck, the "Little Child and Noble Oak," the Montessori School children, and the Wireless Class at Paris Island. In Jasper County there are the several multi-views and the portrait of the Ellis brothers, among others. Hampton County has its railroad work crew with the infant on the tracks, its perfect unit of pictures from the town of Brunson, and the winsome portraits of photographer Robert Lee Cleland and his wife, Elizabeth. Walterboro exhibits the only moonlit scene (made all the more interesting for the fact that it is an artificially created one), the only picture of a civilian hospital, and the only beach card in the book: the entrance to Edisto.

Bamberg County features its mill and its private schools (Carlisle and Voorhees), a parade, and the chief mystery of the book: the question as to the exact location of the "Barbecue Day at Denmark." Allendale combines utility and art, with a picture of theatrical troupers advertising their "Happy Hooligan Tonight" and the sole picture of a municipal electric and water plant. Fairfax offers the image of a monument to women's suffrage pioneer Virginia D.C. Young and an invitation to the opening of a millinery shop—whose proprietor is also named Young. Barnwell has its opera house, Confederate monument, and a rare interior school portrait of a first-grade class.

However else it was being done, then, at least in the form of the modest, low-cost postcard the world—or the friend or relation in the other part of the region, state, or nation—was being shown the unpretentious but substantial glories, the mild progress and modest prosperities, and the storied beauty of Southern Carolina, or what Walterboro editor W.W. Smoak called "this paradise of the South."

As for the actual sales and distribution of postcards in the region, one can say generally that the quantity and the quality—though certainly not their historic value—were diminished in comparison with those produced for the Charleston market. Naturally, in a region which was largely agrarian, the opportunities for marketing, and thus some of the incentive for producing, the picture postcard were not the same as those in the city. The work of such high-quality firms as the Detroit Publishing Company, Raphael Tuck and Sons of London, or Frankfurt's Rosenblatt Lithographic Institute—all of which produced Charleston cards—does not appear among surviving samples from this region. Nor was there an event like the South Carolina Inter-State and West Indian Exposition, held in Charleston in 1901–1902, to spur early production of postcards in Southern Carolina.

Although early Pioneer (pre-May 1898) issues featuring South Carolina images have yet to surface anywhere outside of Charleston, a small series of Private Mailing Cards featuring Beaufort scenes, dating to about 1900, did exist. These few locally printed halftone issues carry pictures of the town's National Cemetery, waterfront, and Sea Island Hotel. Thus, the postcard would begin to function for Beaufort the way it did for Charleston: as a means whereby tourists, commercial travelers, and military personnel—as well as hometown residents—could show the place where they were visiting, or were serving in the Marines or Navy, or permanently lived.

Furthermore, some high-quality images of Beaufort were later produced by two of the leading postcard manufacturers of the period: Knackstedt and Näther of Hamburg and the Albertype Company of Brooklyn. Beaufort, of course, had the advantage not only of being Southern Carolina's principal coastal port, military center, railroad terminal, and commercial hub, but also of being intrinsically photogenic as a quaint and charming place. It is not surprising that the native New Yorker who would become a lifelong resident of Beaufort, Charles G. Luther, recognized the visual potential of his adopted home and proceeded to publish—and to sell in his drugstore—many of the town's finest postcards.

Beyond Beaufort, postcard jobbers provided some high-quality imported postcards for Port Royal, Denmark, Blackville, and Williston. These were obtained from Paul C. Trouche, the Charleston wholesale and retail stationery firm which contracted with German printers to produce South Carolina view-cards. But in general, fewer jobbers were attracted to the rural towns in the back districts, whose drug and general mercantile stores stocked mostly small numbers of commercial postcards. These were often obtained from mail-order houses as limited, low-budget orders. One such firm was the Factory to Consumers Company of Knoxville, which sold a limited issue of Beaufort's "Baptist Parsonage" to members of that church (see below). Another was C.U. Williams of Bloomington, Illinois, who placed advertisements in national and regional publications to which two Southern Carolina merchants, Burckhalter's Drug Store of Barnwell and C.M. McTeer's General Merchandise Store in Hardeeville, responded—probably about the same time (*c.* 1914). These retailers often sent off poorly produced amateur pictures to be copied, and they received back murky halftone images to be sold.

Because of the pronounced demographic differences between the urban environs of Charleston in Volume One and the mainly rural domain of this one, fewer cards produced by the great international publishing houses exist for Southern Carolina. Having said this, however, it must also be stated that the visual resources which survive in postcard form for this area are unsurpassed in historic value by any other body of photographs documenting the life of these "Seven Sisters" during the first third of the twentieth century.

In the final analysis, the credit for this record must go to the local amateur and studio photographers, who took pictures of persons, places, and events in their communities and then published them in limited postcard issues either for commercial purposes or simply for private distribution. It is chiefly because of them that we have the visual riches which are here.

Again, it is our wish that the casual reader and viewer as well as the serious historian may profit from what is found in these pages and that they may enjoy what they discover in them.

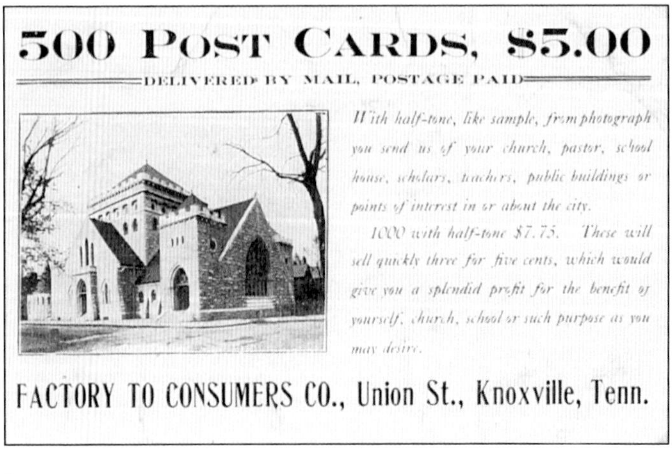


**DOMESTIC ADVERTISING SAMPLE CARD.** (Halftone, 3 1/2" x 5 3/8", Factory to Consumers Co., Knoxville, TN; *c.* 1906.) This mail-order company advertised in regional publications and permitted small orders of halftone view cards. Their customers, found in most Southern states, often submitted amateur photographs which produced very modest results.

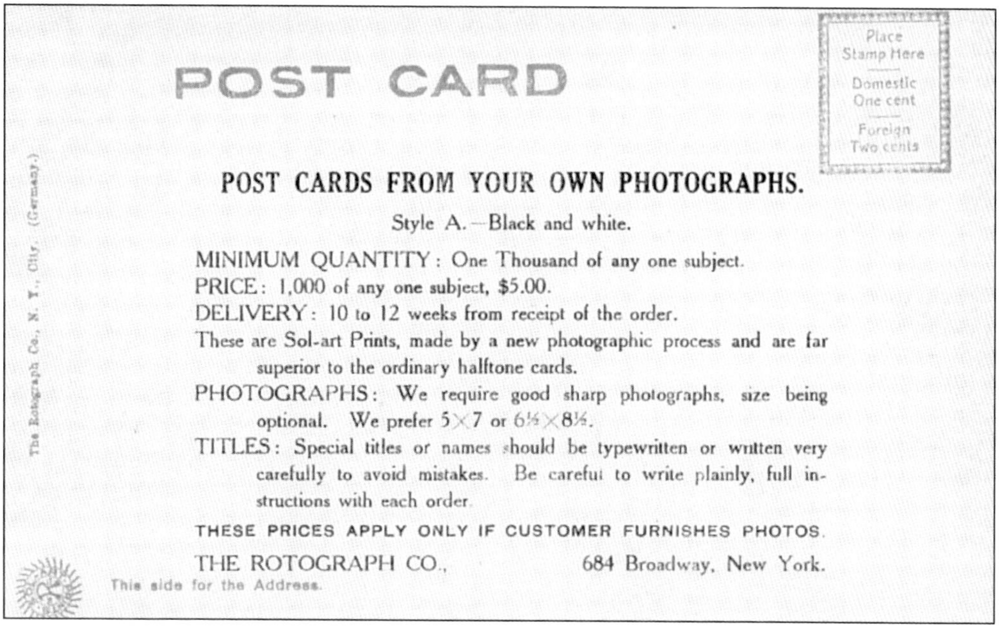

POST CARD

Place Stamp Here
Domestic One cent
Foreign Two cents

The Rotograph Co., N. Y., City. (Germany.)

**POST CARDS FROM YOUR OWN PHOTOGRAPHS.**

Style A.—Black and white.

MINIMUM QUANTITY: One Thousand of any one subject.
PRICE: 1,000 of any one subject, $5.00.
DELIVERY: 10 to 12 weeks from receipt of the order.
These are Sol-art Prints, made by a new photographic process and are far superior to the ordinary halftone cards.
PHOTOGRAPHS: We require good sharp photographs, size being optional. We prefer 5×7 or 6½×8½.
TITLES: Special titles or names should be typewritten or written very carefully to avoid mistakes. Be careful to write plainly, full instructions with each order.
THESE PRICES APPLY ONLY IF CUSTOMER FURNISHES PHOTOS.
THE ROTOGRAPH CO., 684 Broadway, New York.
This side for the Address.

**Import Advertising Sample Card.** (Collotype, 3 1/2" x 5 1/2", [Knackstedt and Näther Co., Hamburg, Germany, pre-1898]; Rotograph Co., New York, NY, importer; *c.* 1906.) The Rotograph Company, a subsidiary distributor of the Knackstedt and Näther Company from 1905, created a collotype process which was a refined monochrome photogelatin process—using a light-sensitive solution of gelatin, potassium bichromate, and ammonia that created a thin surface film of fine granular particles—which precluded the use of halftone screens and permitted sharp, accurate details. Charles G. Luther's Drugstore in Beaufort stocked both the postcards from before the fire of 1907 and the post-1907 issues from this source. The postcard shipment noted in his advertisement in the *Beaufort Gazette*, June 20, 1907, consisted of a series of 13 pictures—1,000 per subject for $65 in addition to shipping—which was ordered in March 1907 and may well have included pre- and post-fire images. Fourteen series codes have been documented on Beaufort cards. The protectionist Payne-Aldrich Tariff Act of 1909 placed on the common import view-card trade closed the Rotograph Company's import business.

# *Acknowledgments*

*South Carolina Postcards: Southern Carolina*, like the first book in this series, is the result of the interest and assistance of many persons. Again, we wish to thank Allen H. Stokes, Henry Fulmer, and Beth Bilderback of the South Caroliniana Library, University of South Carolina, for their invaluable support. Other Midlands and Upcountry residents who made essential contributions were Davie Beard, Paul L. Howle, Paul Jeter, Lois Whisnant, Sylvia Whitney, and Les Winn.

For their generous loan of postcards or provision of information we hereby express our appreciation to the following persons living in or otherwise related to these "Seven Sister Counties": (Allendale) Walker R. Harter, Robert J. Karrer, Henry and Libby Peeples Laffitte, Mr. and Mrs. H.M. Loadholt and friends, Mrs. Henry Madden, Austin Sheheen Jr.; (Bamberg) Caroline E. Boyd, H. Hayne Crum, Mrs. Andrew Peeples, Nyles Rowell, Carol Varn; (Barnwell) Bob and May Ackerman, Barnwell Museum, the Baxley family, Posey Belcher, Bettye Ackerman Jaffe, Ellen Jenkins, Louis O'Gorman, Pauline Zidlick; (Beaufort) Beaufort Museum, Charleston Museum, Fred B. Christensen, Niels Christensen III, A. Duncan Fordham, Coazell Frazier, Dorothy Gnann, Ian Hill, Herbert and Harriet Keyserling, A. Mills Kinghorn, Liz Lee, Alfred Lengnick, Mr. and Mrs. William Mixon, Eugene Norris,

Parris Island Museum, Wyatt B. Pringle, Larry Rowland, Bill Sammons, Frederick W. (Willie) Scheper III, Muriel W. Smalley, Gerhard Spieler, Lee Stevenson, Charles Stockell, Anne Paul Stork, Dwight Stuckey, Carol Tuynman, Laura Von Harten, Betty L. Waskiewicz, Marguerite Waterhouse-Broz, Steve Wise, Henry Wrigley; (Colleton) Fannie Adkins, Sherry Cawley, John S. Hiott, Eunice Jackson, Henry W. Moore, Bud Price, Mrs. J.F. Riddle; (Hampton) Betty Ruth Crews, Sam Crews, Jim Dreyfuss, W.B. Hadwin, Hampton County Historical Museum, J.M. Hogarth, Montague Laffitte, Tom Lawton, Elizabeth Cleland Peeples, Mildred B. Rivers, Fred Whitten, Robert G. Wiggins III, Julia Youmans, Mildred L. Youmans; (Jasper) Dave Bormes, Rosemary Hunt, Jasper County Historical Society, Dick McTeer, Wofford Malphrus, Barbara Pinckney, Curtis L. Smart, and Elizabeth Ellis Taylor.

As always, we are grateful to the Arcadia office and editorial staff, and especially to Mark Berry and Sarah Maineri.

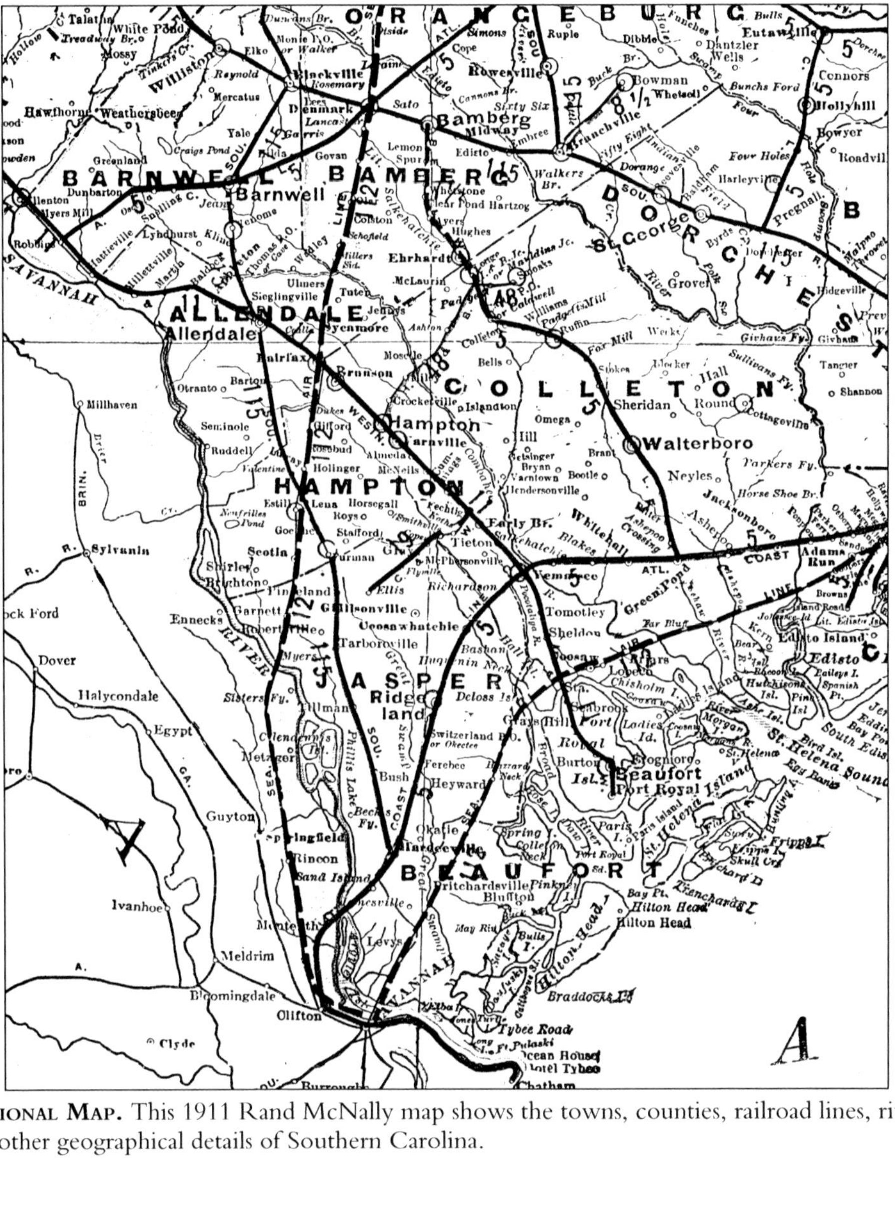


**Regional Map.** This 1911 Rand McNally map shows the towns, counties, railroad lines, rivers, and other geographical details of Southern Carolina.

# *One*

# Beaufort County

The region's strong old anchor, Beaufort County exemplifies Southern Carolina's topographical beauty, long and diverse history, and socio-economic complexity. The county is comprised of 702 square miles distributed over several peninsulas and some 65 islands and has as its seat the second oldest town in South Carolina: Beaufort, founded in 1711.

On the following pages can be seen the visual evidence of the "Beaufort Style," certainly as this term denotes a distinctive architectural blending of Georgian, Colonial, Greek Revival, and Spanish elements. But it also suggests the juxtaposition of coastal mariculture and inland cotton and truck farming; military investment and resort development; Northern initiative and Southern expansiveness; blacks and whites individually and in community; and a glorious and burdened past and an insistent present.

"Come to Beaufort!" wrote N.L. Willett in 1929. "Land of Ancient Shrines . . . . Land of queenly islands. Land of the sea island Negro and of Spirituals and Praise-houses . . . . Land of sunshine and mild climate and rich muck soil and the Truckers' Paradise. Land of spectacular history . . . ."

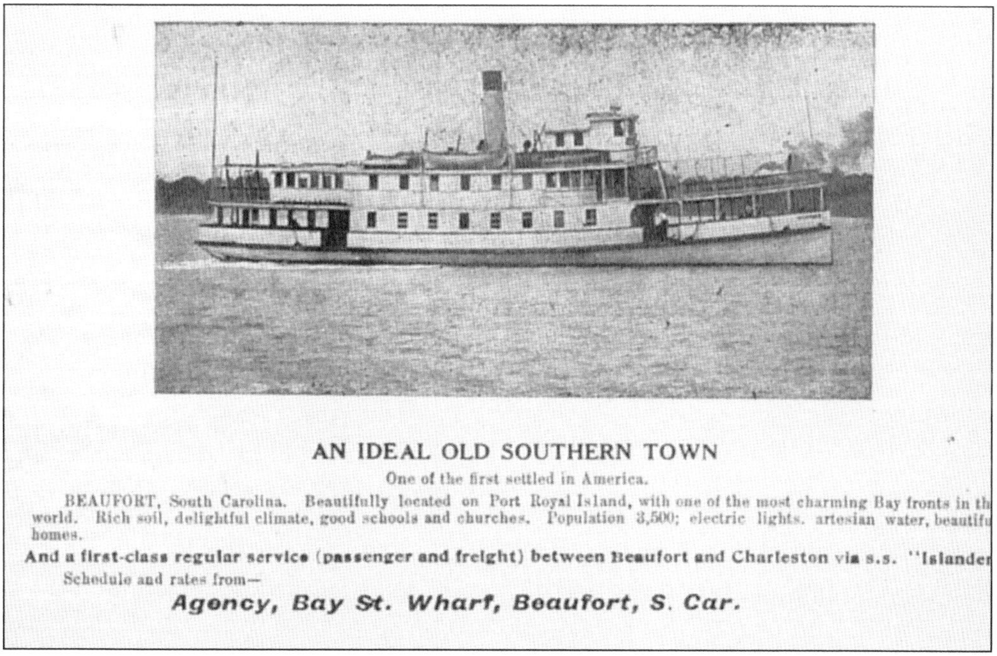


**An Ideal Old Southern Town, Beaufort, South Carolina.** (Halftone, 3 1/2" x 5 4/10"; *c.* 1908.) Traditional local maritime commerce and the relatively new industry of tourism meet in this early promotional postcard issued by a steamship company advertising Beaufort as "an ideal old Southern town" and its own "first-class regular service (passenger and freight) between Beaufort and Charleston." The vessel portrayed here is presumably the steamship *Islander* mentioned on the card. Beaufort was the largest Southern Carolina town, with a population of 3,000 in 1910.

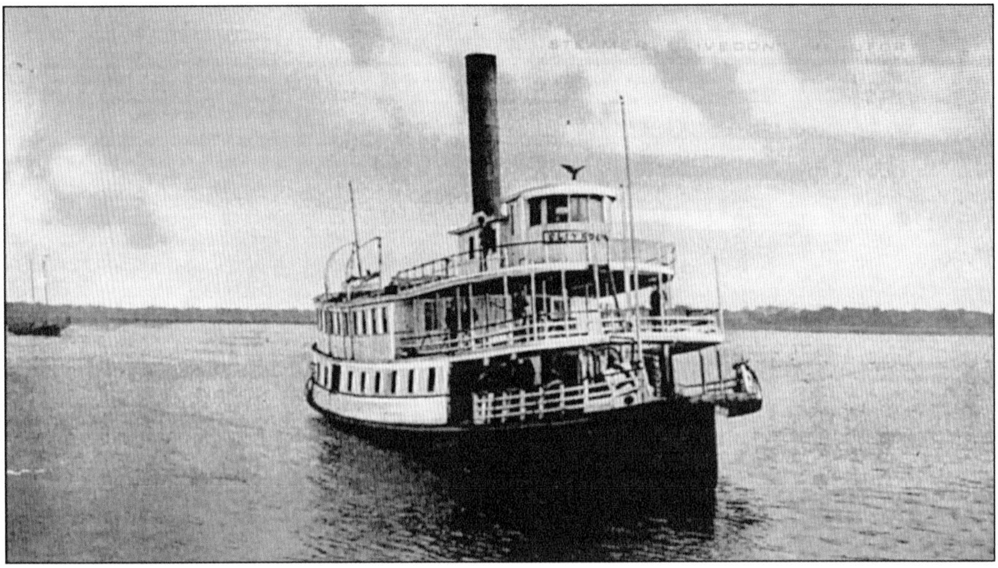

**Steamer Clivedon, Beaufort.** (Color Lithography, 3 1/2" x 5 1/2", unknown German printer; American News Co., #AA4728, New York, NY, importer; 1908.) The screw-propelled *Clivedon*, distinguishable by the eagle ensign on its pilothouse, was one of two vessels operated for many years by the Beaufort and Savannah Line to provide the essential transportation link between the two towns—the other ship being the 1885 Charleston-built side-wheeler *Pilot Boy*. When standard Georgia-Carolina ferry service began on July 29, 1914, with three trips each way daily between Savannah and Beaufort, "immediate large use . . . by automobilists" was anticipated.

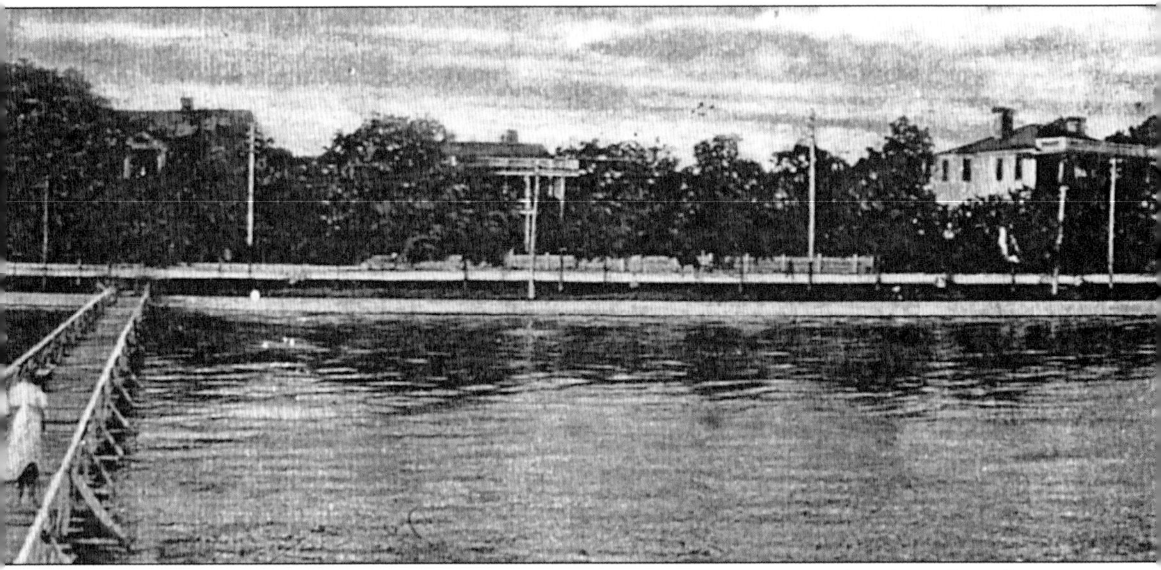

**Water View, Beaufort, S.C.** (Collotype, 3 1/2" x 11", [Knackstedt and Näther Co., Hamburg, Germany]; Rotograph Co., #65324, New York, NY, importer]; *c.* 1907.) "The city of Beaufort has some four thousand five hundred inhabitants," wrote journalist and naturalist James Henry Rice in the *Beaufort Gazette*, February 27, 1920, "and on the whole Atlantic front, from Maine to Florida, there is no spot of such pictured charm . . . ." The easy proximity of beauty and utilitarianism, of business and pleasure, characteristic of the town, is captured in this

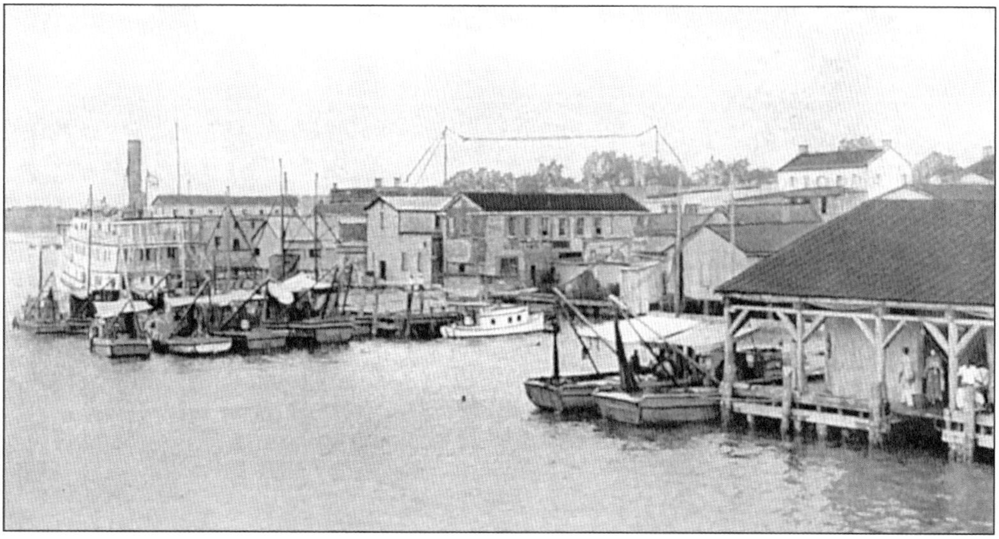

**SCENE ON THE WATERFRONT, BEAUFORT, S.C.** (Color Lithography, 3 1/2" x 5 1/2", Curt Teich Co., #106849, Chicago, IL; *c.* 1921.) Seen here tied up at the docks in this northwesterly view of the waterfront taken from the Beaufort River are the various kinds of vessels which reflected the activity of the river port during this period. Among them were shrimp trawlers and small fishing boats, launches, and (at left) the Savannah steamer. A typical 1918 sailing schedule called for one or the other of the boats to leave Beaufort daily (except Sundays) at 7:30 a.m. and to leave Savannah at 10:00 a.m. (except Saturday). A message on the back of this card, sent in August 1918, reads as follows: "Had a nice ride on a steamer Sunday but not the *Clivedon*."

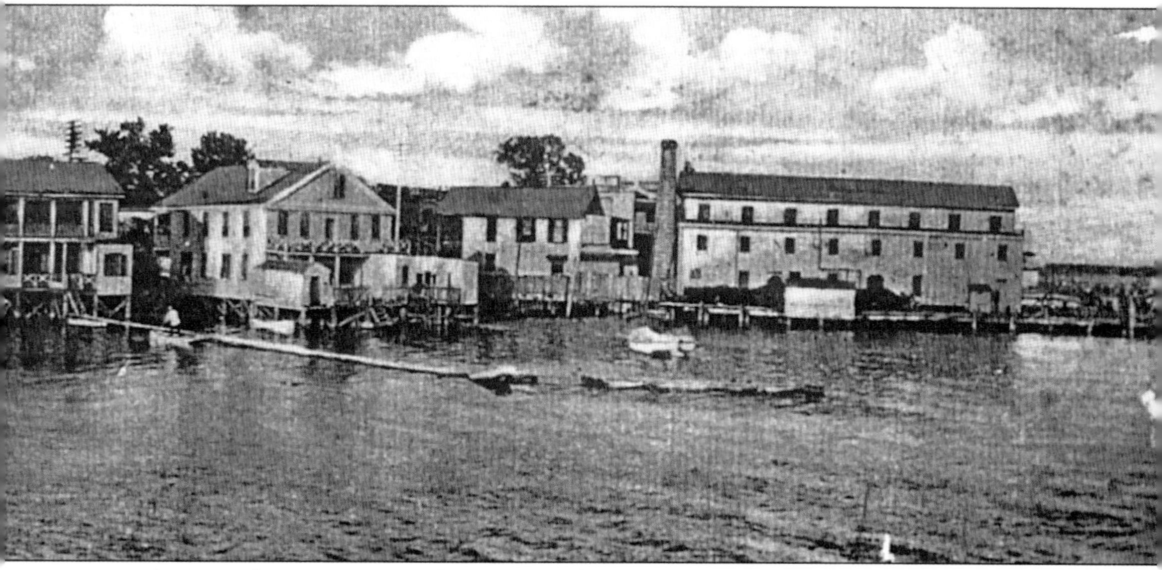

panoramic view of its eastern waterfront. At the far left leisure timers make their way along the Sea Island Hotel's wooden promenade out to its bathhouse on the river. At the far right William P. Waterhouse's imposing 1890s ginnery and general storage warehouse rise over the water. Immediately to its left, on Bay Street, is the old Western Union telegraph office. In the middle of the picture, at the corner of Bay and Charles, across from commercial properties whose backsides front the river, stands the stately George Elliott House, built about 1840.

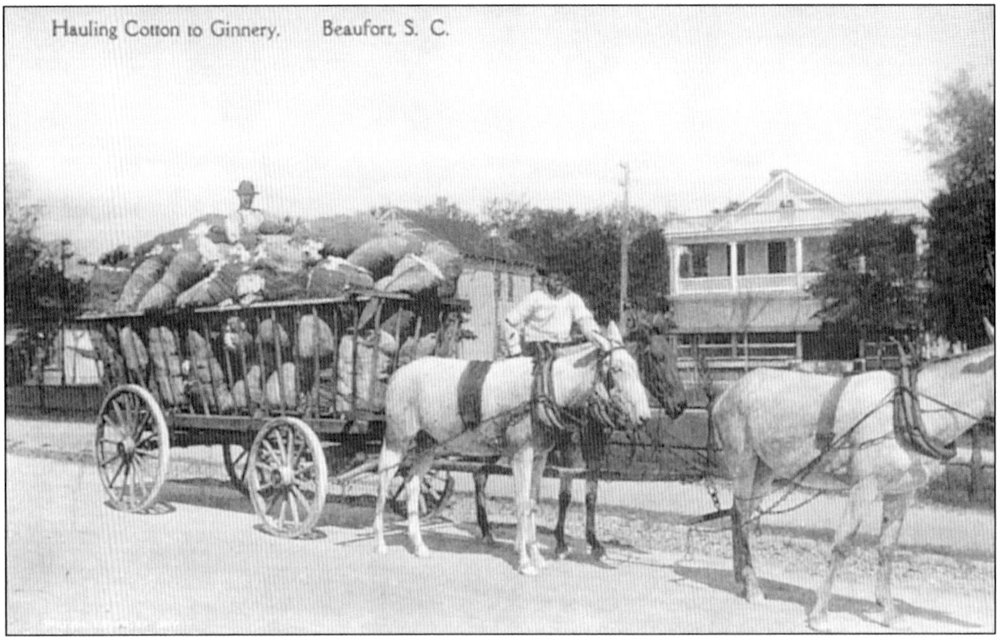


**HAULING COTTON TO GINNERY, BEAUFORT, S.C.** (Hand-Colored Collotype, 3 1/2" x 5 1/2", Albertype Co., Brooklyn, NY; C.G. Luther's Drugstore, Beaufort, sponsor; *c.* 1915.) After the demise of Beaufort's flourishing phosphate industry following the great hurricane of 1893, the county once again depended upon cotton, fish, and timber as economic mainstays. In 1911, Beaufort County ginned 9,904 bales of cotton—the largest number ever remembered being reported for the county—valued at $350,000. Mule-drawn cotton wagons would have been a familiar sight on town and country roads for the first several decades of the twentieth century.

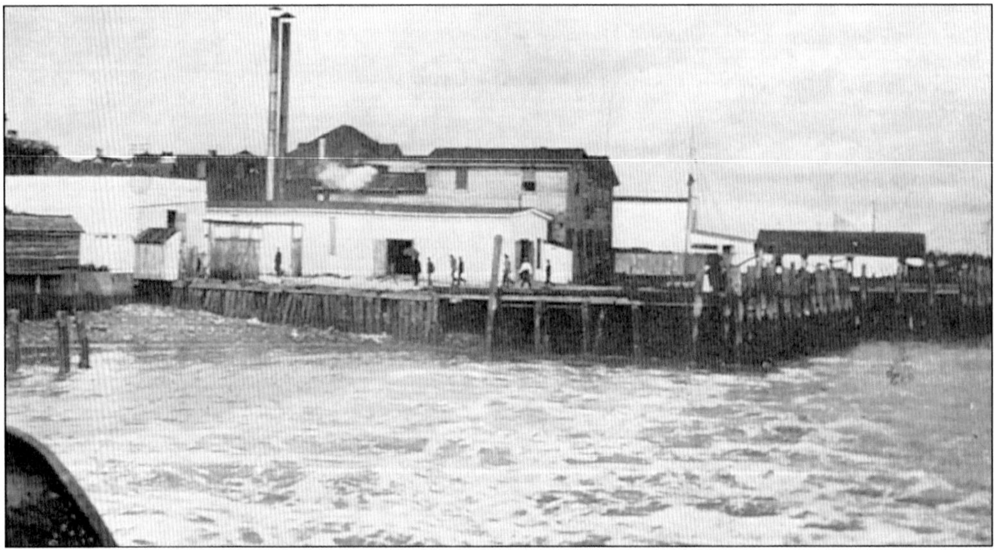

**SAVANNAH STEAMER LANDING, BEAUFORT.** (Halftone, 3 1/2" x 5 4/10", [United View Co., Newark, DE]; 1911.) This view of the Beaufort waterfront shows not only the location of the old Savannah steamer landing, but also some of the structures which once fronted the river. Of the two buildings in the center of the picture, the taller one reportedly housed the Chero-Cola bottling works at one time. The one in front was a warehouse.

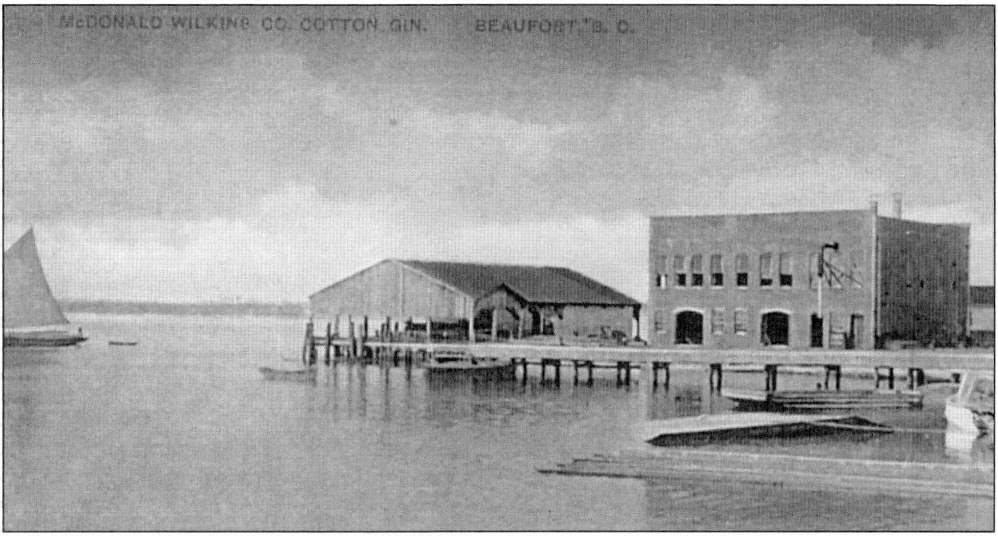


**McDonald [sic] Wilkins Company Cotton Gin, Beaufort, S.C.** (Hand-Colored Collotype, 3 1/2" x 5 1/2", Albertype Co., Brooklyn, NY; C.G. Luther's Drugstore, Beaufort, sponsor; *c.* 1912.) The large brick Macdonald-Wilkins gin-house, which once stood on East Bay near Carteret, was built in 1911. At this time the company also repaired the wharf and enclosed and covered part of it for use as a warehouse, which was later acquired by the Keyserling family. The People's Bank eventually bought and demolished the building in order to use the space for parking. The shed-like structure to the left has been identified as the shrimp dock.

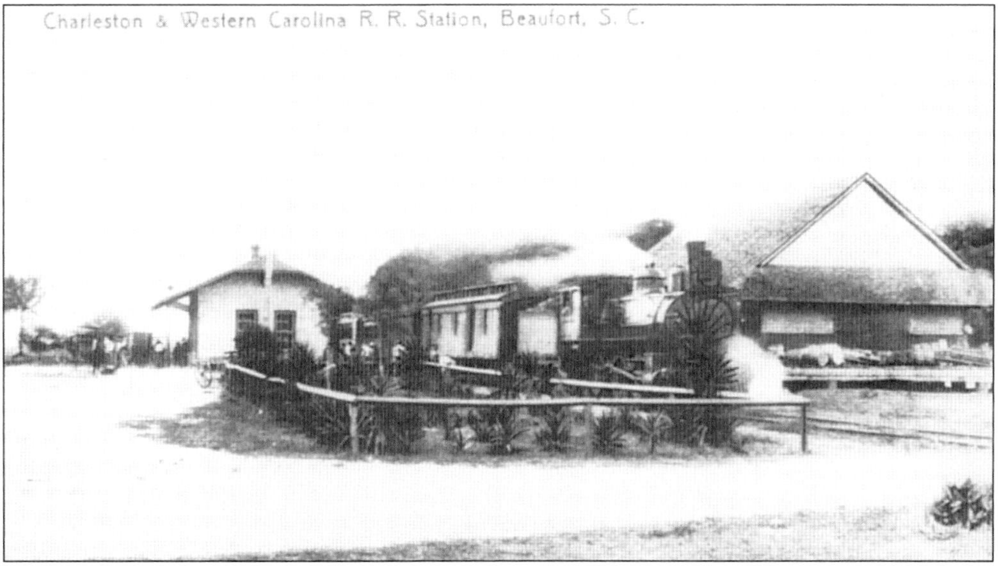


**Charleston & Western Carolina Railroad Station, Beaufort, S.C.** (Collotype, 3 1/2" x 5 1/2", [Knackstedt and Näther Co., Hamburg, Germany]; Rotograph Co., #64554, New York, NY, importer; 1910.) This view of the old Charleston & Western Carolina Railroad (C&WC) station, which stood on the west side of town at the foot of Depot Street, was taken facing south from the Hay Street crossing. The freight depot is to the right. After the station had been remodeled and repaired in 1912, the editor of the *Beaufort Gazette* remarked on September 7 that "we are no longer ashamed to have tourists come here." This passenger station was replaced by a new one in the late 1920s.

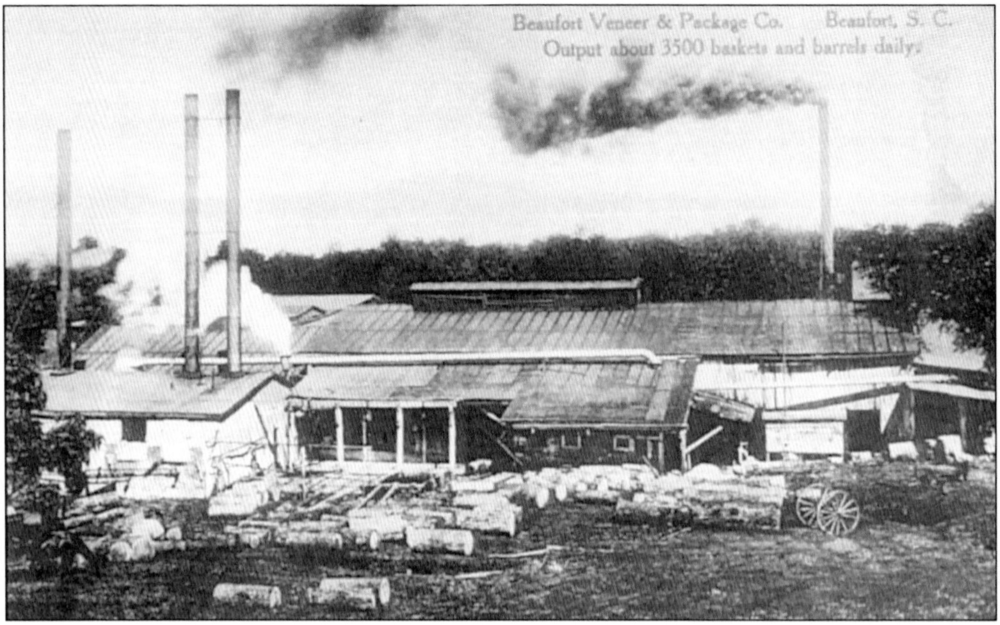


**Beaufort Veneer & Package Co., Beaufort, S.C.** (Hand-Colored Collotype, 3 1/2" x 5 1/2", Albertype Co., Brooklyn, NY; C.G. Luther's Drugstore, Beaufort, sponsor; *c.* 1916.) "The first decade of the 20th century saw Beaufort County depending on cotton and seafoods and her timber products once again," J. Ed McTeer wrote in *Beaufort Now and Then* (1971). Among the local commercial wood manufacturing ventures was the Beaufort Veneer and Package Company, which turned out about 3,500 baskets and barrels daily.

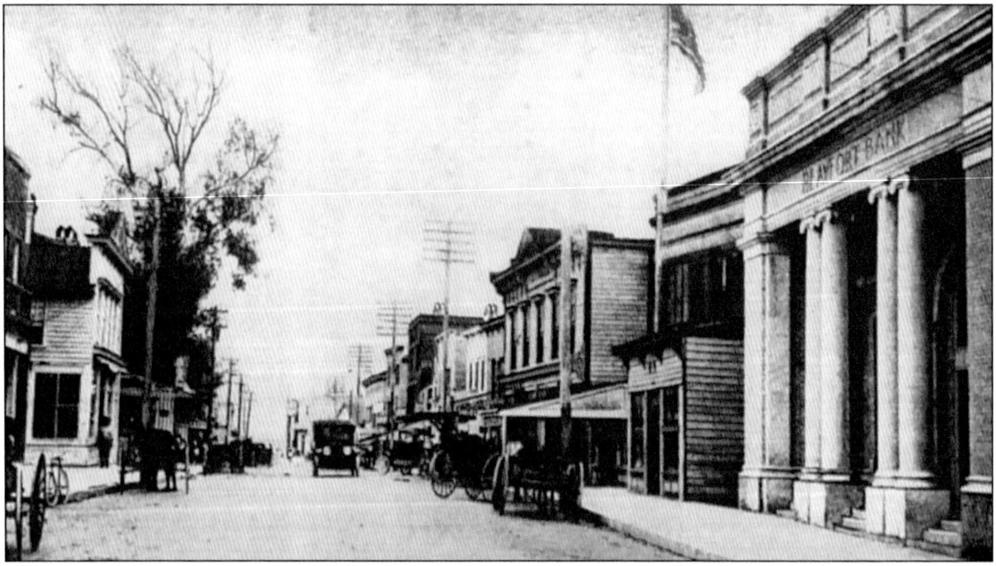

**Bay Street, Beaufort, S.C.** (Hand-Colored Collotype, 3 1/2" x 5 1/2", Albertype Co., Brooklyn, NY; C.G. Luther's Drugstore, Beaufort, sponsor; *c.* 1914.) In 1913 the Beaufort Bank bought from Mrs. Scheper the property on which the old Post Office stood and erected the building at the right in this view looking east on Bay Street. The Custom House is probably flying the flag seen here. Years later the bank was used as a movie theater. In 1998, it stood at 926 Bay as the Bank Waterfront Grill and Bar.

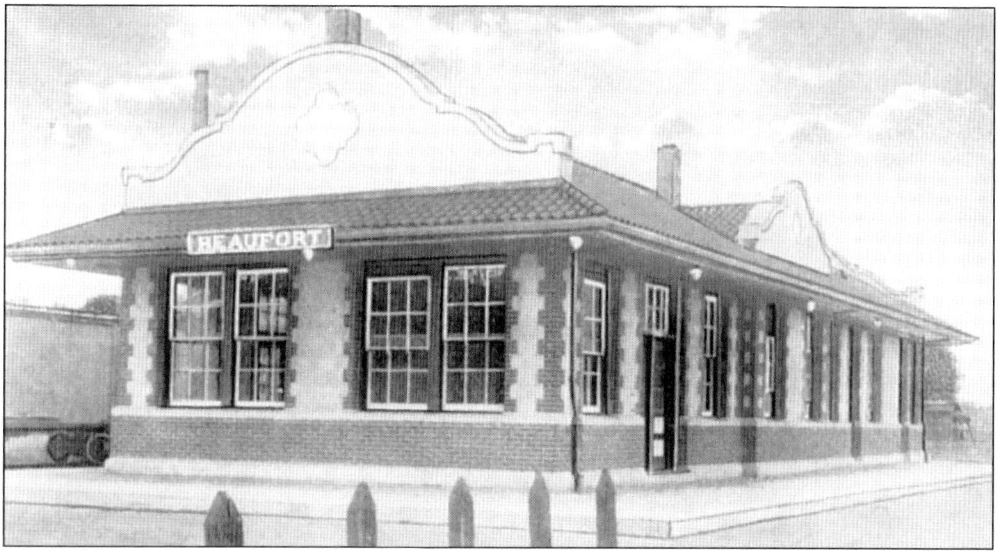


**C & WC Passenger Depot, Beaufort, S.C.** (Color Lithography, 3 1/2" x 5 1/2", Curt Teich Co., #106845, Chicago, IL; *c.* 1929.) The foundation of this "new" Charleston & Western Carolina Railroad passenger depot can still be found among the weeds at the foot of Depot Road. Featuring pseudo-Dutch architectural embellishments, it is believed to have been constructed in the late 1920s and demolished in 1974.

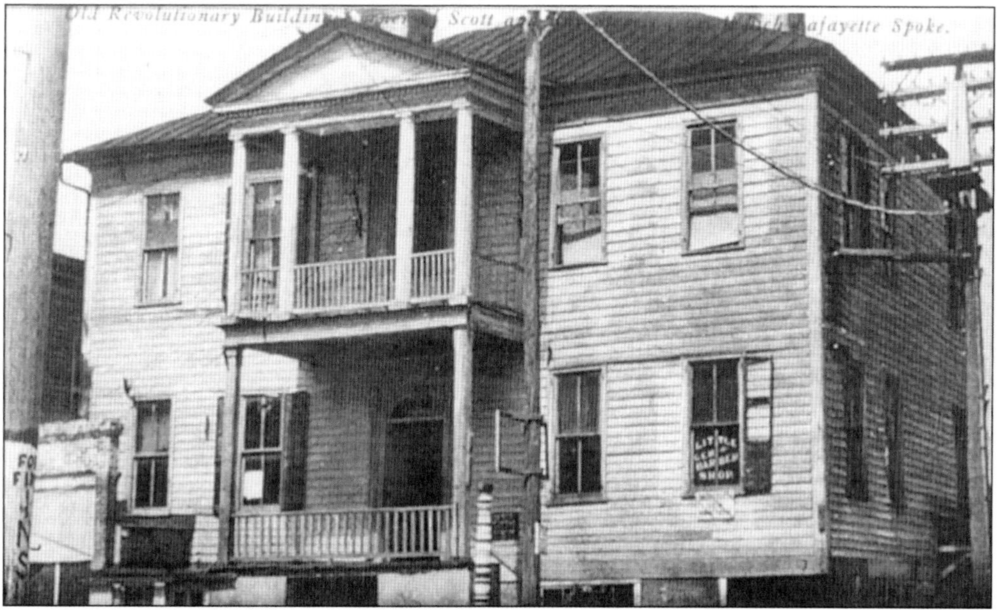

**Old Revolutionary Building, Beaufort, S.C.** (Collotype, 3 1/2" x 5 1/2", American News Co., New York, NY, importer; *c.* 1912.) Through the years the John Mark Verdier House, 801 Bay Street, has capitalized on the claim that on his 1825 visit to Beaufort the Marquis de Lafayette addressed the citizenry from its portico. Built by Verdier about 1790, the two-story residence erected on a tabby foundation has been carefully preserved and today houses a museum and the offices of the Historic Beaufort Foundation. It once served as Federal headquarters (Civil War), a fish market, and law and telephone offices. It has been on the National Register of Historic Places since 1971 and was restored in 1976.

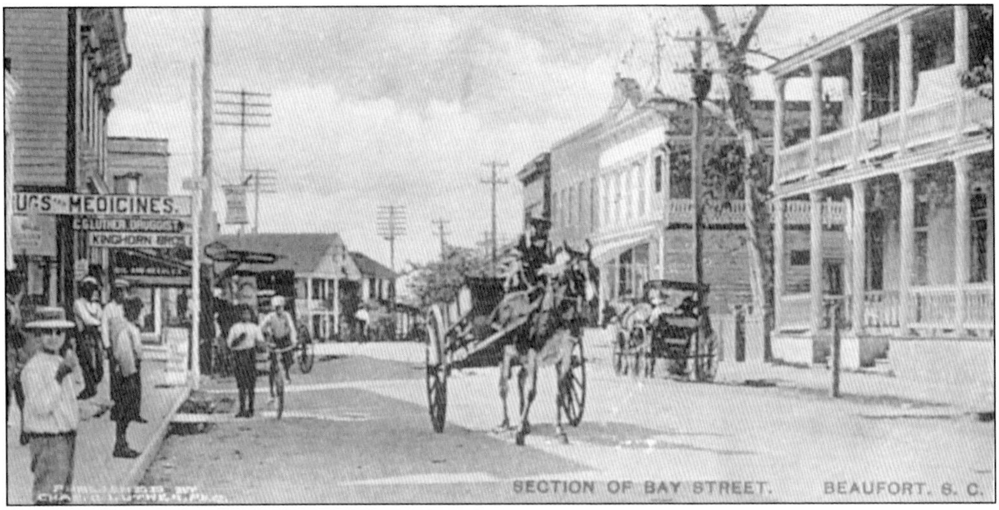


**SECTION OF BAY STREET, BEAUFORT, S.C.** (Hand-Colored Collotype, 3 1/2" x 5 1/2", Albertype Co., Brooklyn, NY; C.G. Luther's Drugstore, Beaufort, sponsor; *c.* 1912.) Animal-drawn vehicles and the bicycle are the principal means of transportation in this view of Bay Street, looking west. To the left are signs indicating the location of Dr. Charles G. Luther's Drugstore and the grocery store belonging to the Kinghorn Brothers.

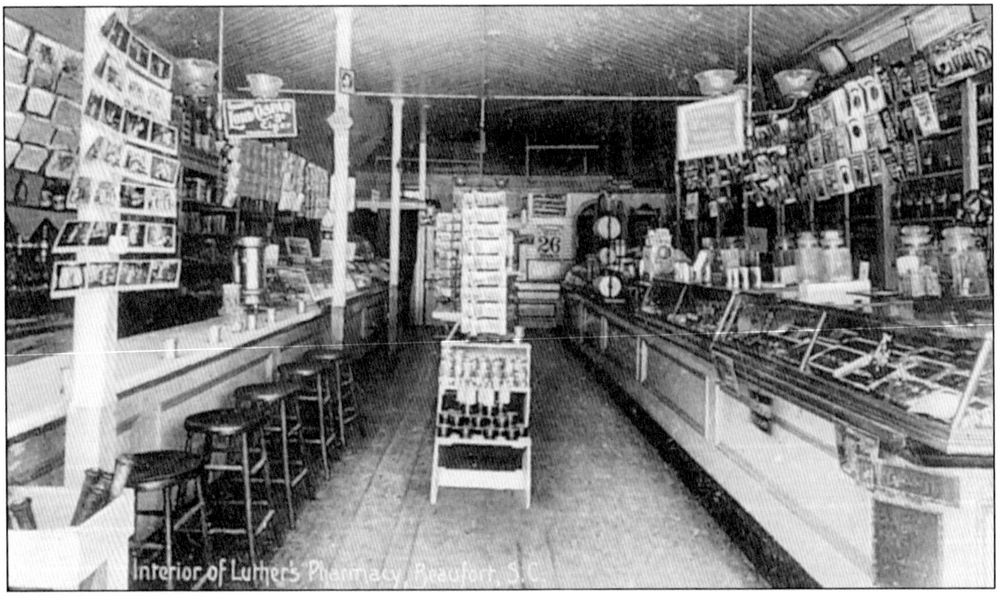


**INTERIOR OF LUTHER'S PHARMACY, BEAUFORT, S.C.** (Collotype, 3 4/10" x 5 4/10", [Knackstedt and Näther Co., Hamburg, Germany]; A.M. Simon, #12655, New York, NY, importer; C.G. Luther's Drugstore, Beaufort, sponsor; *c.* 1908.) New York native Charles G. Luther (1876–1960), a Navy pharmacist who had served in the Spanish-American War, was stationed at Paris Island in 1901. By 1906, with $4,000 borrowed from an aunt, he had purchased Elliott's Pharmacy and had begun operating the drugstore which would occupy him until 1941, when he sold it to his nephew, Dr. Julius C. Long. Known as "the poor man's doctor" of Beaufort, Luther is remembered for his inability to turn anyone away from the store. The cards seen here in this rare interior scene no doubt include some of the many views he published of Beaufort (see page 9).

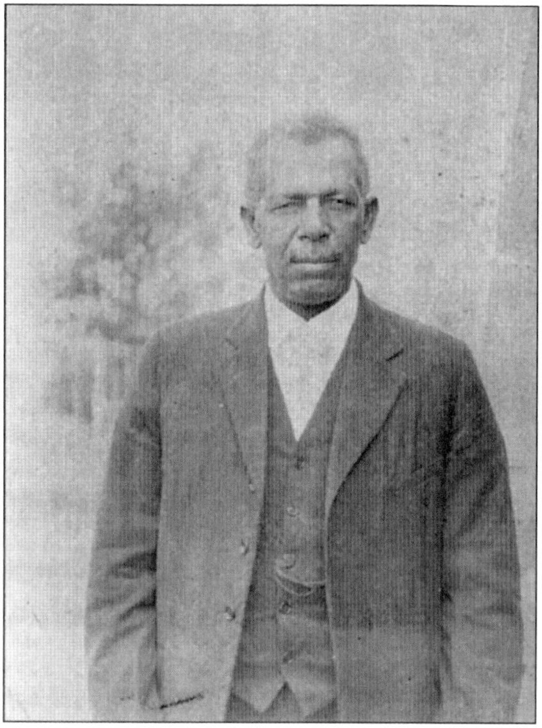

**[Portrait of Samuel Washington.]** (Photoprint, 5" x 3 1/2"; *c.* 1918–22.) Beaufort native Samuel Washington (*c.* 1870–1954) owned and operated a grocery store in "The Neighborhood" at the corner of Duke and Charles Streets, where he was also known for his provision of fine shrimp-fishing nets. He was a member of First African Baptist Church. His daughter, Muriel Washington Smalley, lives in a home erected on the family property on Charles Street.

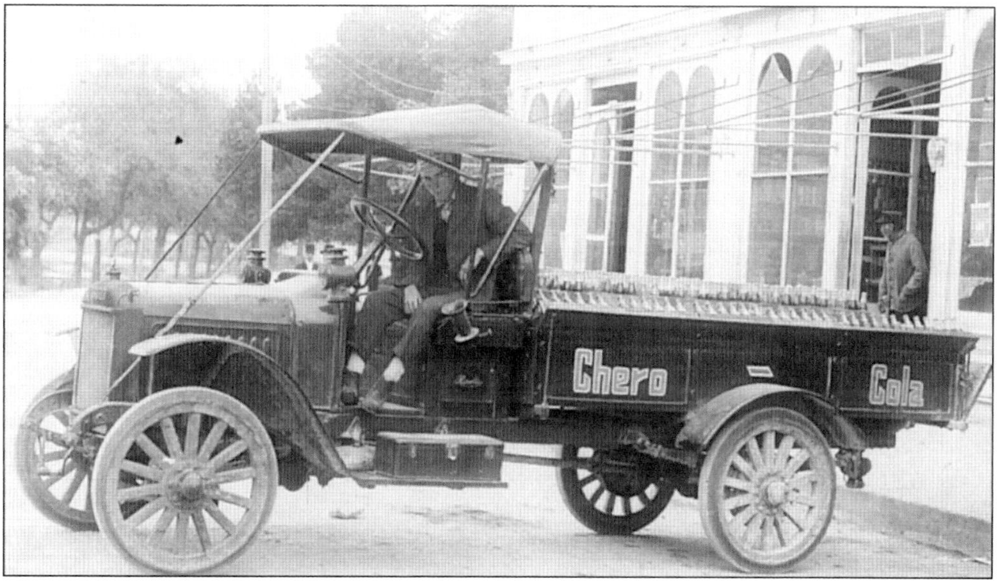


**[Charles Chin Sang and His Chero-Cola Truck.]** (Photoprint, 3 1/2" x 5 1/2"; *c.* 1910–18.) The only known surviving picture of Beaufort's early Chinese-American merchant and bottling entrepreneur, Charles Chin Sang (1842–1927), this postcard shows him standing in the doorway of his Bay Street establishment, along with the Chero-Cola delivery truck and its driver, probably a young relative. Sang had come to Beaufort about 1899 from Charleston, where he was a grocer as early as 1877. He eventually returned to Charleston and is buried in St. Laurence Cemetery there.

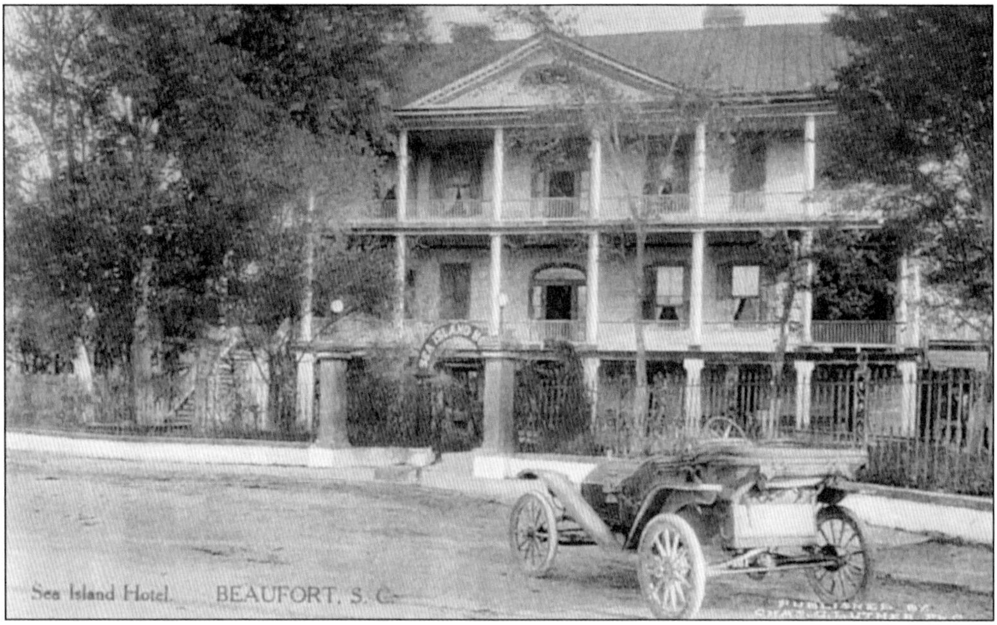


**SEA ISLAND HOTEL, BEAUFORT, S.C.** (Hand-Colored Collotype, 3 1/2" x 5 1/2", Albertype Co., Brooklyn, NY; 1913.) The Sea Island Hotel, once on the northeast corner of Bay and Newcastle Streets, was erected *c.* 1820 as Scotsman George Mosse Stoney's home, later served as General Saxton's Civil War headquarters, and finally became a commercial hotel for some 80 years. It was razed in 1959 and replaced by the Sea Island Motel in 1960.

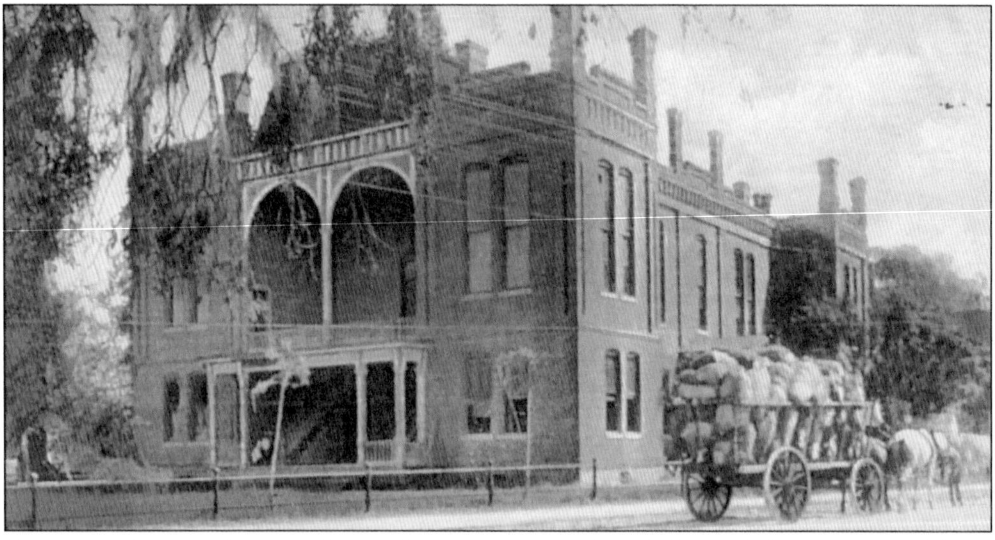

**BEAUFORT COUNTY COURT HOUSE, BEAUFORT, S.C.** (Hand-Colored Collotype, 3 1/2" x 5 1/2", Albertype Co., Brooklyn, NY; C.G. Luther's Drugstore, Beaufort, sponsor; 1912.) The present gleaming white 1930s Federal Deco-style edifice at 1503 Bay, between Monson and Bladen Streets, which was dedicated as a United States courthouse on November 9, 1994, bears little resemblance to the eclectic Romanesque structure above, upon which the radical remodeling was performed in 1936. This courthouse, whose cornerstone was laid with Masonic rites on November 29, 1883, replaced the original one lost to fire: the four-story, residential "Barnwell Castle," in which Lafayette had been entertained on his visit to Beaufort in 1825.

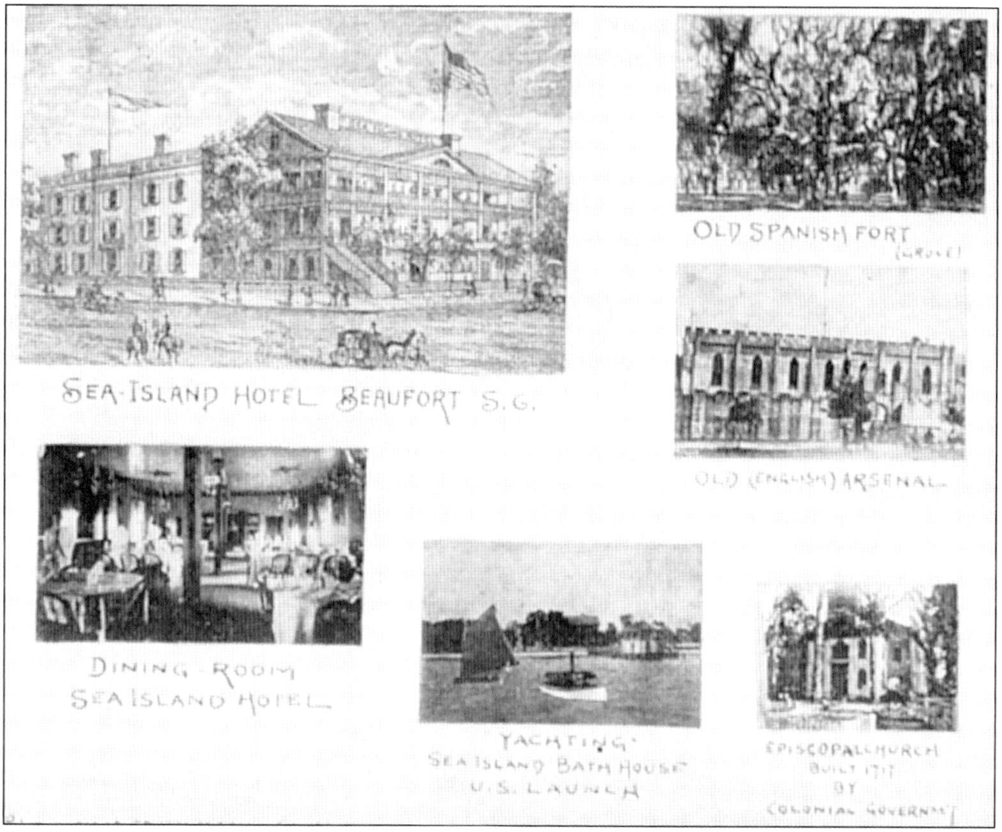


**MULTI-VIEW, SEA ISLAND HOTEL, BEAUFORT, S.C.** (Halftone, 3 1/2" x 5 1/2", Adolph Selige Publishing Co., St. Louis, MO; M. Edward Wilson, Savannah, GA, photographer; *c.* 1906.) The fact that half of the images on this early (1906) multi-view card represent the Sea Island Hotel and its property suggests that it was published as a promotional item for the hotel. The other three views were chosen to highlight some other historical sights of Beaufort: the Old Spanish Fort, the Arsenal, and St. Helena's Episcopal Church.

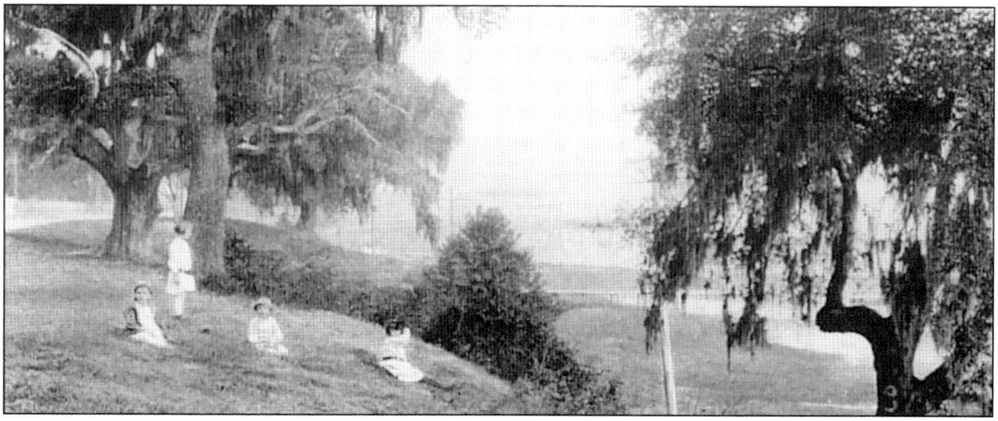

**TWO OF GOD'S WONDERFUL CREATIONS. THE LITTLE CHILD AND NOBLE OAK, BEAUFORT, S.C.** (Hand-Colored Collotype, 3 1/2" x 5 1/2", Albertype Co., Brooklyn, NY; C.G. Luther's Drugstore, Beaufort, sponsor; *c.* 1916.) Marjorie McLeod Fordham (b. 1911), standing, is pictured here with some playmates near her home along The Bluff on Bay Street.

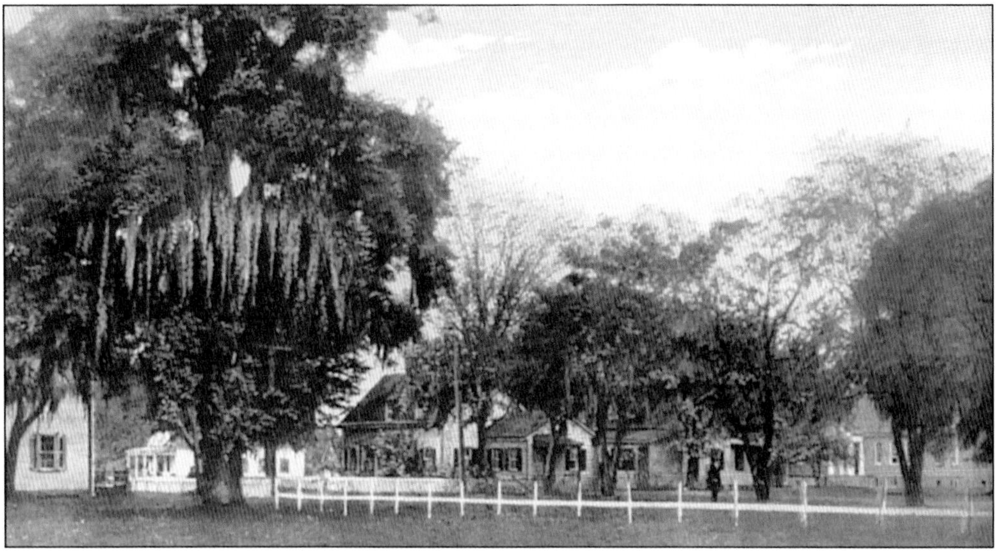

**MATHER[']S INDUSTRIAL SCHOOL FOR NEGRO GIRLS, BEAUFORT, S.C.** (Color Lithograph, 3 1/2" x 5 1/2", Curt Teich Co., #106842, Chicago, IL; *c.* 1929.) The Mather School, once located on the harbor side of Ribaut Road on property now occupied by the Technical College of the Lowcountry, was founded in 1868 by Rachel Crane Mather of Boston. Beginning in 1882, it was operated by the Woman's American Baptist Home Mission Society and offered young black women instruction in the arts of home-making, teaching, and gardening. The school grew in size to a 12-building complex and the status of a junior college before closing in 1968, when it was sold to the state "for the educational benefit of all races."

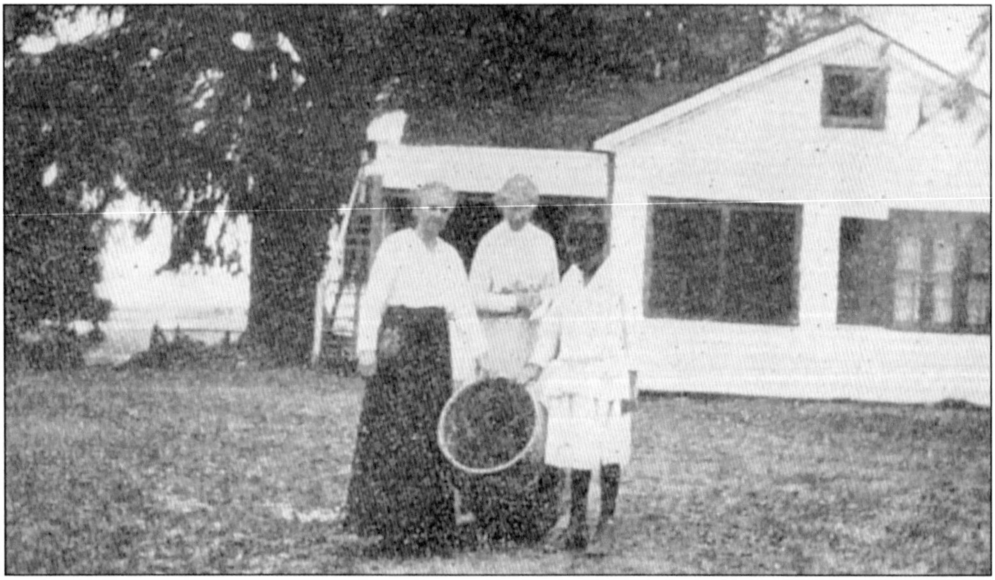

**WHO WILL FILL IT? [MATHER SCHOOL, BEAUFORT, S.C.]** (Halftone, 3 3/8" x 5 1/2"; 1928.) A note, dated February 23, 1928, typed on the back of this card thanks a Mrs. Baldwin and "the Circle" for "the nice new rug and new quilt and other things which you sent to us." It continues as follows: "We hope to save the new things towards helping to furnish the new building. We are also glad for the things for the Saleshouse as its stock is getting low toward the end of our cold winter."

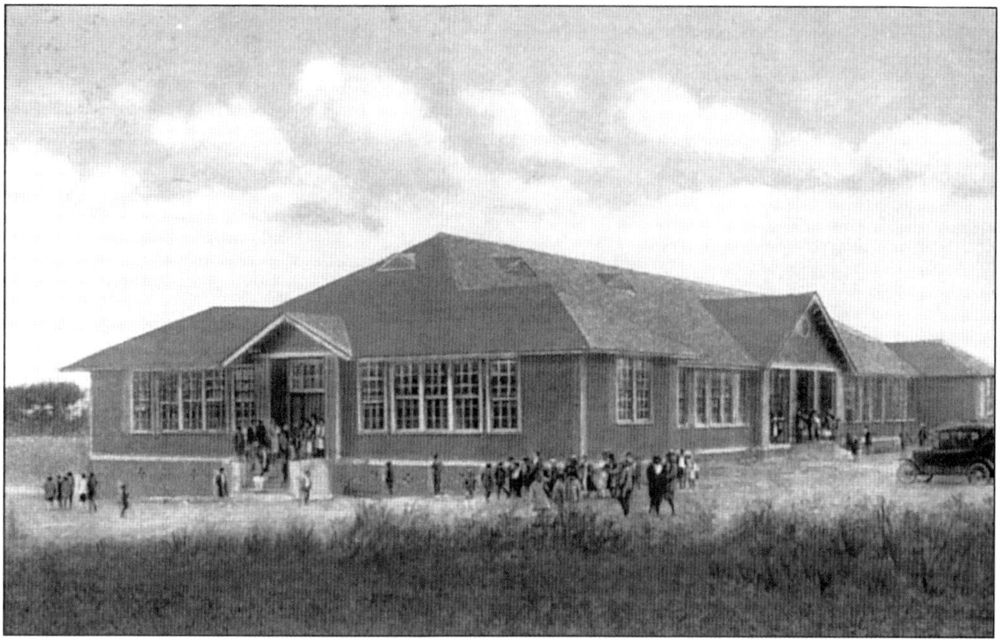

**New Negro Public School, Beaufort, S.C.** (Color Lithography, 3 1/2" x 5 1/2", Curt Teich Co., #106843, Chicago, IL; *c.* 1933.) In 1925, Beaufort opened a new school for black students, located on the western side of town on property bordered by Ribaut Road and Boundary Street. It was named for Civil War hero and political leader Robert Smalls. When it burned in 1932, it was replaced by the brick structure above, which served as a high school and then a junior high school until it was destroyed by fire on April 2, 1965. The Beaufort County governmental administrative complex now occupies the site.

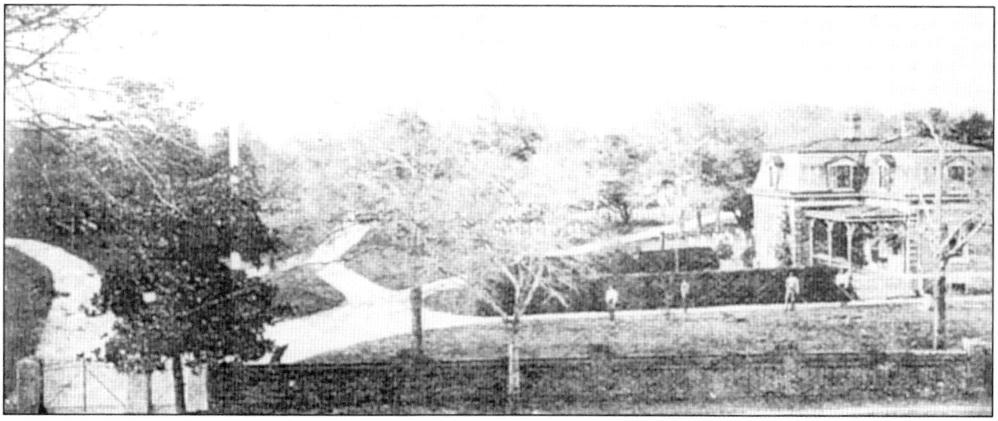

**National Cemetery, Beaufort, S.C.** (Halftone, 3 1/4" x 5 1/2"; *c.* 1900.) This private mailing card featuring a view of the 29-acre National Cemetery, 1601 Boundary Street, is probably the earliest item in the present volume. The cemetery would have been of national as well as regional interest: more than 7, 000 Union and 117 Confederate dead are buried in the cemetery, which was established in May 1868. Captain Niels Christensen (1840–1909), superintendent from 1870 to 1876, beautified it by planting trees, shrubs, and flowers, turning it into a favorite resort both for Beaufortonians and out-of-town visitors. For three or four years he kept a peacock at the cemetery.

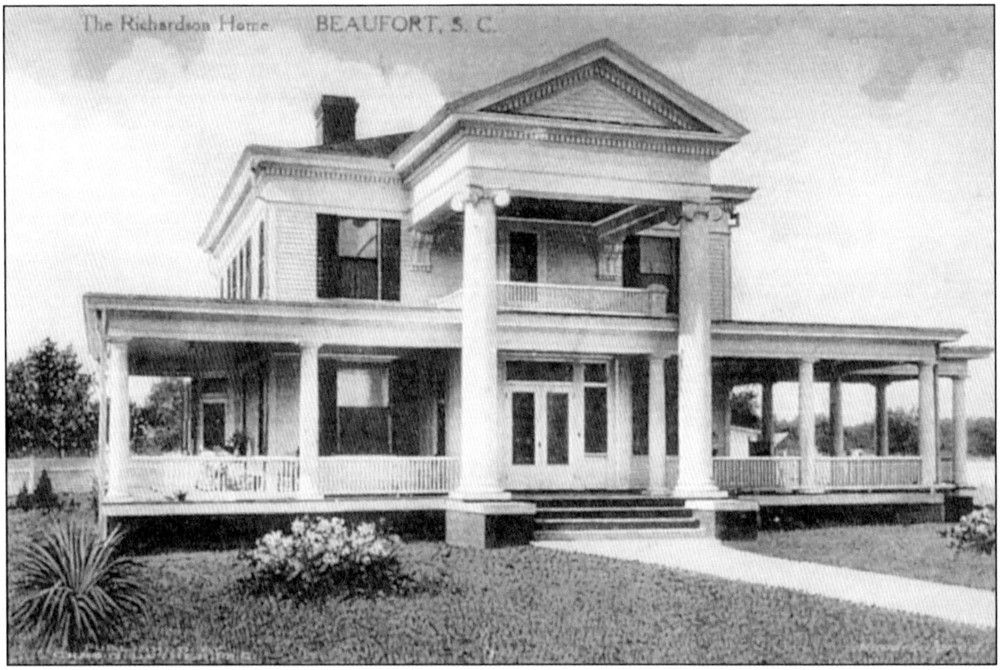


**The Richardson House, Beaufort, S.C.** (Hand-Colored Collotype, 3 1/2" x 5 1/2", Albertype Co., Brooklyn, NY; C.G. Luther's Drugstore, Beaufort, sponsor; *c.* 1920.) The Richardson Home, also called the Barnwell House, once stood off Pidgeon Point Road on Barnwell Bluff, facing the water. It served as the Pius X Center of St. Peter's Catholic Church from 1957 until 1986, when the congregation relocated to Lady's Island. In the late 1980s, the house was moved to Charles Street (1307).

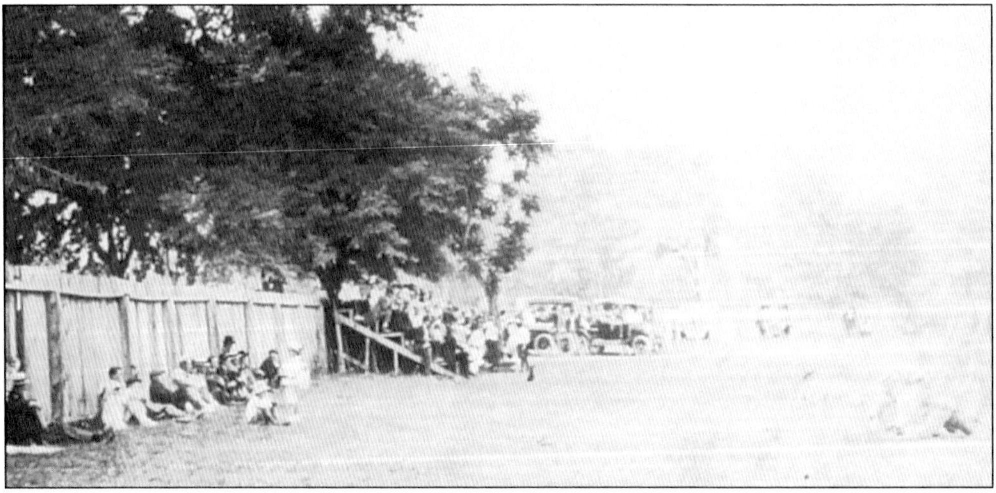

**[Spectators at a Baseball Game.]** (Photoprint, 3 1/2" x 5 1/2"; 1914.) Believed to have been taken in 1914, this unusual view of a baseball game in progress may very well have been of the one between the Beaufort city team and the Naval Station played "at the park" on Field Day, May 22. A boat carried local baseball fans down to the Naval Station when the games were played there (the *Beaufort Gazette*, May 14, 1914). This one-of-a-kind amateur picture was probably taken by a spectator at the game who then had the local camera shop develop the film and make prints on postcard stock.

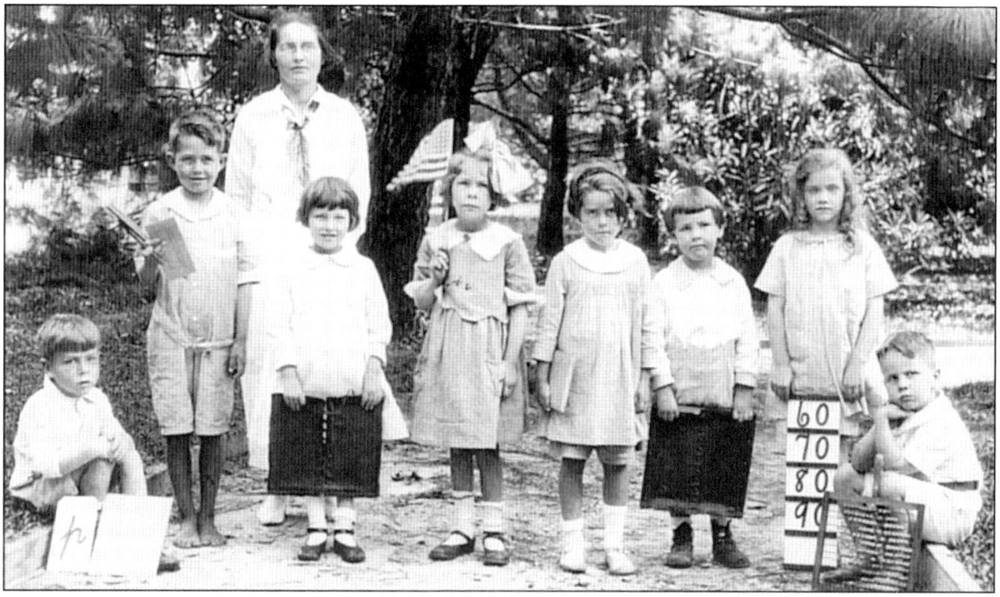

**[Montessori School Portrait.]** (Photoprint, 3 1/2" x 5 1/2"; 1919.) The children in this rare Montessori School picture, presumably taken in the yard of the Christensen residence about 1919, have been identified as (left to right) Herbert Keyserling, Niels Christensen, Marguerite Waterhouse, Caroline Eve, Anne Christensen, Alfred Lengnick, Anne Paul, and Dick Bray. The teacher seen here with the children is believed to be Miss Winnie Christensen. Each student holds some educational device, learning tool, or symbol. The lacing boards held by Marguerite Waterhouse and Alfred Lengnick were used in learning to lace and tie shoes.

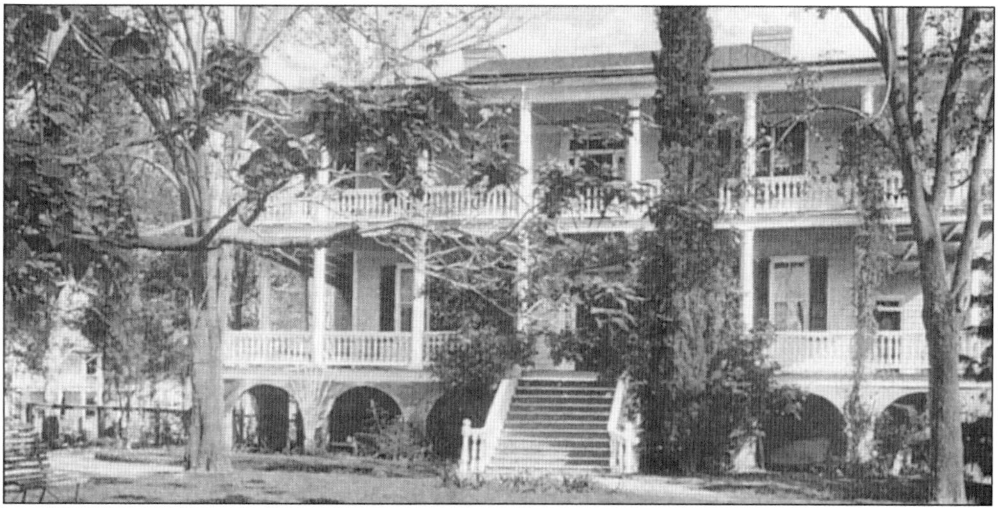

**Christensen's Residence, Beaufort, S.C.** (Hand-Colored Collotype, 3 1/2" x 5 1/2", Albertype Co., Brooklyn, NY; C.G. Luther's Drugstore, Beaufort, sponsor; 1915.) The Christensens' residence, 411 Bayard Street, is believed to have been built in the early 1800s as a parsonage for the Reverend Thomas E. Ledbetter, for many years a minister with the Beaufort Methodist Mission. In 1881, it was purchased by Captain Niels Christensen, a Dane who had come as a young man to Beaufort while serving in the Union army and later returned as superintendent of the National Cemetery. He is said to have designed the garden and planted its unusual trees and shrubs.

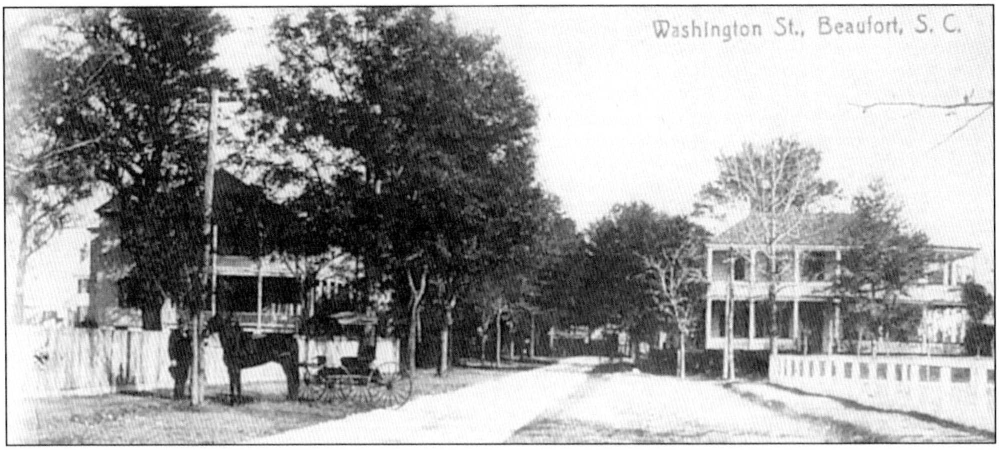


**WASHINGTON STREET, BEAUFORT, S.C.** (Collotype, 3 1/2" x 5 1/2", [Knackstedt and Näther Co., Hamburg, Germany]; Rotograph Co., #65242, New York, NY, importer; *c.* 1907.) Washington Street is actually the street running in front of the two edifices in the middle of this picture and can only be seen as it crosses New Street, which extends into the center of the card from the lower left. The home visible in the distance at the right is Chaplin Court, erected before the Civil War by John Chaplin, who was the father of 22 children. Remodeled in 1931, the Court underwent a restoration in the late 1990s. The campus of the University of South Carolina at Beaufort now occupies the property seen to the left.

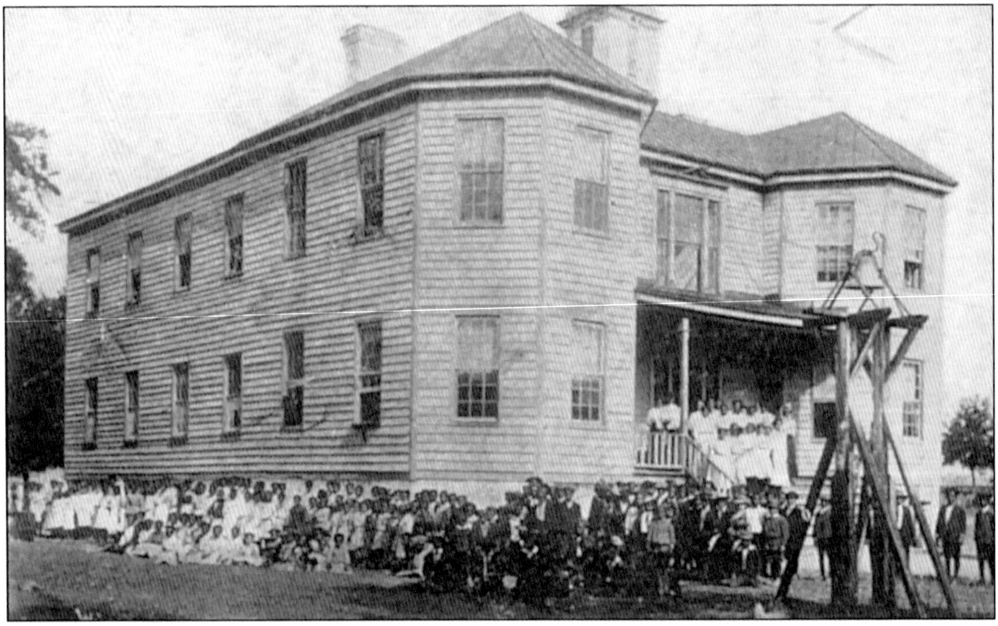

**COLORED PUBLIC SCHOOL, BEAUFORT, S.C.** (Halftone, 3 1/2" x 5 1/2", [Tanner Souvenir Co., New York, NY]; C.G. Luther's Drugstore, Beaufort, sponsor; M. Edward Wilson, Savannah, GA, photographer; 1907.) The school shown here once stood facing Washington Street on the site of the present USC-Beaufort Performing Arts Center. It had been built as a residence by Col. William Fuller (1794–1857) and his wife, Margaret Guerard Fuller (1794–1848), sometime after their marriage in 1828, on property inherited from her father. Reportedly purchased by the school board in 1893, the house was doubled in size and utilized as a school for African Americans until 1925, when it was torn down and replaced by a new school building.

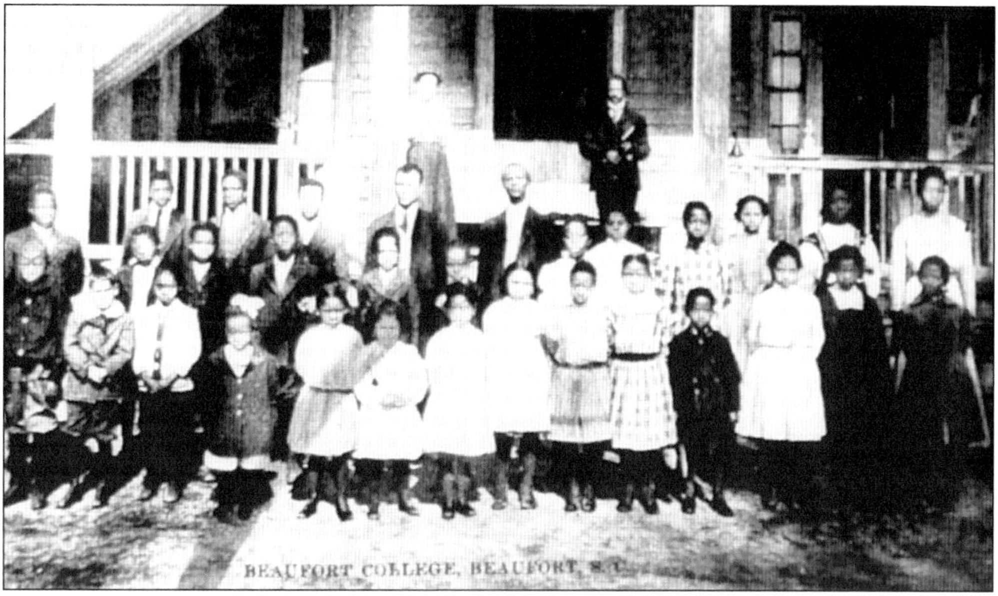


**BEAUFORT COLLEGE, BEAUFORT, S.C.** (Collotype, 3 1/2" x 5 1/2", unknown German printer; American News Co., #AA4734, New York, NY, importer; 1908.) This group portrait of pupils and staff of "Beaufort College" may have been made outside the one-story frame auxiliary building which once stood on Block 31 next to the "Colored Public School," facing Washington Street near the corner of Carteret. The block is now part of the campus of the University of South Carolina at Beaufort.

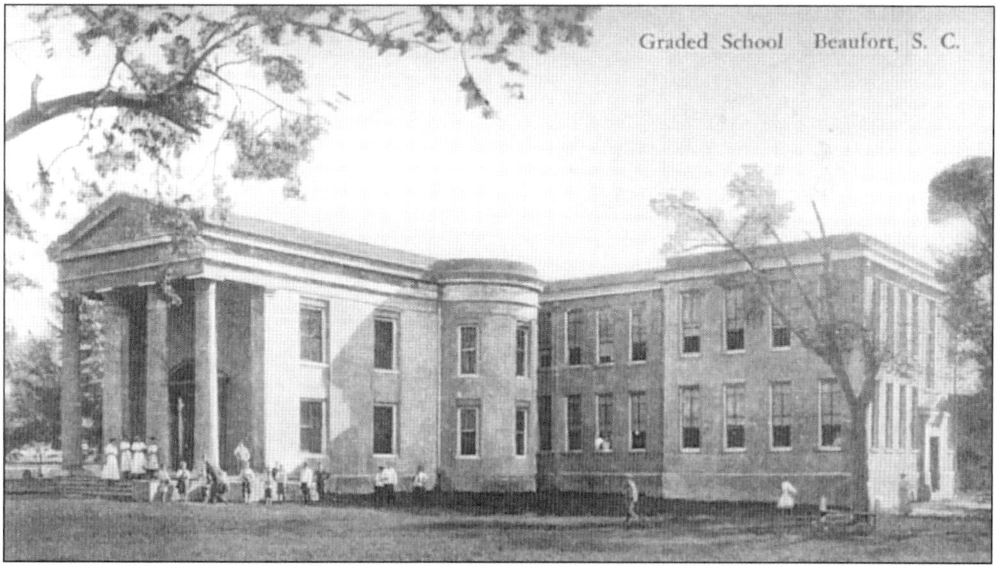


**GRADED SCHOOL, BEAUFORT, S.C.** (Hand-Colored Collotype, 3 1/2" x 5 1/2", Albertype Co., Brooklyn, NY; *c.* 1915.) This simple late Greek Revival edifice was erected in 1852 as a boys' school and is generally referred to as the Old Beaufort College Building. During the Civil War it was used by Federal military personnel; afterwards, by the Freedman's Bureau. Wings were added to the building in 1909, during the early days of its life as a grammar school (*c.* 1904–1940). These were removed after 1957, when it became the centerpiece of the Beaufort campus of the University of South Carolina, at 800 Carteret Street.

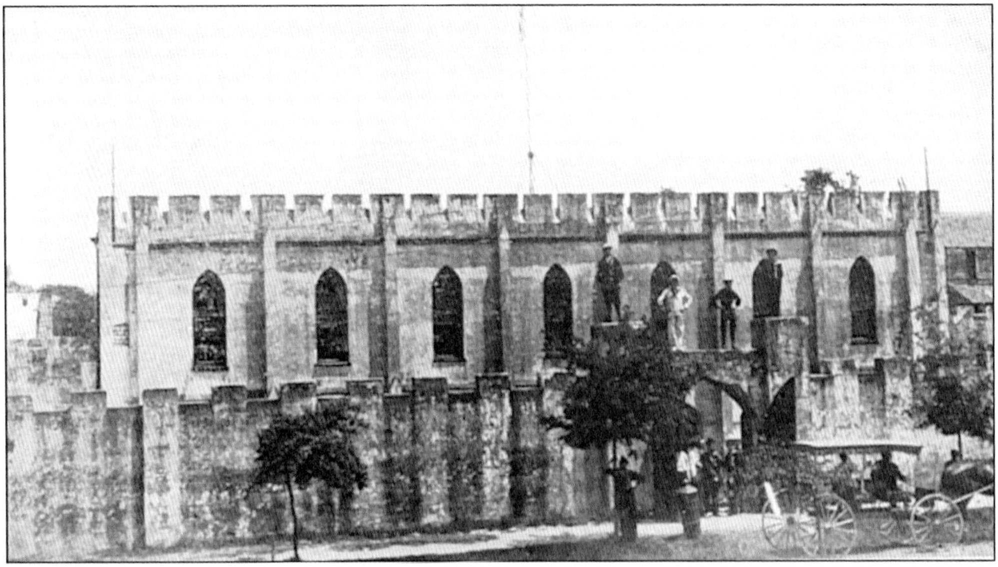

**B.V.A. Arsenal, Beaufort, S.C.** (Halftone, 3 1/2" x 5 1/2", [Tanner Souvenir Co., New York, NY]; C.G. Luther's Drugstore, Beaufort, sponsor; *c.* 1906.) The castellated neo-Gothic Beaufort Arsenal is believed to have been constructed in 1795 on the site of the town's first courthouse. It was rebuilt in 1852 after severe fire damage to its upper story. For many years the Arsenal was home to the Beaufort Volunteer Artillery, the fifth oldest military unit in the United States. Remodeled and furnished by the Women's Civic League during World War I, it became known as the Beaufort Sojourners' Club and served as a recreation center for enlisted men from Paris Island. Today the Arsenal, as the Beaufort Museum, houses a small but valuable collection of historical artifacts and relics of local and regional importance.

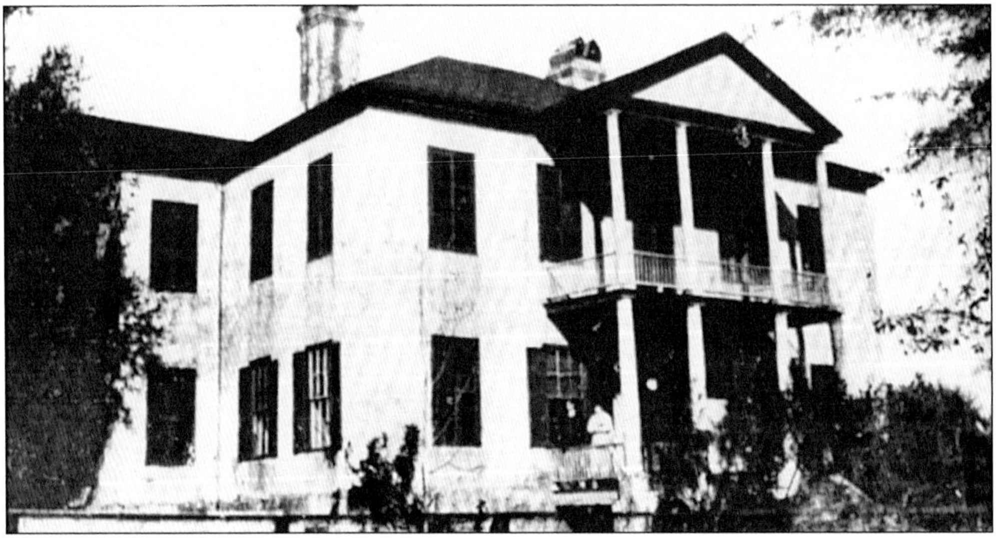

**Baptist Parsonage, Beaufort, S.C.** (Halftone, 3 1/2" x 5 1/2", [Factory to Consumers Co., Knoxville, TN]; 1908.) Beaufort Baptists bought this house on Washington Street early in the twentieth century and used it as the parsonage until 1913, when the decision was made to erect one "on their new lot at the corner of Carteret and Port Republic Streets" (the *Beaufort Gazette*, March 14, 1913). It still stands as the first house on the right-hand side of Washington as one turns west off Carteret.

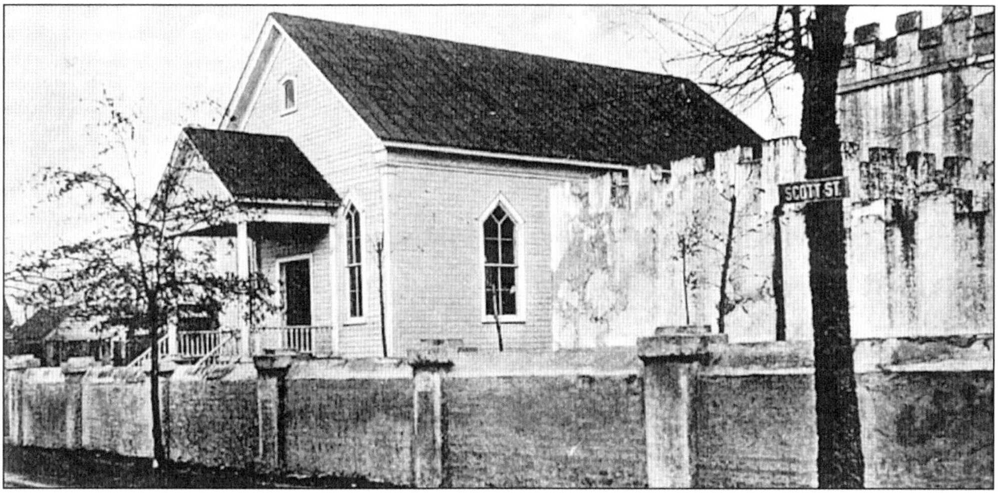


**BETH ISRAEL CONGREGATION SYNAGOGUE, BEAUFORT, S.C.** (Collotype, 3 1/2" x 5 1/2", unknown German printer; American News Co., #AA4729, New York, NY, importer; C.G. Luther's Drugstore, Beaufort, sponsor; *c.* 1908.) On Sunday, February 3, 1907, Mr. P.M. Epstein, president of the Beth Israel congregation, announced to the members that a prominent architect had been in town and taken to the lot purchased as a synagogue site. The architect reportedly said he would draw up plans and have it finished as soon as possible. The simple, unpretentious frame synagogue on Scott Street stands next to the Arsenal. Services are still held—on Friday evenings at 8:00.

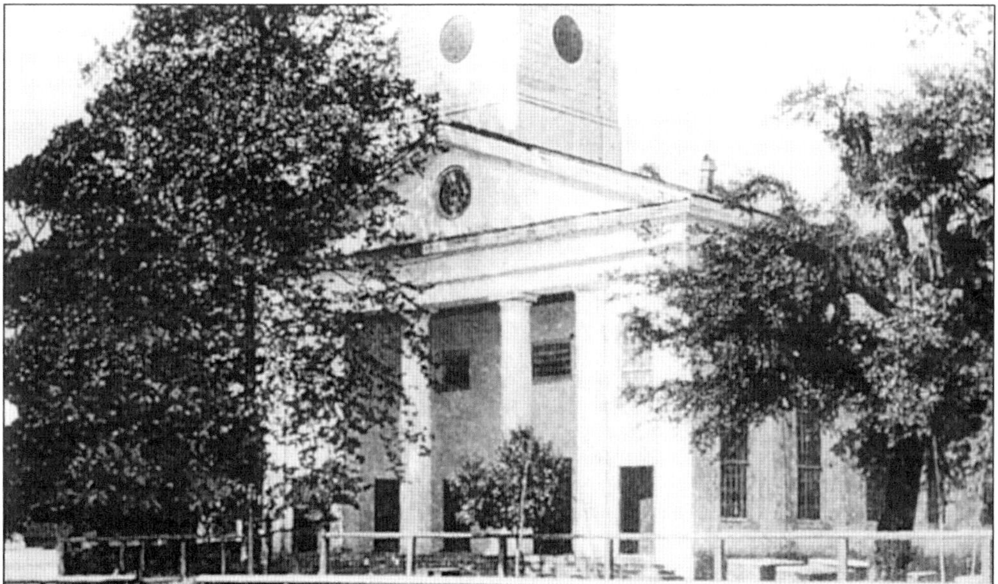

**BAPTIST CHURCH, BEAUFORT, S.C.** (Collotype, 3 1/2" x 5 3/8", [Knackstedt and Näther Co., Hamburg, Germany]; Rotograph Co., #10243, New York, NY, importer; 1907.) The Baptist Church of Beaufort, on Charles between King and Prince Streets, with its well-proportioned Greek Revival exterior finished in white stucco, was completed in 1844. During the Civil War, when Beaufort was a Southern hospital center for Federal troops, this church was used as Hospital 14. Some of the graves in the churchyard bear dates from the early 1800s. The congregation had been organized in 1780.

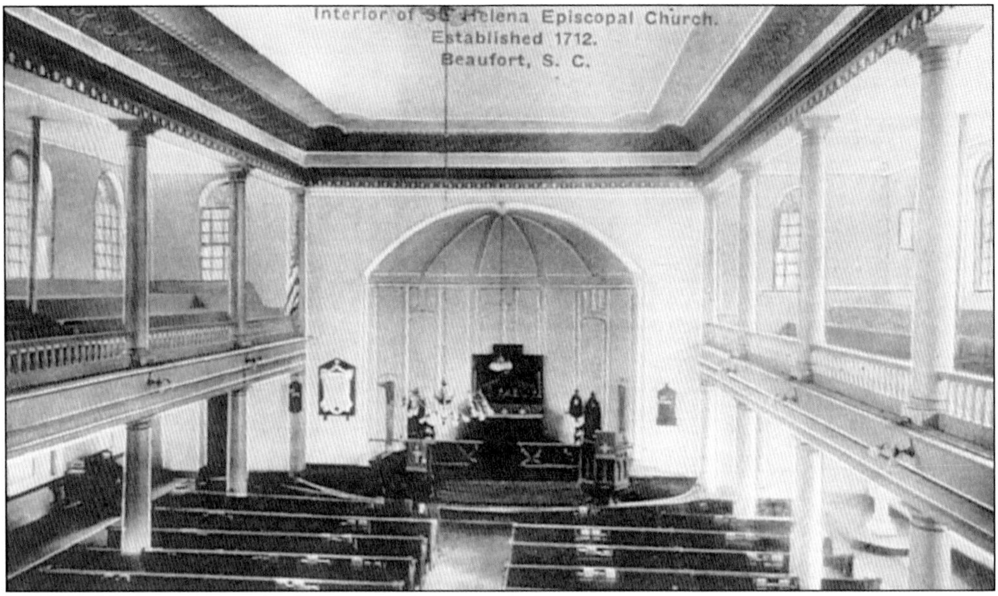


**Interior of St. Helena Episcopal Church. Established 1712. Beaufort, S.C.** (Hand-Colored Collotype, 3 1/2" x 5 1/2", Albertype Co., Brooklyn, NY; C.G. Luther's Drugstore, Beaufort, sponsor; *c.* 1918.) The interior of St. Helena's is characterized by the simple elegance of its colonial style, manifested in the placement and detail of the columns, cornices, and balustrade. Federal troops used the church as a hospital during the Civil War. The altar was given by the crew of the USS *New Hampshire*, which was based at Beaufort sometime after that conflict.

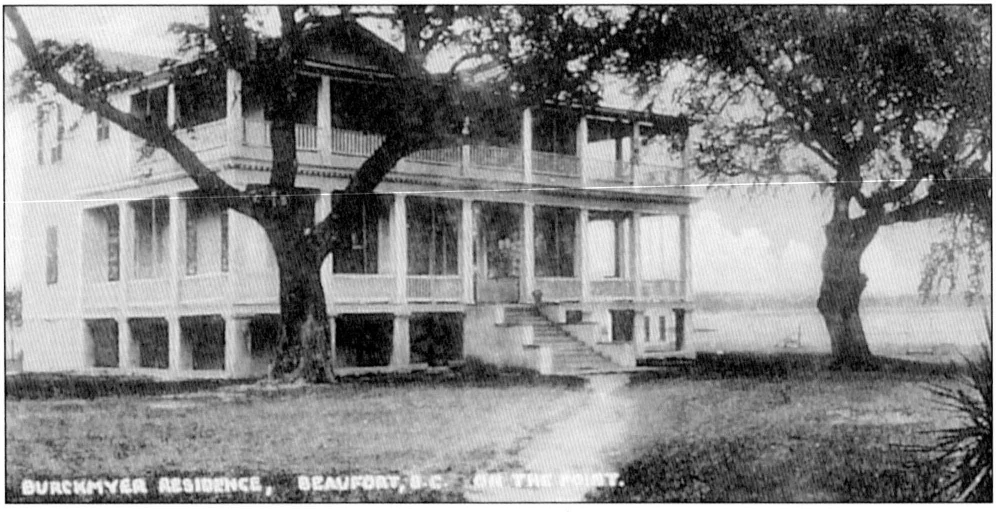


**Burckmyer Residence, on The Point, Beaufort, S.C.** (Color Lithography, 3 1/2" x 5 3/8", American News Co., New York, NY; *c.* 1914.) Owned by the Burckmyer family during this period, the large frame residence at 1 Laurens Street had been built *c.* 1856 as a summer home for St. Helena planter Edgar Fripp. During the Civil War it was used as one of Beaufort's many federal hospitals. Originally constructed as an Italianate villa, with a central tower and a one-story piazza wrapping three sides, it was remodeled after the hurricane of 1893, when the second-story piazza seen here was added. From the 1920s to the early 1970s, "Tidalhold" was a popular guest home. It was restored as a private residence in 1973.

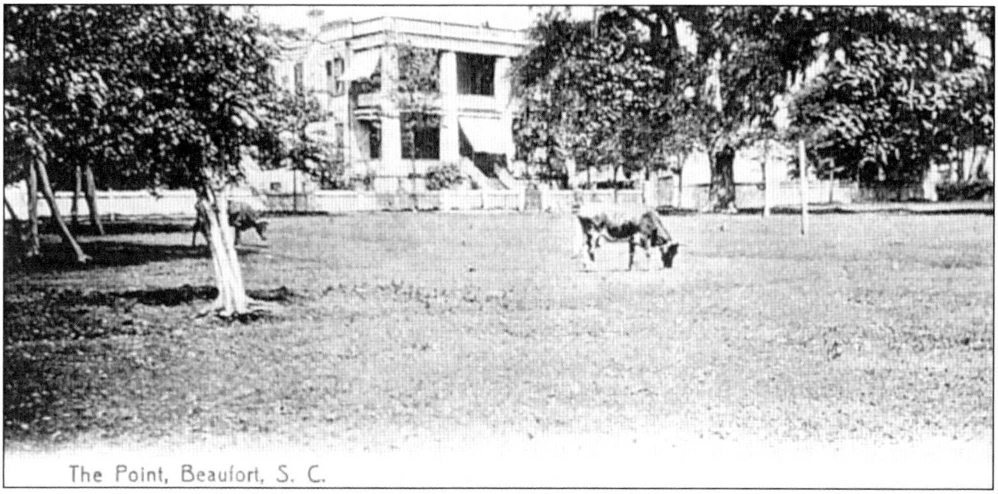


**The Point, Beaufort, S.C.** (Collotype, 3 1/2" x 5 3/8", [Knackstedt and Näther Co., Hamburg, Germany]; Rotograph Co., #59137, New York, NY, importer; 1907.) The Berners Barnwell Sams House, 201 Laurens Street, was built in 1852 and is characterized by its intricate brickwork and huge Doric columns, which support double piazzas across the front. At one time it served as the rectory for St. Helena's Episcopal Church, and during the Civil War it was used as a hospital. In this picture cows graze on the Green, which was also used as a playing field by the children living in this section of The Point.

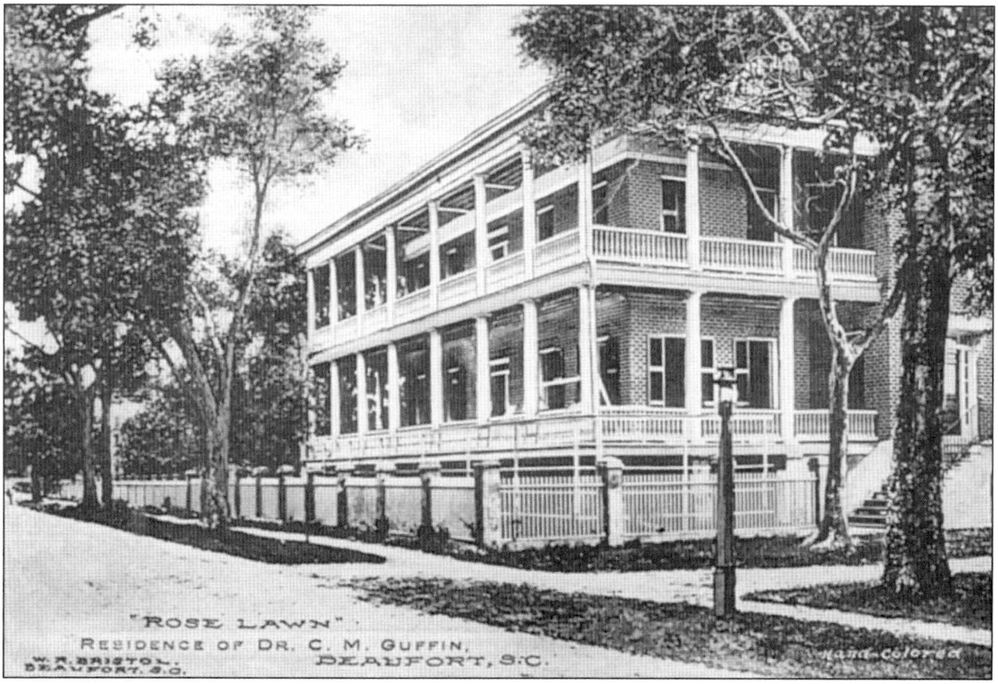


**"Rose Lawn," Residence of Dr. C.M. Guffin, Beaufort, S.C.** (Hand-Colored Collotype, 3 1/2" x 5 1/2", Albertype Co., Brooklyn, NY; *c.* 1920.) Called here "Rose Lawn," the Guffin House, or Johnson House, can still be seen on The Point at the corner of Pinckney and Hancock. It is now painted white.

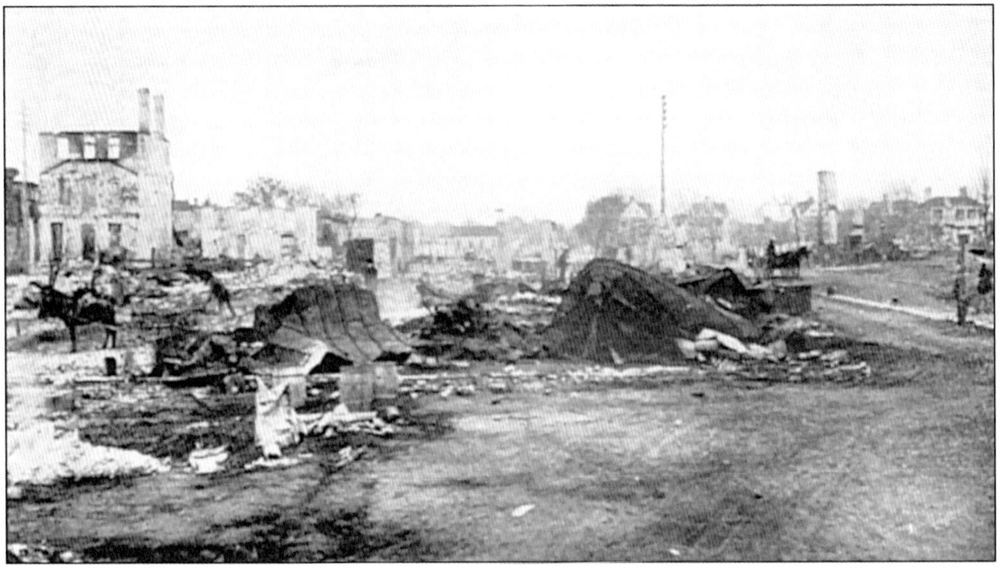

**Fire Ruins from Scheper's Wharf, Beaufort, S.C.** (Halftone, 3 1/2" x 5 1/2", [Tanner Souvenir Co., New York, NY]; C.G. Luther's Drugstore, Beaufort, sponsor; 1907.) The scope of the disastrous fire which broke out in Beaufort on Saturday afternoon, January 19, 1907, is caught in this view looking north from the corner of Bay and Carteret, where it was first discovered near buildings connected with F.W. Scheper's store. Considered the "most serious conflagration that ever visited the old town," it was spread northwest and eastward by brands of fire and flaming cotton fibers carried by high winds onto the flammable shingle roofs of businesses and residences. Over 40 buildings were destroyed at an estimated loss of $175,000. In the distance are the Arsenal and the Presbyterian Church.

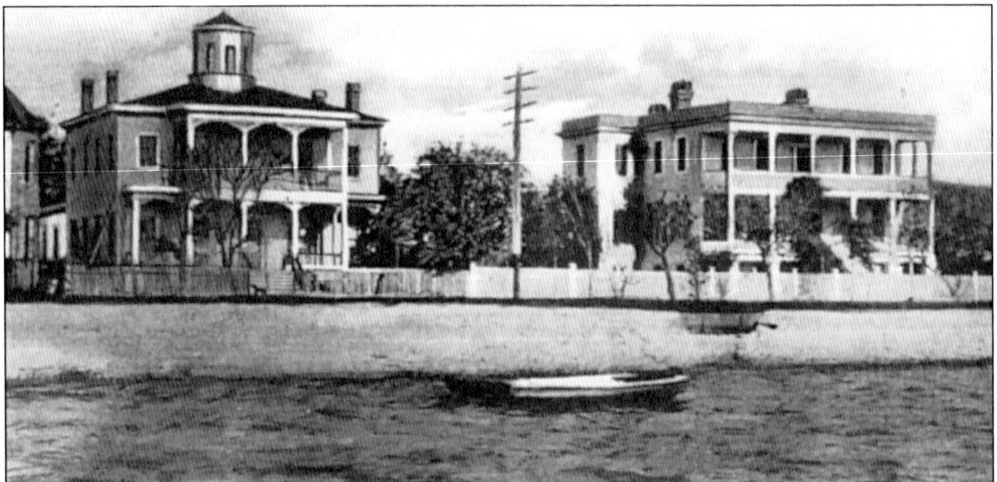

**Water Front, Beaufort, S.C. [Before Fire].** (Collotype, 3 1/2" x 5 1/4", [Knackstedt and Näther Co., Hamburg, Germany]; Rotograph Co., #A53614, New York, NY, importer; 1906.) This pre-1907 card shows, at left, the two-story clapboard house which burned in 1907 and was replaced in 1909 by the concrete stone block Victorian residence at 607 Bay erected by William Joseph Thomas. The Waterhouse home, at right, built by Lewis Reeve Sams in 1852, was reportably saved from the fire by the bucket-brigade efforts of the Waterhouse cotton gin workers, who also used wet blankets to beat out the flames.

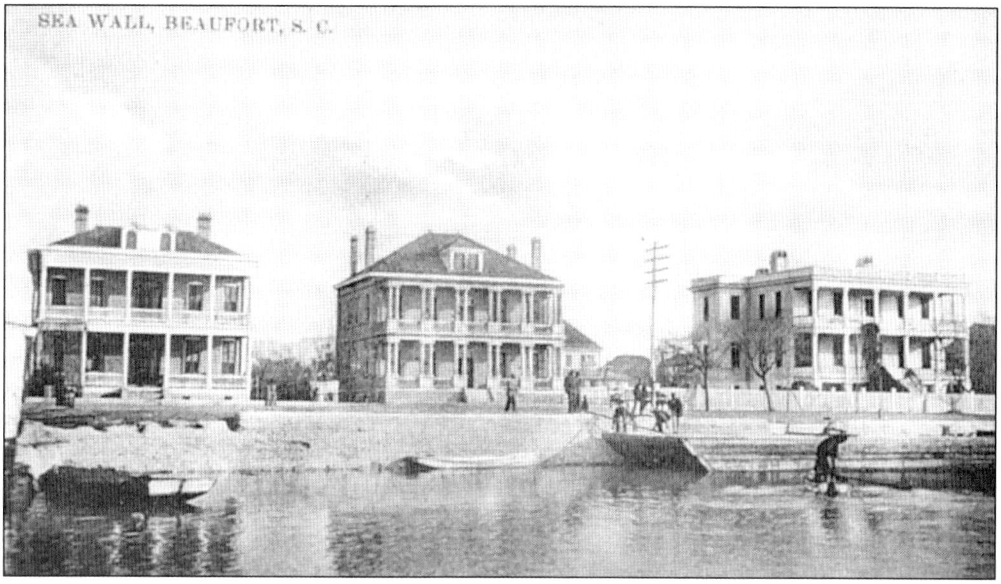


**SEA WALL, BEAUFORT, S.C.** (Collotype, 3 1/2" x 5 1/2", unknown German printer, American News Co., #AA4727, New York, NY, importer; *c.* 1909.) The view of the Thomas House here, the middle of the three residences, indicates that this picture was made during or after 1909, when it was rebuilt after the fire of 1907. The three original families on this block—the Fullers, the Elliotts, and the Samses—built the sea wall, made of oyster shell, and, according to *A Guide to Historical Beaufort* (1978), deeded the lots across from their homes to the town, with the provision that nothing would ever be built on them.

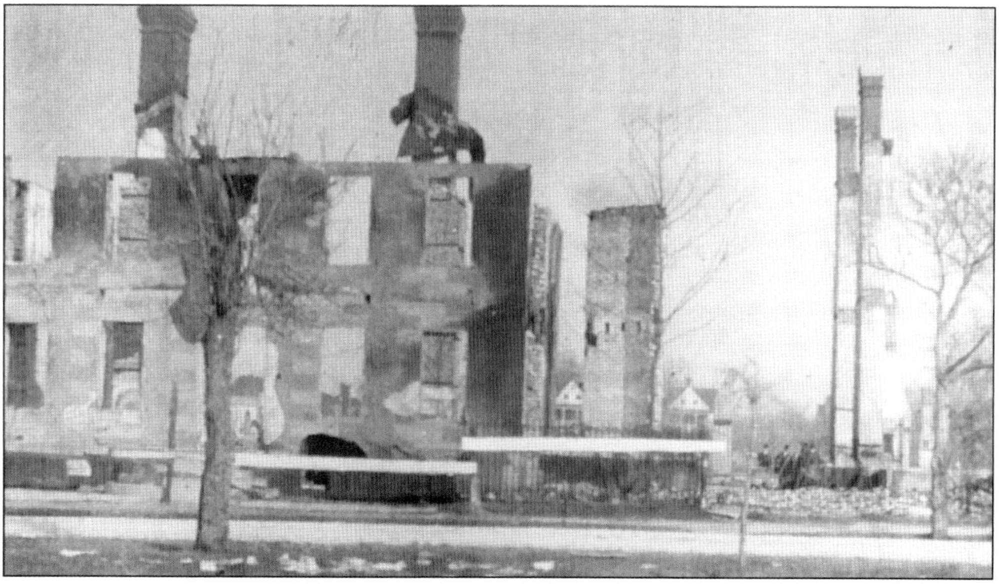

**[1907 FIRE SCENE, WALLACE HOUSE, BAY STREET.]** (Photoprint, 3 1/2" x 5 1/2"; 1907.) After the 1907 fire, this gutted hulk was all that remained of the two-story Federal tabby home which had once belonged to Dr. Thomas Fuller and stood on the northeast corner of Bay and Carteret Streets. It was replaced with the Beaufort-style Wallace House, which features fine Victorian period millwork. In recent years this edifice at 611 Bay has been adapted for use as shops and apartments.

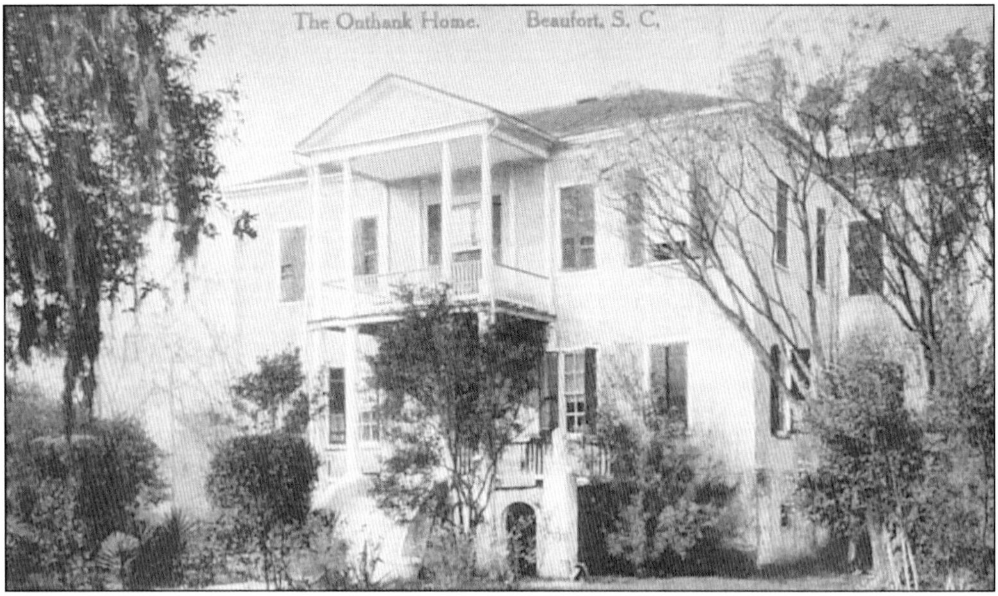


**THE "ONTHANK HOME," BEAUFORT, S.C.** (Hand-Colored Collotype, 3 1/2" x 5 1/2", Albertype Co., Brooklyn, NY; C.G. Luther's Drugstore, Beaufort, sponsor; *c.* 1918.) The Thomas Fuller home, at 1211 Bay Street, was built *c.* 1786 with 18- to 20-inch-thick walls made of "tapia real," a building material first used by the Spanish and created from a mixture of crushed oyster shells, lime, and sand. Fuller, a merchant and planter, was the father of the noted Baptist minister Richard Fuller. Also called the "Onthank Home," as here, it was constructed in such a way that all the rooms have the advantage of a southern exposure. Identified as the Tabby Manse, it has been on the National Register of Historic Places since 1971.

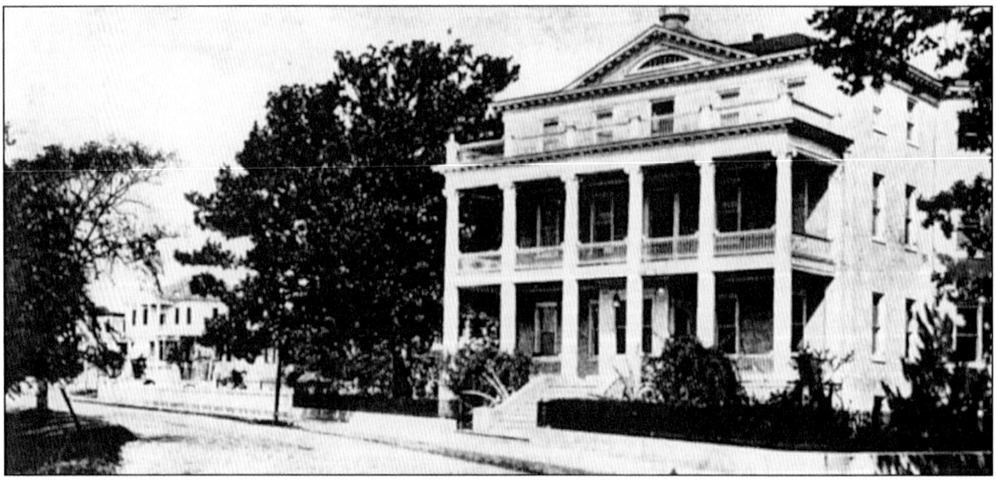

**THE ANCHORAGE, BEAUFORT, S.C.** (Collotype, 3 1/2" x 5 1/2", [Stengel & Co., Dresden, Germany]; H.L. Woehler, #1780, Buffalo, NY, importer; *c.* 1907.) This three-story tabby house at 1103 Bay Street, built by William Elliott I before the Revolutionary War, was not known as "The Anchorage" until it was given that name by Admiral Lester A. Beardslee (d. 1903), the former Port Royal Naval Station commandant who retired to Beaufort, bought the home, and spent $80,000 remodeling it. Its best-known occupant was author, sportsman, agriculturist, and Unionist William Elliott III (1788–1863). Saved by Historic Beaufort Foundation, it is now on the National Register of Historic Places.

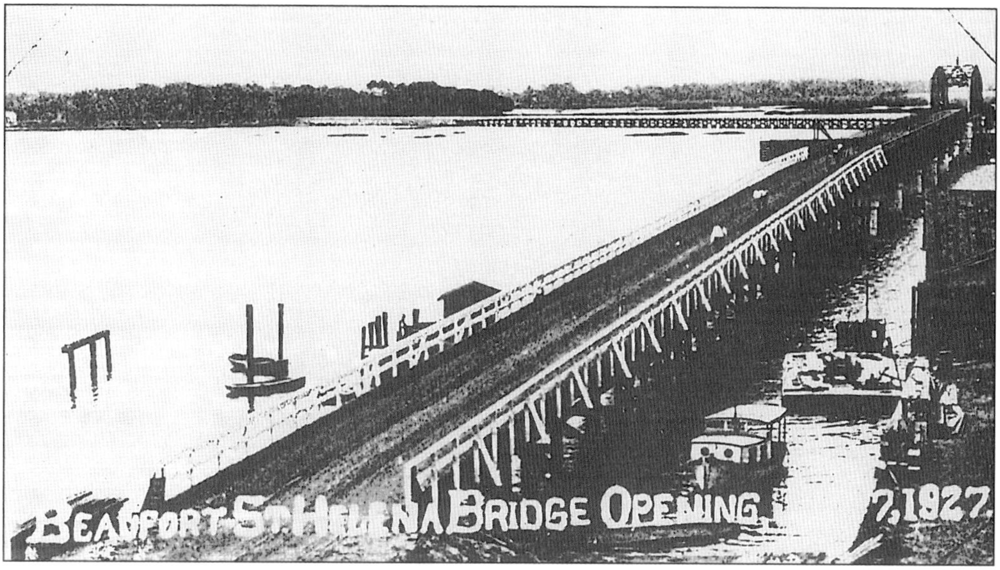


**BEAUFORT-ST. HELENA BRIDGE OPENING.** (Photoprint, 3 1/2" x 5 1/2"; 1927.) The .7-mile-long, $350,000 Beaufort-St. Helena Bridge, hailed as "one of the most beautiful structures in the state" and the fulfillment of "a dream of a quarter of a century," was opened on July 7, 1927, with a two-day celebration which featured parades, oratory, barbecue, music, dancing, and "general glad-handing" among the 3,000 visitors who attended. The Richard V. Woods Memorial Bridge replaced this one in 1971.

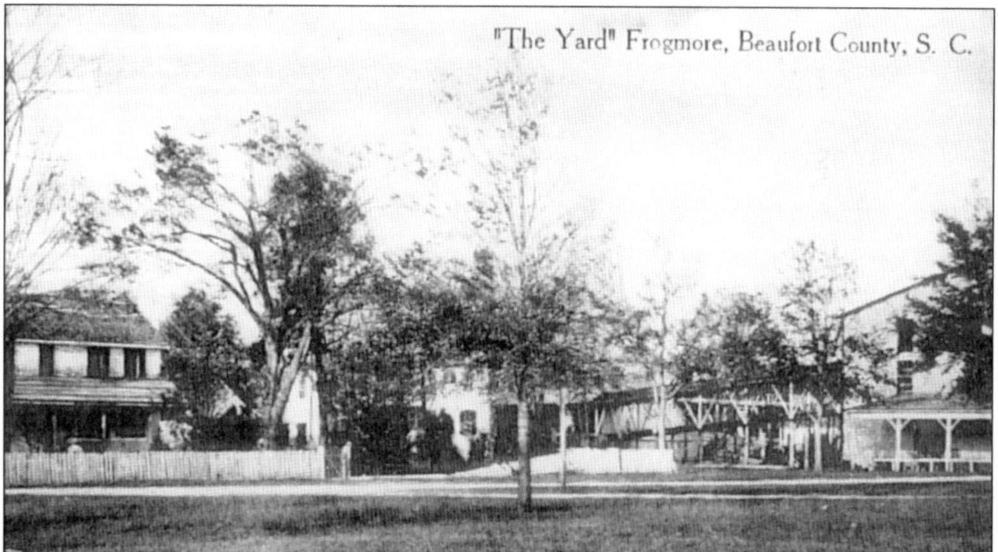


**"THE YARD," FROGMORE, BEAUFORT COUNTY, S.C.** (Collotype, 3 1/2" x 5 3/8", Illustrated Post Card Co., New York, NY, importer; 1910.) Fuller's Place, or the Yard, near the center of St. Helena Island, was the location not only of the residence of Dr. Robert Fuller (at the left), but also of a large cotton gin and a huge store right at the landing point. According to historian Edith M. Dabbs, the Yard was a shipping point for much of the island's cotton. She describes the home as facing the water where schooners came in to load produce to be delivered to the ocean-going steamers at Savannah or Charleston.

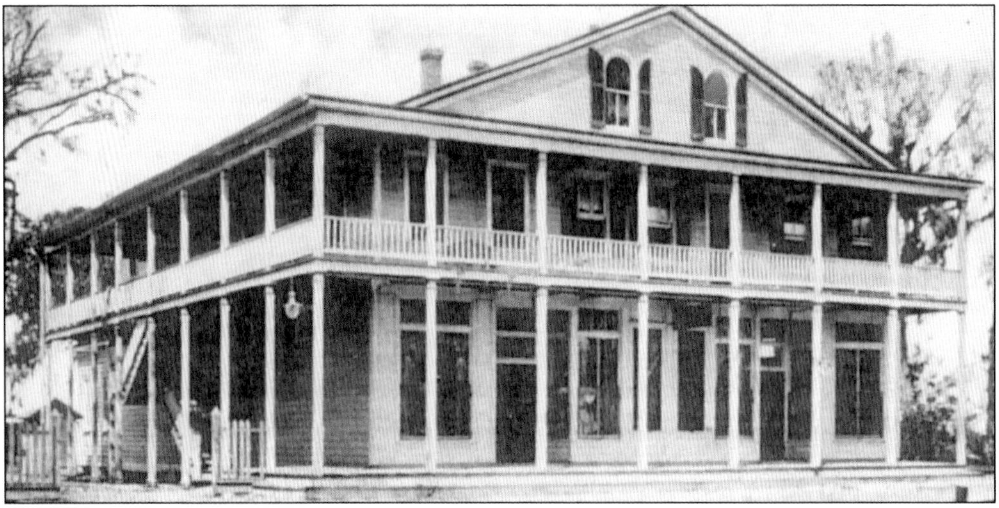

**"THE CORNER STORE," FROGMORE, BEAUFORT COUNTY, S.C.** (Collotype, 3 1/2" x 5 3/8", Illustrated Post Card Co., New York, NY, importer; *c.* 1910.) Still standing on Highway 21 East at Frogmore, the two-story Victorian Commercial-style store built *c.* 1877 by James Ross Macdonald (d. 1917) later became known as Sutcliffe Grocery and Hardware. Macdonald, who as a young man had come south from Rhode Island for his health, bought Frogmore Plantation after the death of Penn School teachers Laura Towne and Ellen Murray. Macdonald's store today houses the Red Piano Too Art Gallery.

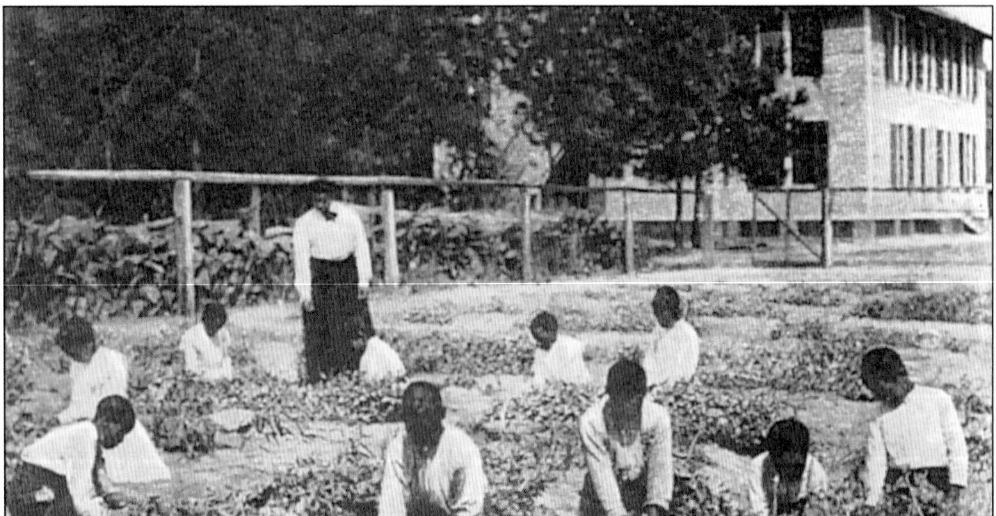

**FROM PENN SCHOOL, ST. HELENA ISLAND, S.C.** (Collotype, 3 1/2" x 5 1/2"; 1911.) The picture postcard was a perfect, inexpensive means of publicizing the architecture, way of life, achievements, and needs of an institution like Penn Normal, Industrial, and Agricultural School, located 8 miles from Beaufort on St. Helena Island. Founded in 1862 as a school for freed slaves, Penn became the center for promoting black islanders' education, welfare, health, and heritage. When P.W. Dawkins became the school's superintendent of industries early in the twentieth century, he made the 90-acre school farm a demonstration model and mandated the teaching of practical agriculture to all older pupils, most of whom were destined to become engaged in some phase of the small-farm economy which supported St. Helena.

**Near Penn School, St. Helena Island, S.C.** (Collotype, 5 1/2" x 3 1/2"; 1911.) Edith Dabbs in *Face of an Island* (1970) identifies the woman in this picture as Mrs. Green, shown standing in front of her home adjoining Penn School property at the waterfront. The photograph was taken by Connecticut native Leigh Richmond Miner (1864–1935), whose work is the focus of Mrs. Dabbs's book.

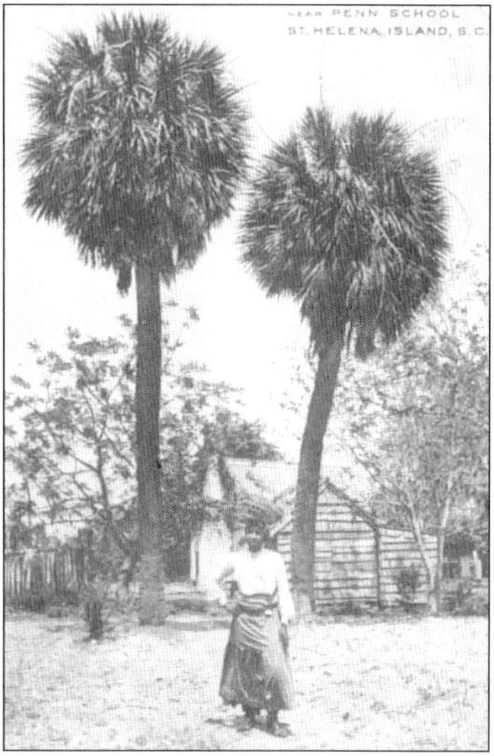


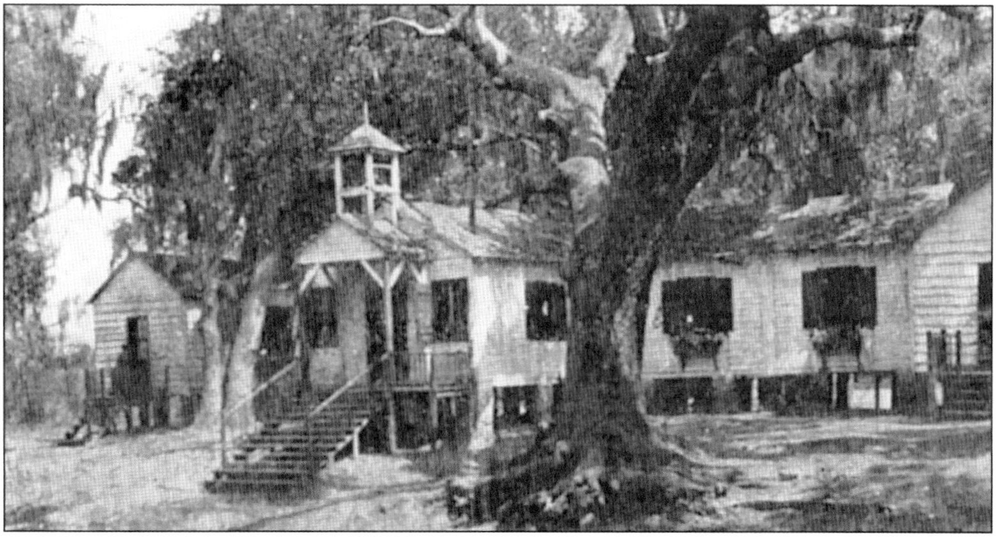

**First School Building, Penn School, St. Helena Island, S.C.** (Halftone, 3 1/2" x 5 1/2", *c.* 1915.) Seen here, with later additions, is the original schoolhouse at Penn (actually the second in the South erected for the purpose of teaching the freedmen), situated in a field opposite Brick Church and assembled from three small one-room army surplus houses purchased in Boston and shipped south by boat in 1864. In 1903, one of the school's founding teachers, Ellen Murray, would write that the building, "enlarged, propped up and mended," was "still our schoolhouse." Edith Dabbs says in her 1983 book, *Sea Island Diary*, that it practically collapsed of old age after serving continuously for 40 years.

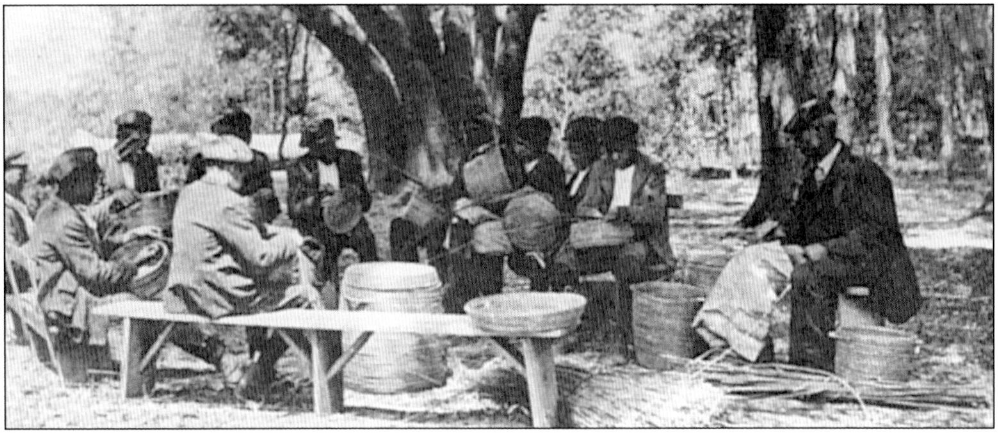

**MAKING BASKETS AT PENN SCHOOL, ST. HELENA ISLAND, S.C.** (Collotype, 3 1/2" x 5 1/2"; 1911.) Baskets had always been essential to the residents of isolated St. Helena, where since plantation times the people had made and used them as their basic containers and carriers. The ancient art and science of making baskets was kept alive at Penn through the services of craftsmen who passed down their skills from generation to generation. Edith Dabbs mentions two such teachers at the school: Alfred Graham, who learned basket-making from his granduncle who had brought it from Africa, and his grand-nephew George Brown. Their baskets were considered excellent.

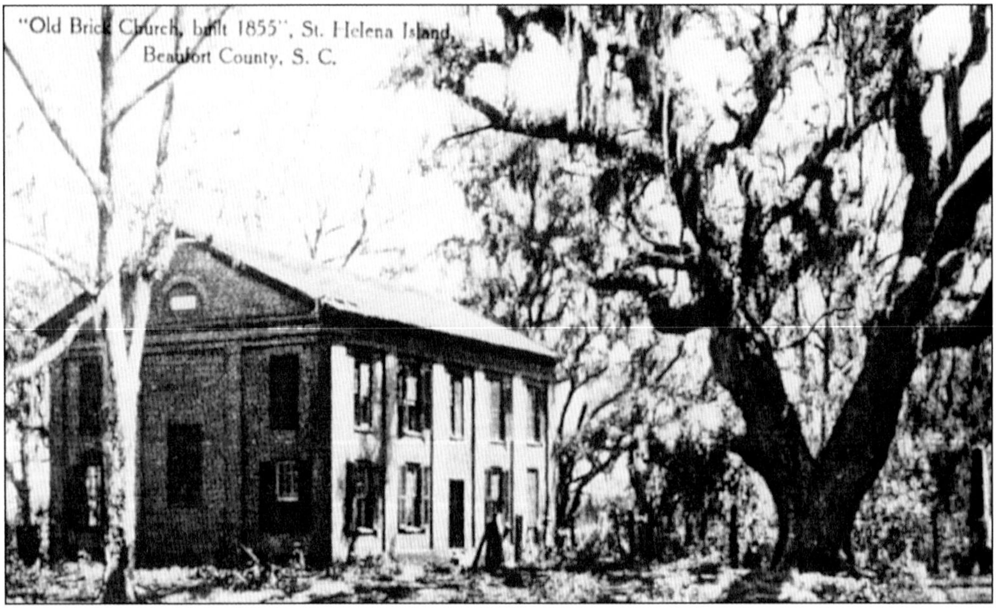


**"OLD BRICK CHURCH, BUILT IN 1855," ST. HELENA ISLAND, BEAUFORT COUNTY, S.C.** (Collotype, 3 1/2" x 5 3/8", [Illustrated Post Card Co., New York, NY, importer]; 1911.) Located on Road 45, Central Baptist Church, or St. Helena Baptist Church—"Brick Church," as it is best known—is a part of the Penn Center National Historic Landmark District. Built in 1855 by Baptist planters on the island, this rectangular, gabled, two-story brick church replaced an old wooden structure on the same site, John Fripp's Corner Plantation. Deserted at the coming of the Civil War by its white members, the church was adopted by the freedmen and during Reconstruction became the center of education and political as well as religious activities for the community of freed slaves and Northern missionaries and abolitionists.

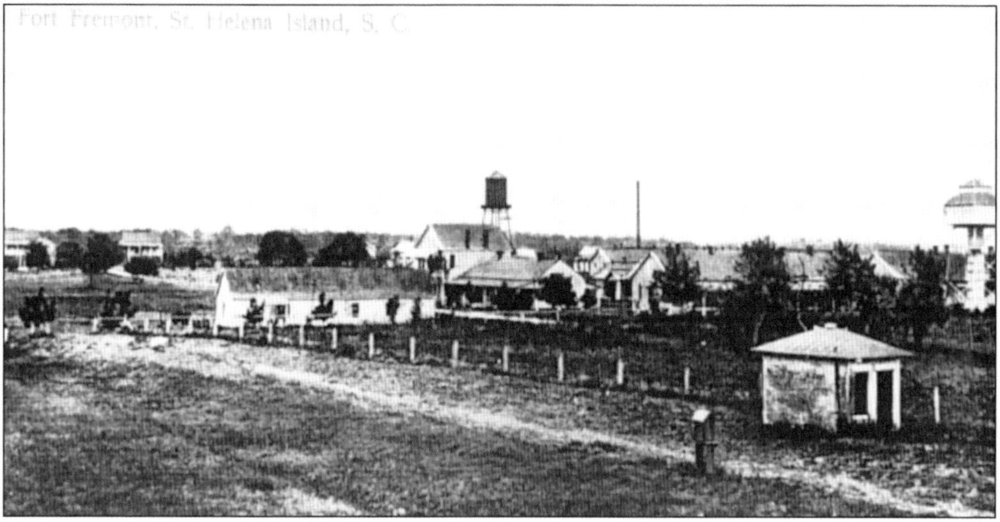


**Fort Fremont, St. Helena Island, near Beaufort.** (Hand-Colored Collotype, 3 1/2" x 5 3/10", [Knackstedt and Näther Co., Hamburg, Germany]; A.M. Simon, #15 513, New York, NY, importer; C.G. Luther's Drugstore, Beaufort, sponsor; *c.* 1909.) Fort Fremont, named for the Savannah-born, Charleston-educated military topographer John Charles Fremont, was hastily erected on St. Helena Island in 1898 as a fortification of Port Royal Sound in the face of threats of a major conflict with Spain. The fort continued to be garrisoned with artillerymen until 1911, when it was decommissioned. In 1930, the remains of the fort were sold to Frederick H. Barnes of Long Island, who lived there until 1946. The property was later developed into a summer resort.

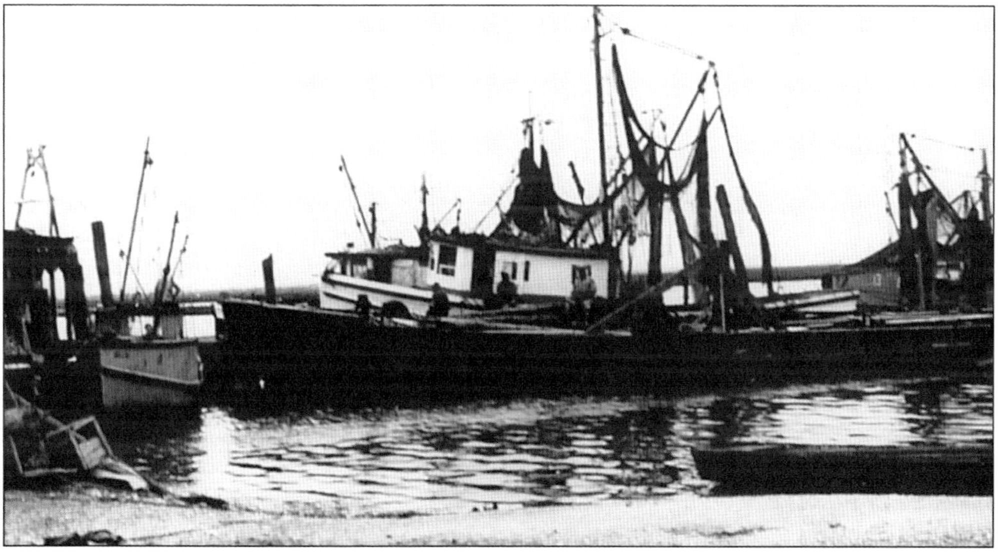

**Shrimp Boats at Coffins Point, Frogmore, S.C.** (Master photograph, halftone, 3 1/2" x 5 1/2", [Curt Teich Co., Chicago, IL]; Asheville Post Card Co., Asheville, NC; *c.* 1928.) The two ocean-going, gas-powered St. Augustine trawlers shown here, center and right, with their nets suspended aft, are tied up on Coffin Creek, on the northeastern end of St. Helena Island near the shrimp-rich waters off Egg Bank. In 1928, Beaufort was the center of the state's fledgling shrimping industry with 96 licensed shrimp boats and nets (as opposed to 13 for Charleston and 3 for Georgetown), an increase of 46 over 1927. The craft at left appears to be a converted yacht.

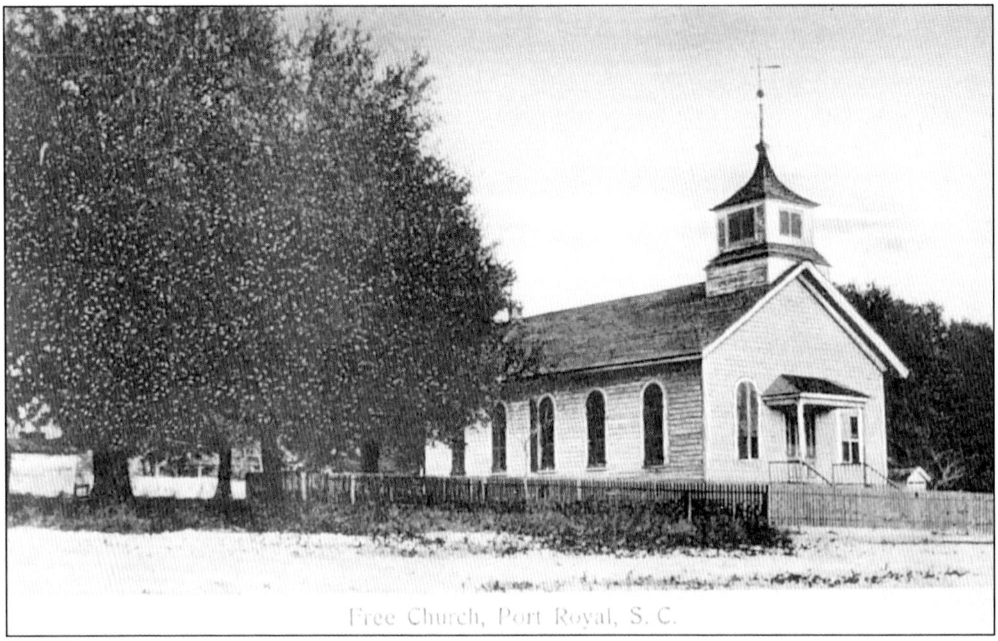


**FREE CHURCH, PORT ROYAL, S.C.** (Hand-Colored Collotype, 3 1/2" x 5 1/2", unknown German printer; Paul F. Trouche, Charleston, SC, importer; 1908.) Port Royal had an estimated population of 500 in 1910. Its Free Church, used by several worshipping communities down through the years, still stands—minus the picket fence—off Paris Avenue on Eleventh Street. It now functions as the Port Royal Playhouse.

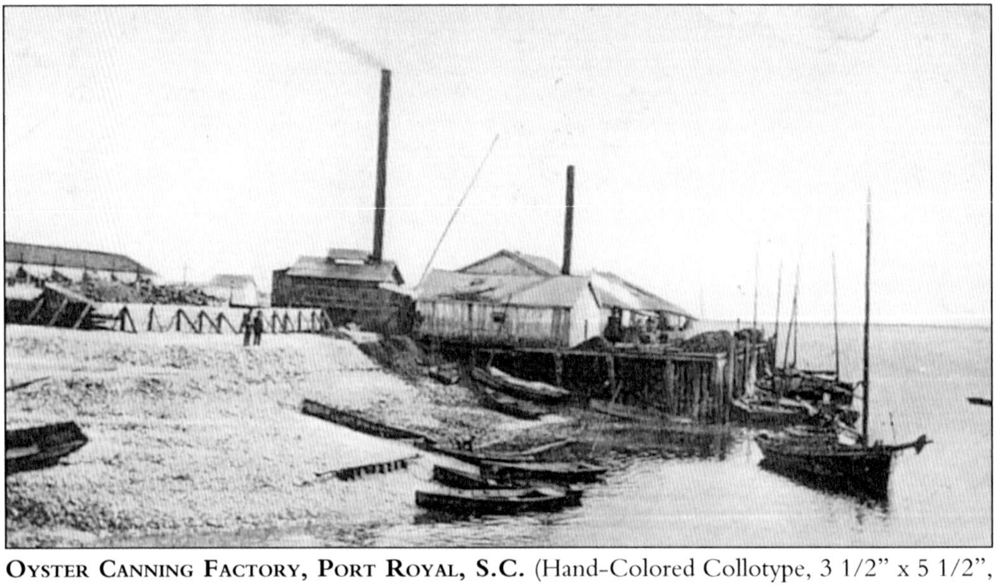

**OYSTER CANNING FACTORY, PORT ROYAL, S.C.** (Hand-Colored Collotype, 3 1/2" x 5 1/2", unknown German printer; Paul F. Trouche, Charleston, SC, importer; 1911.) From 1903 to 1917, the L.P. Maggioni Company operated an oyster factory at Port Royal. In 1911, when this card was sent, Beaufort County collected revenues of $4,281 out of a statewide industry total of $10,588 (see "Trade Conditions in Beaufort," the *Beaufort Gazette*, September 7, 1912). Today at the west end of Eleventh Street a seafood market continues to operate, and nearby the Dockside Restaurant overlooks the shrimp boat docks of Battery Creek.

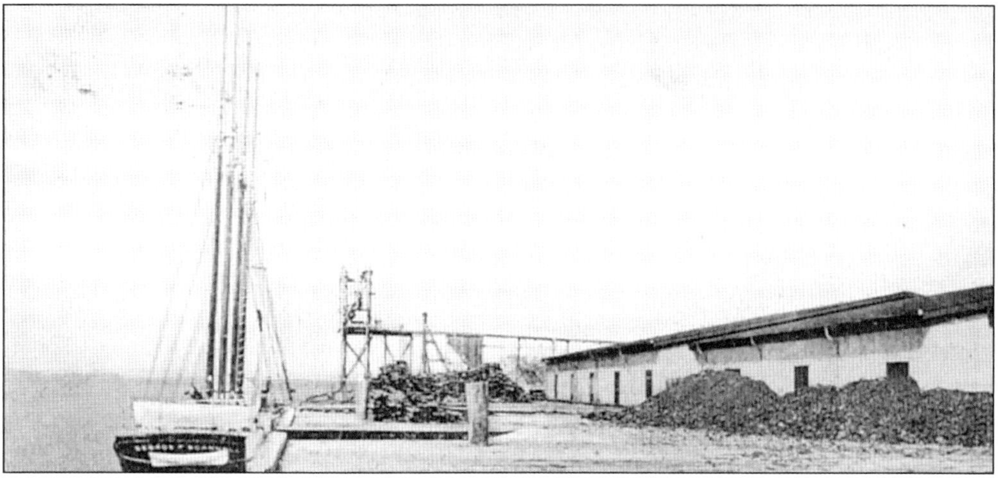

**C. & W.C. Wharf, Port Royal, S.C.** (Hand-Colored Collotype, 3 1/2" x 5 1/2", unknown German printer; Paul F. Trouche, Charleston, SC, importer; 1912.) The schooners seen tied up here at the Charleston & Western Carolina wharf at Port Royal represent the residue of a flourishing nineteenth-century maritime trade centered here, even though the village never developed into the projected "new city of the south"—as the terminus of the shortest railway line to be built from the Mississippi to the Atlantic. Port Royal and Beaufort saw their maritime interests, both commercial and naval, subverted to those of Charleston and Savannah, even though Port Royal laid claim to having the finest natural harbor south of Chesapeake Bay. The building pictured here is gone, and the waterfront property, now Pier 21, is owned by the State Ports Authority.

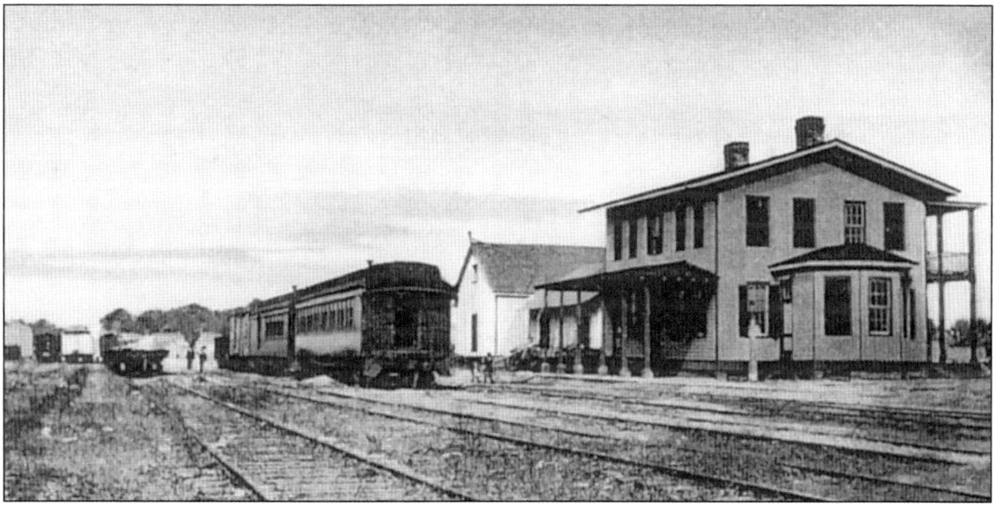

**C. & W.C. Station & Yard, Port Royal, S.C.** (Hand-Colored Collotype, 3 1/2" x 5 1/2", unknown German printer; Paul F. Trouche, Charleston, SC, importer; 1912.) This relatively large, two-story frame station was a modestly impressive one for the eastern land-sea terminus of the Charleston & Western Carolina Rail Road, whose hopes of seeing Port Royal become the most important city on the South Atlantic Coast never materialized. "The C. & W.C. R.R. has signified its intention of doing everything possible to facilitate the resumption of export work through this harbor," a journalist reported in a front-page article in the *Beaufort Gazette*, October 22, 1920, on the special occasion of the docking at Port Royal of the 3,000-ton SS *Summerleaf* with cargo from Germany.

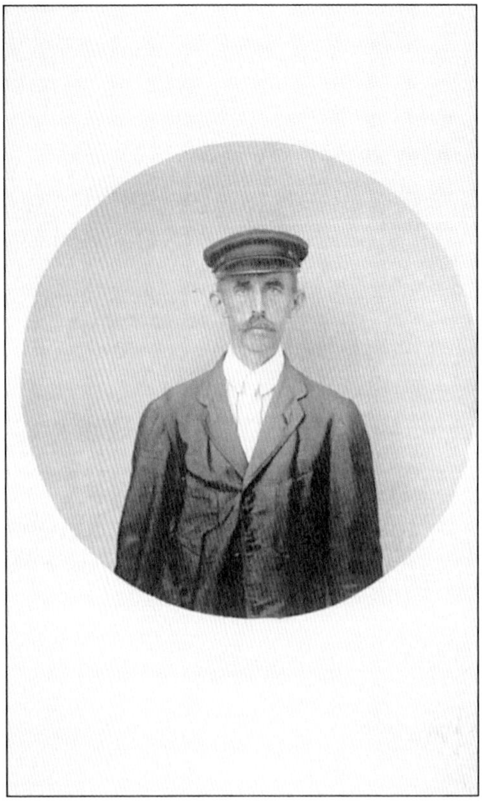

**[Portrait of Frederick William Scheper Jr., Port Royal, S.C.]** (Photoprint, 5 3/8" x 3 3/8"; *c.* 1918.) Beaufort-born Frederick W. Scheper Jr. (1872–1955) succeeded his German emigrant father in running the family store in Port Royal and became one of the town's leading merchants. A pre-World War I store letterhead identifies his functions as those of ship chandler, wholesale and retail grocer, and dealer in hay and grain. Scheper also served as agent for the Propeller Tow Boat Company of Savannah and Pilot Boat No. 1, and in October 1907, he was appointed postmaster of Port Royal. He is said to have owned one of the first automobiles in the Beaufort area. The Port Royal postcards, imported by Paul E. Trouche and used in this section on the town, were sponsored by and sold at the Scheper store.

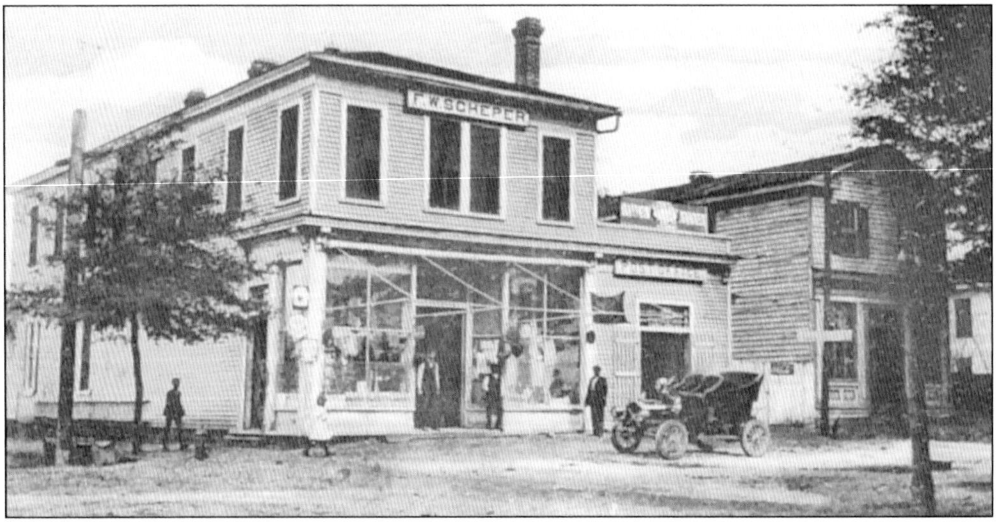


**F.W. Scheper's Store, Port Royal, S.C.** (Hand-Colored Collotype, 3 6/10" x 5 4/10", unknown German printer; Paul E. Trouche, Charleston, SC, importer; 1908.) This *c.* 1908 picture of the northeast corner of Paris Avenue and Eighth Street in Port Royal shows the two-story white frame store of F.W. Scheper (1842–1913), which remained in business from about 1885 to 1955. The one-story building next to it is the post office, in front of which may be parked one of F.W. Jr.'s cars. The two-story building at the far right was a pharmacy. The Scheper store was still standing in 1998, in use as a church and a school.

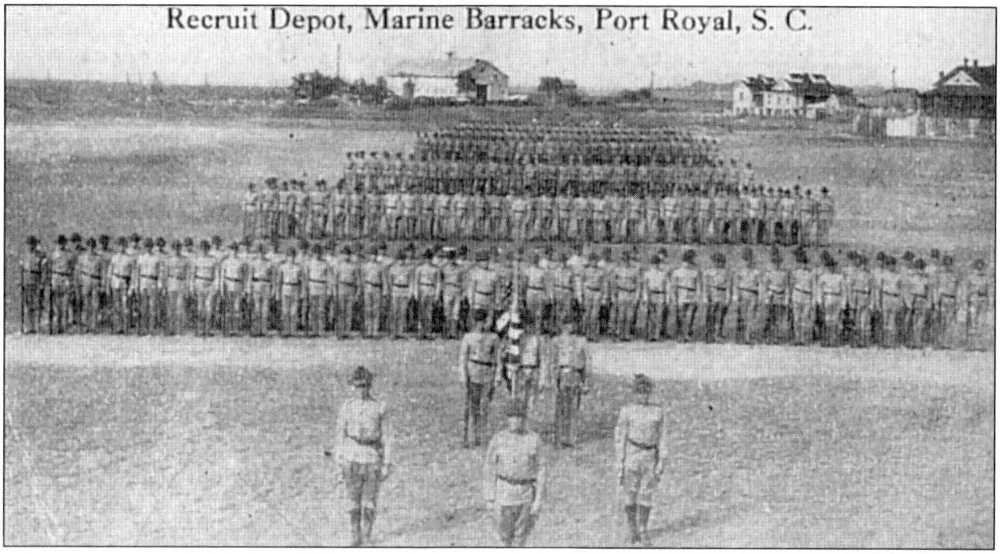


**Recruit Depot, Marine Barracks, Port Royal, S.C.** (Halftone, 3 1/4" x 5 1/2"; 1915.) "South Carolina," wrote Major Edwin N. McClellan in his 1919 monograph *The United States Marine Corps in the World War*, "had close association with the great expansion which the Marine Corps, in common with other components of the Navy, underwent during the war." Two major recruit training depots were set up, at Beaufort and at Mare Island, California. The one at Paris Island, established on November 1, 1915, was the larger of the two, and during the war more than 42,000 men went through the intensive eight-weeks' basic course.

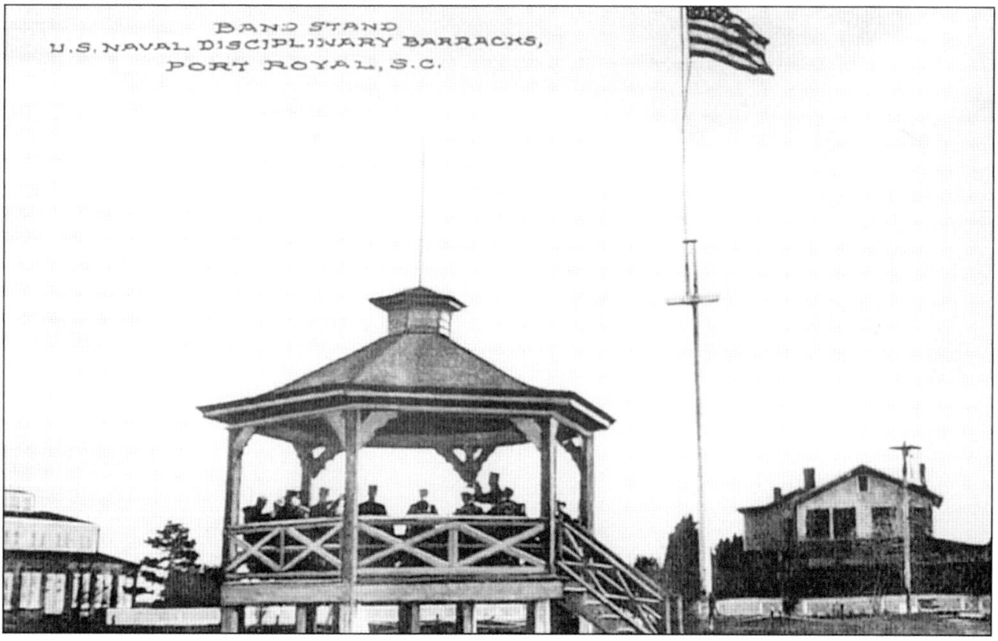


**Band Stand, U.S. Naval Disciplinary Barracks, Port Royal, S.C.** (Collotype, 3 1/2" x 5 1/2", Albertype Co., Brooklyn, NY; *c.* 1918.) Described in current Depot literature as "an octagonal gazebo of Victorian period design," the bandstand still exists on a grass plot across from Quarters One and at the head of the old dry dock on the 2-acre part of the island which has been listed on the National Register of Historic Places.

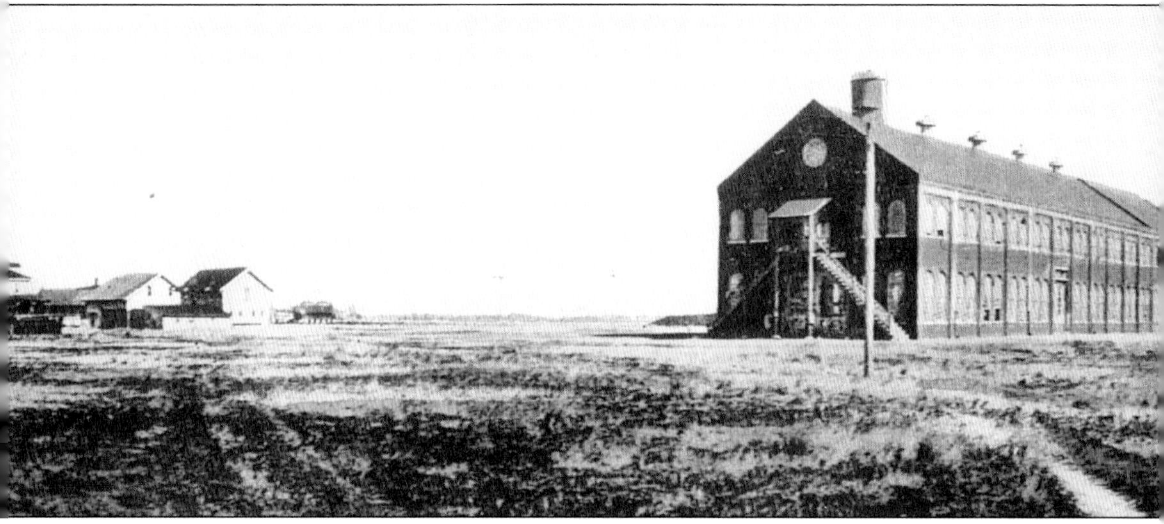

**Pan.[orama] of Naval Station, Port Royal, S.C.** (Hand-Colored Collotype, 3 1/2" x 10 3/4", [Knackstedt and Näther Co., Hamburg, Germany]; A.M. Simon, #15514, New York, NY, importer; 1910.) Parris Island, as Major E.N. McClellan described it in *A Brief History of Parris Island* (1921), is a low-lying piece of land located off the South Carolina coast midway between Charleston and Savannah and opposite Port Royal. It is covered with semi-tropical foliage and is about 10 square miles in area. In 1883, the Federal government purchased the eastern portion of the island for use as a naval coaling and supply station. The completed Naval Station was opened

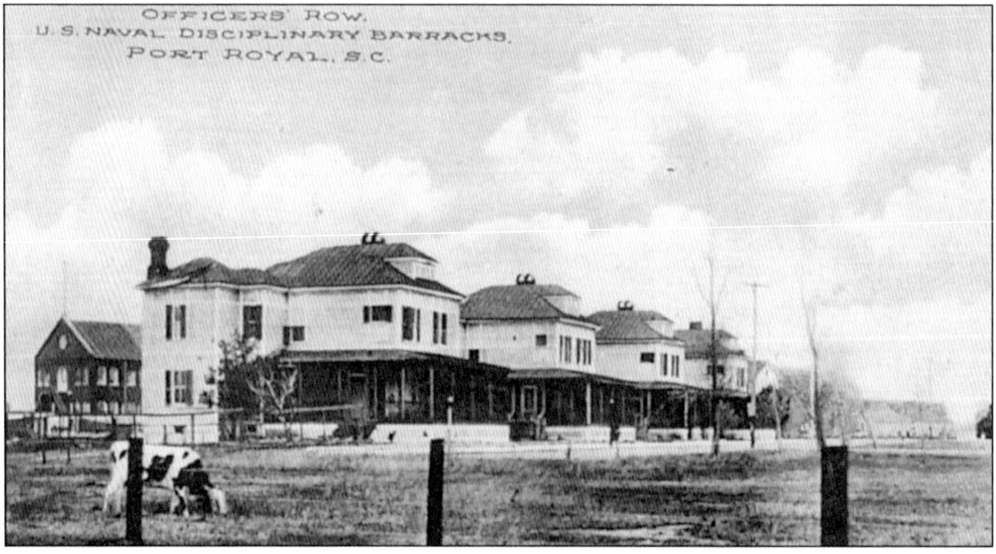


**Officers' Row, U.S. Naval Disciplinary Barracks, Port Royal, S.C.** (Collotype, 3 1/2" x 5 1/2", Albertype Co., Brooklyn, NY; *c.* 1913.) Seen here grazing next to the uniformly built frame officers' quarters, believed to have been erected in the 1890s as part of the old Port Royal Naval Station, is the ubiquitous cow, in what was at the time an immediate, necessary mixing of the military and the agrarian. The view was taken sometime between September 1912 and October 1915, when the facilities on Paris Island were used by the Navy for an experimental detention and probationary establishment. In 1913, about 400 men were stationed at the Disciplinary Barracks.

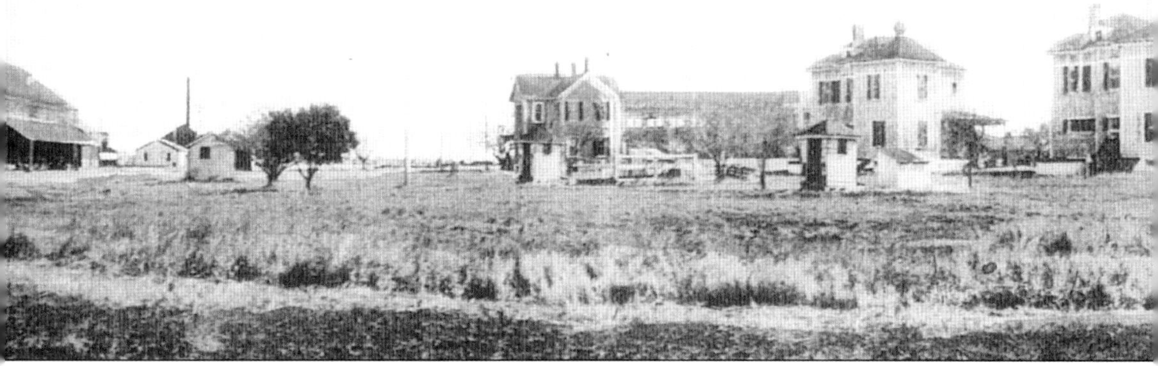

in 1899. In 1891, the first Marine post was established on the island in connection with the Naval Station, when the Navy decided to locate its primary South Atlantic naval base at Port Royal. The dry dock, constructed in 1894–1895, was the only one of its kind on the East Coast south of Norfolk and remained in service until 1910. In 1909, a school for Marine officers was inaugurated on the island and operated there until 1911, when it and a small recruit depot which had been started that year were transferred to Norfolk. This panoramic view of the Naval Station is the only one known to have been published during its critical first decade of the twentieth century.

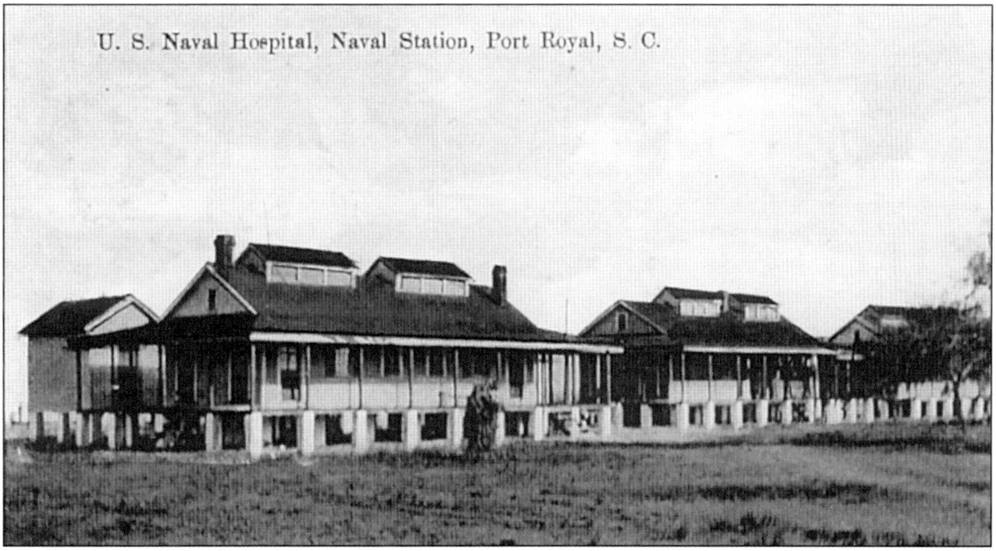


**U.S. Naval Hospital, Naval Station, Port Royal, S.C.** (Hand-Colored Collotype, 3 1/2" x 5 1/2", [Knackstedt and Näther Co., Hamburg, Germany]; A.M. Simon, #16031, New York, NY, importer; 1912.) Built in 1899 to replace its 1891 predecessor destroyed by a storm in 1898, the U.S. Naval Hospital is shown here during the period 1912–1915, when it served the contingent of Marines and Naval personnel at the Disciplinary Barracks. In June 1915, just a few months before the formal establishment of Paris Island as a U.S. Marine Recruit Depot (October 28, 1915), an appropriation of $15,000 was sought for expansion and upgrading of the hospital (see the *Beaufort Gazette*, June 9, 1916).

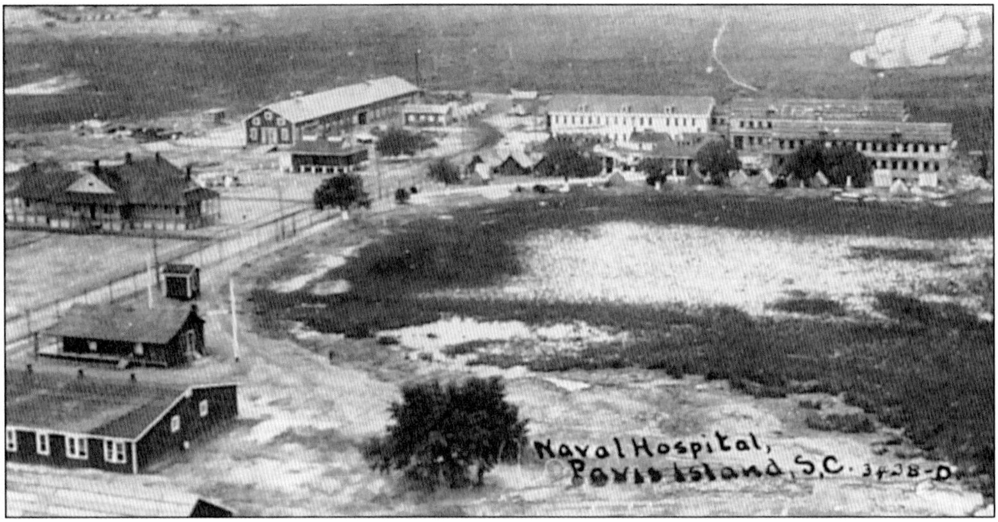


**Naval Hospital, #3438-D, Paris Island, S.C.** (Photoprint, 3 3/8" x 5 3/8"; *c.* 1917.) Looking north, this aerial view probably was meant to show off the 1917 ward expansion of the Naval Hospital (upper right, behind the barely visible old hospital units). Also seen here are the bowling alley (lower left), the non-commissioned officers' mess (left center, above the bowling alley), and the vehicle shed (the long building just above and to the right of the NCO mess). The structure at the far right in the upper part of the picture near the hospital is the mess hall and galley.

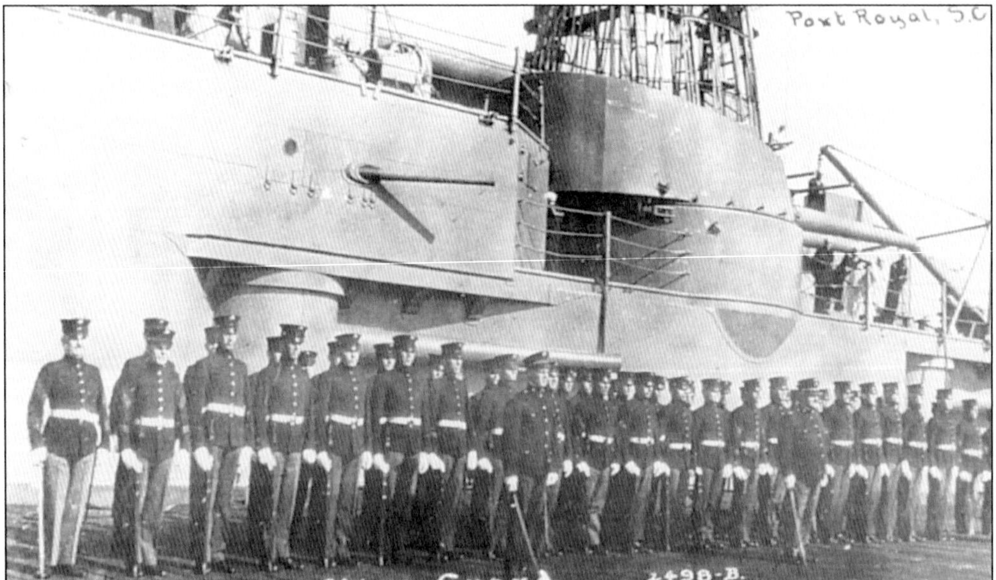


**Ships Guard, Marine Barracks, #2498-B, Port Royal, S.C.** (Photoprint, 3 3/8" x 5 3/8"; *c.* 1917.) According to Major McClellan, Marines and Naval personnel have together been connected with the history of Paris Island since 1861, when as joint Federal forces under command of Flag Officer Samuel Francis DuPont, they took possession of the forts and surrounding territory on Bay Point and Hilton Head. This postcard demonstrates better than most the subsequent mutual dependency of these two branches of the armed services in the area, both often relying upon the presence of the other to do their jobs—and for their jobs.

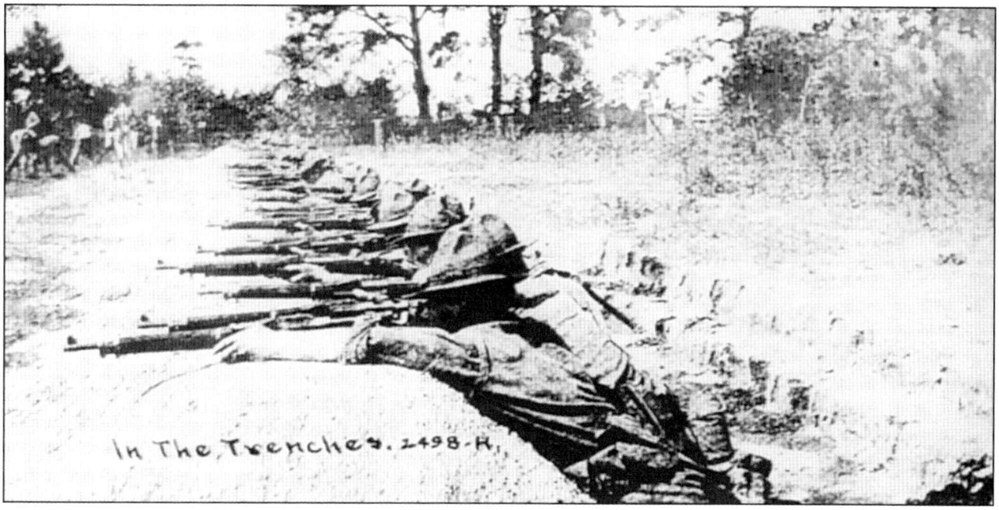


**In the Trenches, #2498-R, Marine Barracks, Port Royal, S.C.** (Photoprint, 3 1/2" x 5 1/2"; *c.* 1918.) "Every morning in Beaufort town," the editor of the *Beaufort Gazette* observed on September 7, 1917, "the rifle practice of the Marines on Paris Island can be heard and the Boches [Germans] will soon have cause to know that this training in marksmanship is not to be scorned." Part of every Marine recruit's basic training was weapons instruction on the rifle range and in the trenches. An expert rifleman could increase his monthly pay by $5.

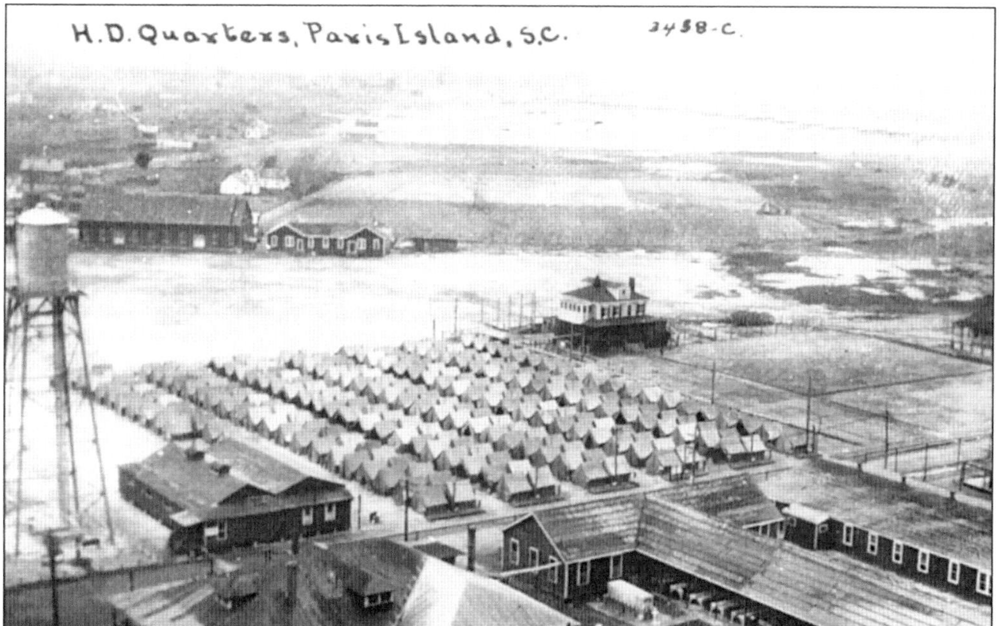


**H.D. Quarters, #3438-C, Paris Island, S.C.** (Photoprint, 3 3/8" x 5 3/8"; *c.* 1917.) In this northwesterly aerial panorama the officers' quarters in the center anchor the rows of enlisted field shelters. Also seen here (moving clockwise, starting at the far right) are portions of the NCO mess and bowling alley, the latrine and scrubbing area, the guardhouse and sick bay, the library, water tank, prison buildings, and laundry (the gabled building with the white trim). The base fence stretches across the photo, top center, beyond which is evidence of the civilian community outside the barracks. The government purchased the whole island in 1917.

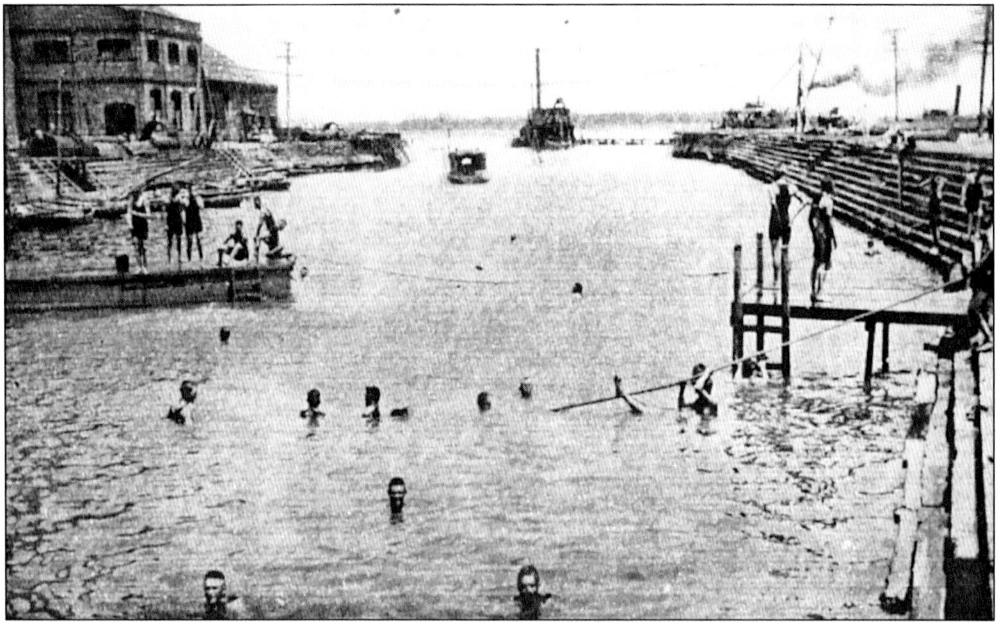

**"The Old Swimmin' Hole" Main Station, U.S. Marine Training Station, Parris Island, S.C.** (Collotype, 3 1/2" x 5 1/2"; *c.* 1920.) "The Old Swimmin' Hole" at the U.S. Marine Training Station appears to have been created by flooding the old timber dry dock, which for many years following its construction in 1895 had been a principal facility of the Port Royal Station. It was some 449 feet long, 66 feet wide, and 26 feet deep.

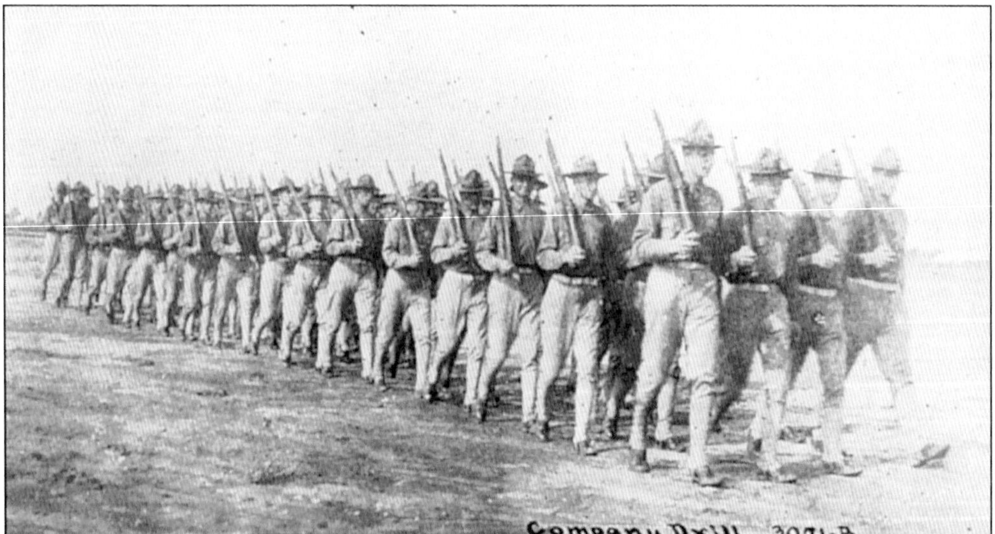


**Company Drill, #3001-B, Marine Barracks, Paris Island, S.C.** (Photoprint, 3 3/8" x 5 1/2"; *c.* 1917.) Paris Island recruits are going through the company drills, which were a part of their required training. On December 1, 1915, there were 9 commissioned officers and 908 men attached to the Marine Barracks (see the *Beaufort Gazette*, December 10, 1915). These coded photoprint sets, taken by Marine photographers, had numerical codes with an A-Z image identifier in each group. The earliest of the five documented codes was #2498 and the latest was #3438 during the *c.* 1917–1920 period.

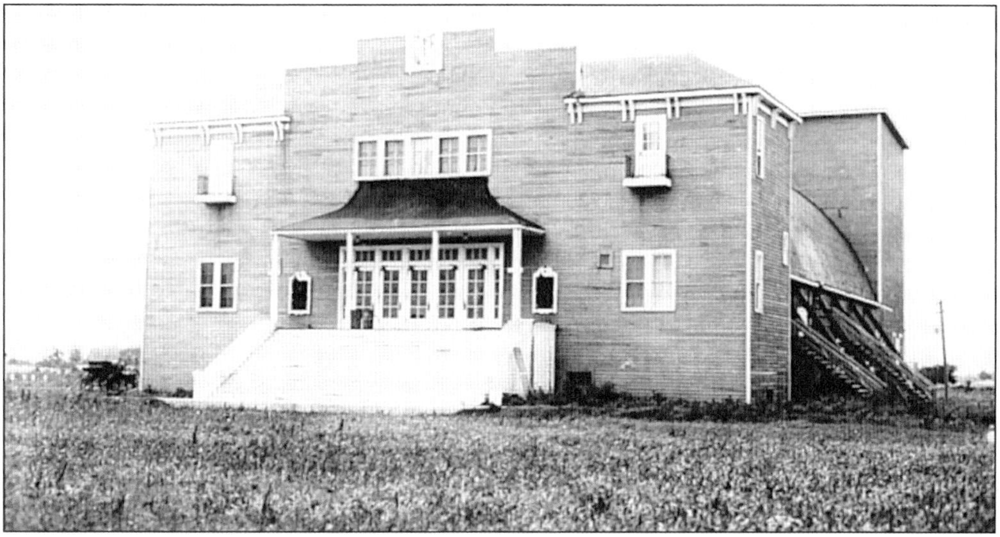

**[Theatre, Parris Island, S.C.]** (Photoprint, 3 1/4" x 5 1/4", *c.* 1922.) As early as 1915, the public was informed that everything possible was being done for the entertainment and amusement of the men stationed at the Recruit Depot, including provision of a "splendid library, free use of the bowling alleys and pool tables, free moving pictures every night" (see the *Beaufort Gazette*, December 10, 1915). The Liberty Theatre (above), 1920–1928, was a general-purpose auditorium erected as part of the Recruit Depot's Civic Center development. It was located in the vicinity of the post inn, base chapel, and the YMCA building.

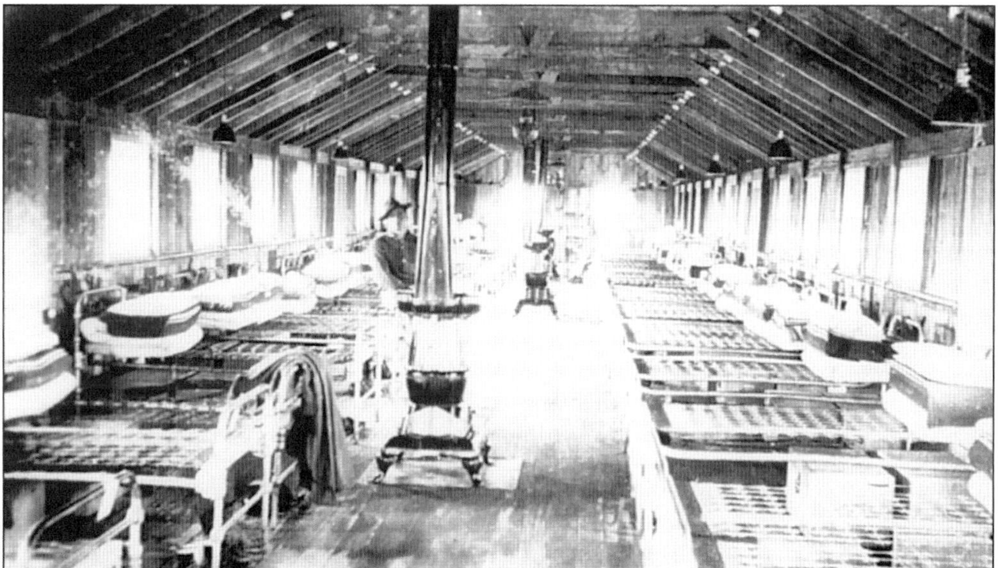

**[Interior Barracks, Parris Island, S.C.]** (Photoprint, 3 1/2" x 5 3/8"; 1920.) This interior view of one of the barracks at Parris Island provides some idea of the housing provided "the soldiers of the sea." The larger of the two great Marine recruit depots (the other being Mare Island, California), Parris Island handled 42,604 men during World War I. Major McClellan also reveals that two units, the Seventh and Eighth battalions, were organized at Parris Island and sent directly to France from South Carolina. This poorly defined uncoded image is probably an amateur picture.

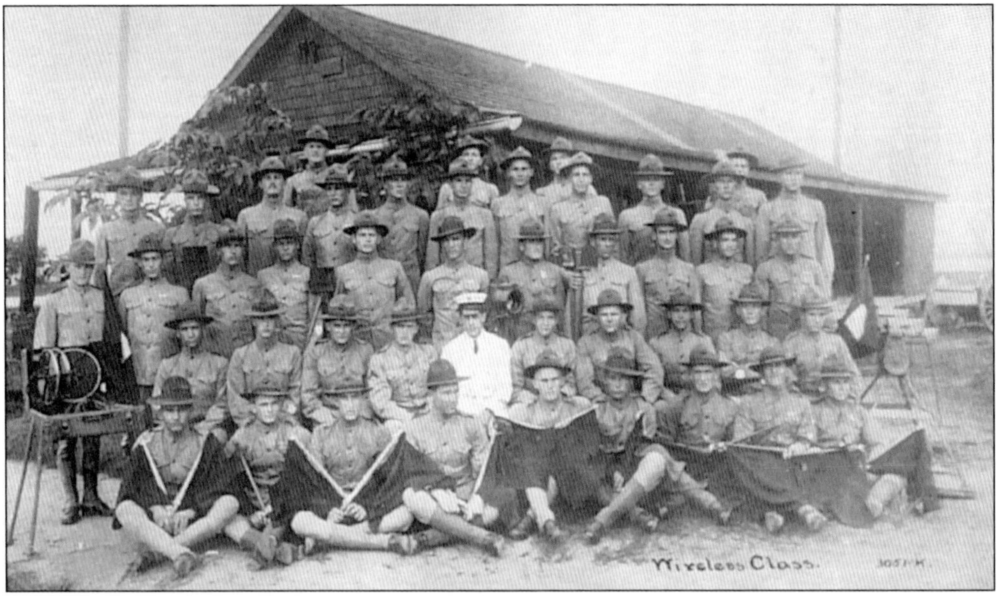


**Wireless Class, #3051-K, Marine Barracks, Paris Island, S.C.** (Photoprint, 3 1/2" x 5 3/8"; *c.* 1917.) *The Southern Auto Guide and Beaufort County Directory for 1918–19* speaks of the Marine Barracks at Paris Island as being the largest recruit depot of the U.S. Marine Corps, accommodating 10,000 to 15,000 men and handling all accepted applicants from east of the Mississippi. It singles out the instruction in firing, trench warfare, and wireless telegraphy as basic components of a 12-weeks' training period.

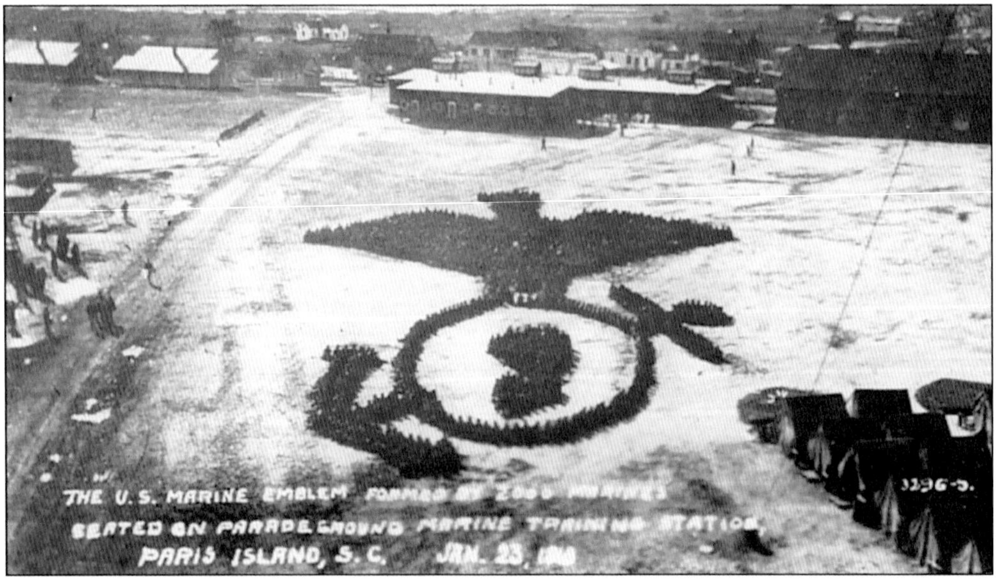


**The U.S. Marine Emblem Formed by 2,000 Marines Seated on the Parade Grounds, Marine Training Station, Paris Island, Jan. 1918.** (Photoprint, 3 1/2" x 5 1/2"; #3296-S, 1918.) Definitely a postcard for the recruit to send home, this novelty conveys the size of the station and of the corps itself in January 1918. The wire visible at right may indicate that the picture was taken from a biplane. On May 3, 1919, the Marine Corps would issue an order mandating that henceforth the correct spelling of the name of the island would be "Parris."

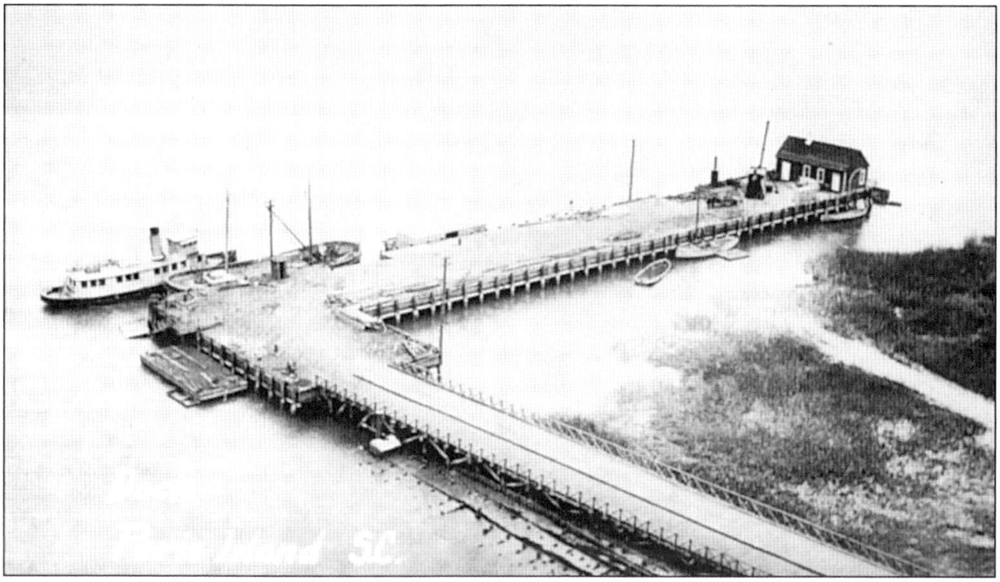

**DOCK—PARIS ISLAND, S.C.** (Photoprint, 3 3/8" x 5 3/8"; *c.* 1918.) An essential part of "Mainside" Paris Island, the dock, or boat landing, on the Beaufort River was the main entry point for personnel and supplies until 1928, when the bridge was built across Archer's Creek, thus connecting the causeway and Horse Island. The large open-sided shed still stands on the dock as a remnant of the structures that were part of the waterside apparatus of an earlier day.

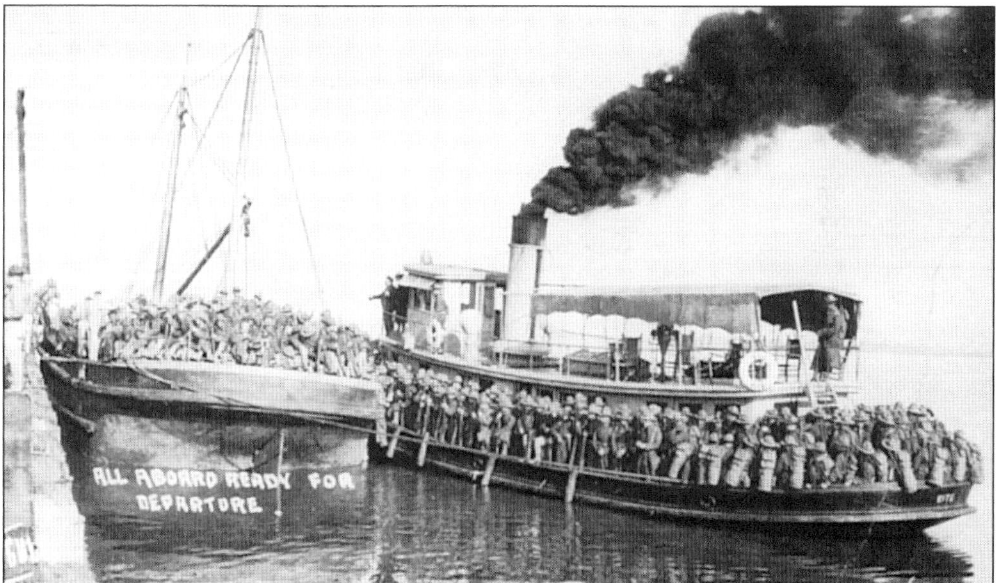


**ALL ABOARD READY FOR DEPARTURE.** (Photoprint, 3 1/2" x 5 1/2", Culp, Marine Photographer; 1918.) The Marines ready for departure on board the USS *Kite* to the right here appear to have embarked via the barge-like vessel to the left. A message on the back of this card, dated January 20, 1918, indicates that these men, fully equipped and ready for field service, were on their way to Quantico, Virginia. There they probably took a short finishing course in the Overseas Forwarding camp. This uncoded card by Culp is likely to have been an independent image made at the departure date and not a part of the normal A-Z series.

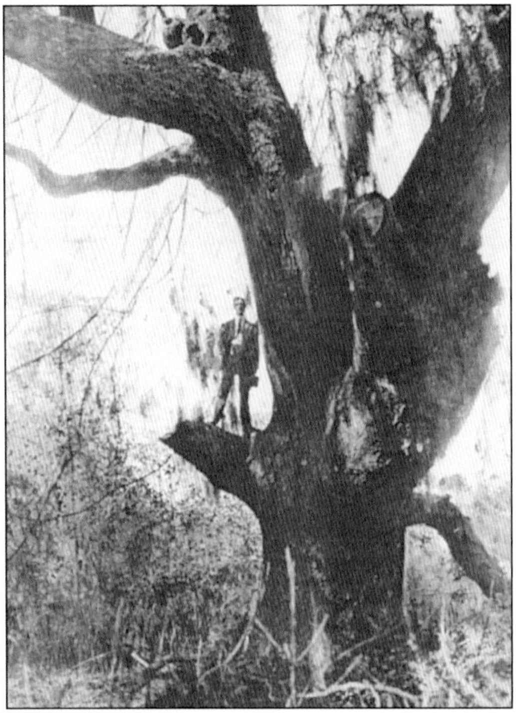

**Giant Oak on Benton Farm near Beaufort, S.C.** (Hand-Colored Collotype, 3 1/2" x 5 1/2", [Knackstedt and Näther Co., Hamburg, Germany]; A.M. Simon, #16032, New York, NY, importer; 1910.) On a Friday in late June 1912, the Baptist Sunday School held its annual picnic at the Benton Plantation on Broad River. "A more beautiful place for a picnic could not have been chosen," wrote an observer in the *Beaufort Gazette* of June 28. One of the great oak trees, whose massive limbs were "hung with flags and streamers and flossy sheens of gray moss," was said to be 30 feet around. C.U.V. Benton, one of the county's major truck farmers, had been particularly successful as a lettuce grower.

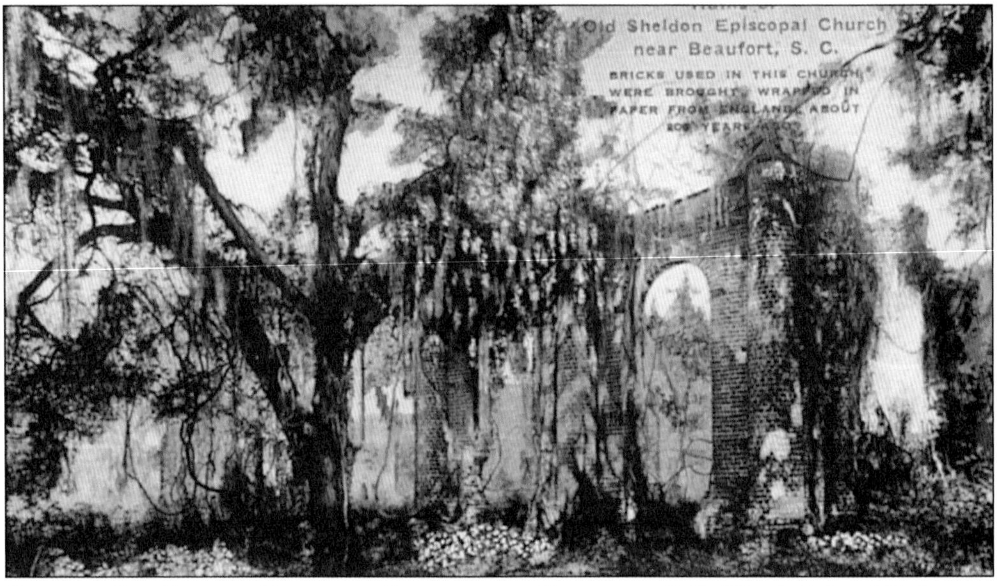


**Ruins of Old Sheldon Episcopal Church near Beaufort, S.C.** (Hand-Colored Collotype, 3 1/2" x 5 1/2", Albertype Co. Brooklyn, NY; C.G. Luther's Drugstore, Beaufort, sponsor; 1920.) Some 16 miles northwest of Beaufort lies Prince William's Parish Church, called Old Sheldon for the ancestral home of the Bull family in Warwickshire, England. Erected in 1745–1748, it was burned by the British in 1779 and rebuilt in 1826, only to be burned again by the Federal army in 1865. Annual services are held on site the second Sunday after Easter. Its burial ground still yields its secrets; among them, these words inscribed on a gravestone: "Because I love this life, I know I shall love the new life better."

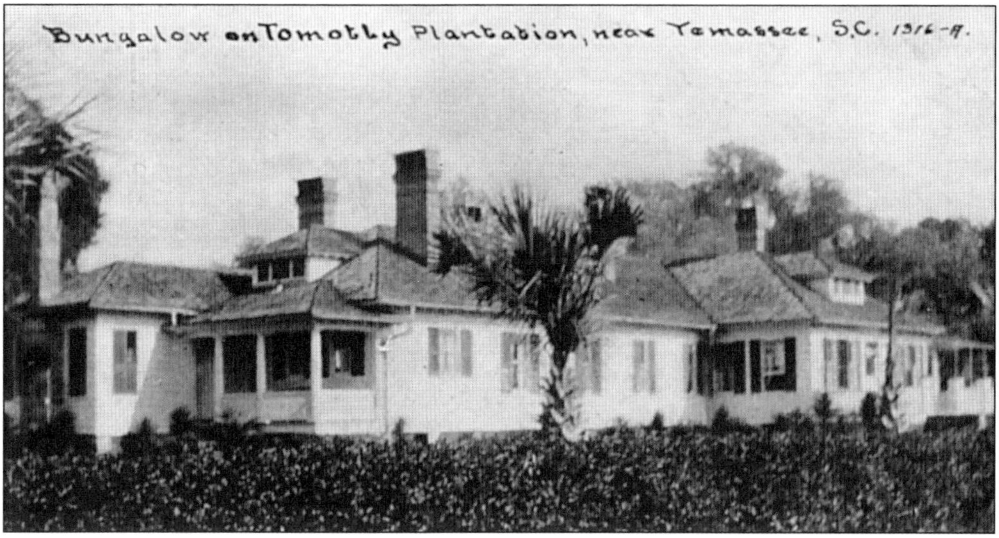


**BUNGALOW ON TOMOTLY [SIC] PLANTATION, NEAR YEMASSEE, S.C.** (Photoprint, 3 1/2" x 5 4/10"; *c.* 1917.) Tomotley Plantation, located about 18 miles northwest of Beaufort, has long been known for its twin live-oak avenues. Of equal interest is the old rice plantation's "bungalow," above, built by Robert H. McCurdy in 1910 as a hunting lodge largely for Northern patrons. This view from the south reveals some of the chimneys which serviced fireplaces in each of the ten bedroom-and-bath units. Restored by the William Mixons, who acquired it in 1990, the huge, rambling structure looks much the same today as when this picture was made *c.* 1916–1917.

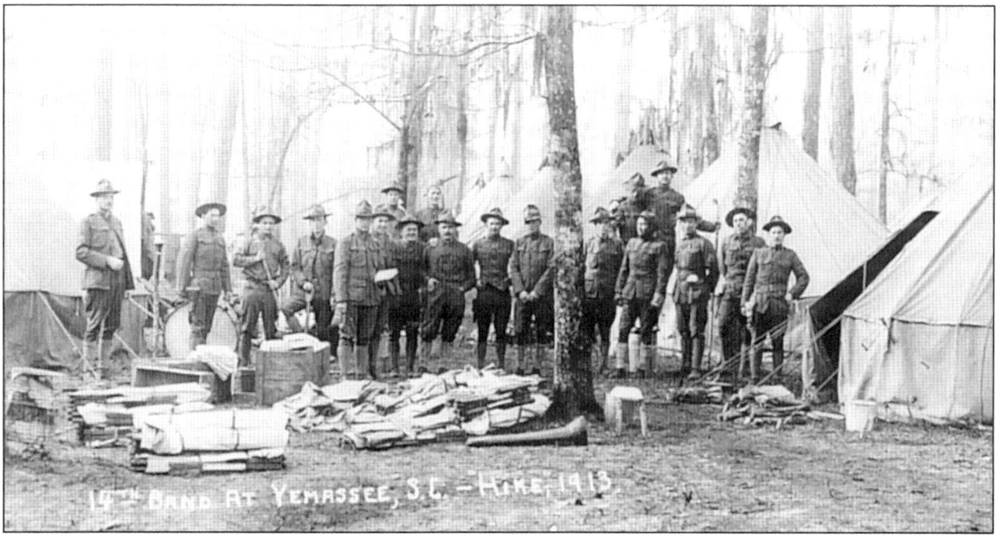


**FOURTEENTH BAND AT YEMASSEE, S.C.—HIKE, 1913.** (Photoprint, 3 3/8" x 5 3/8"; 1913.) It would be said during this period that there were always uniforms—Marine ones especially—to be seen about Yemassee, the little town at the northern edge of Beaufort County, and around its big depot, since the town was the region's railroad trading point for east-west and north-south lines. The military musicians' unit pictured here, identified only as the "14th Band," is indicated as on a "Hike, 1913"—three years before the Marines established a receiving station at Yemassee to facilitate and ease their recruits' train transfers to Paris Island. This portrait was probably taken by an officer to document the hike.

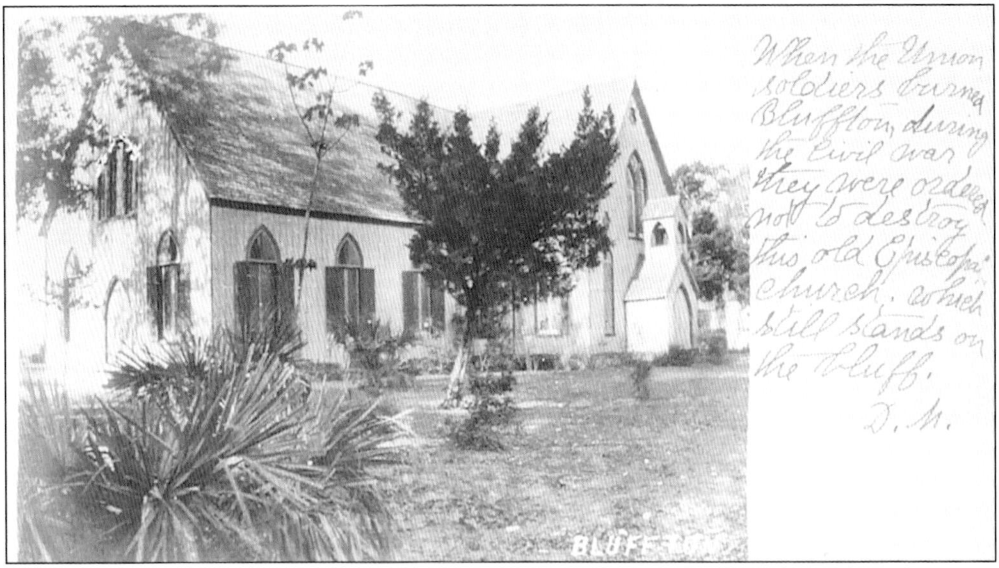


**Old Episcopal Church, Bluffton.** (Photoprint, 3 1/2" x 5 1/2"; *c.* 1907.) The Gothic-Revival Church of the Cross perches high on the bluff in the historic village of Bluffton, long known as a summer resort and artists' colony. Built in 1854 of cypress board-and-batten after an original design by Charleston architect Edward Brickell White, the church is one of the most beautiful in the Lowcountry and continues as the center of an active parish. It was saved from being burned in 1861 by the timely arrival of Confederate troops.

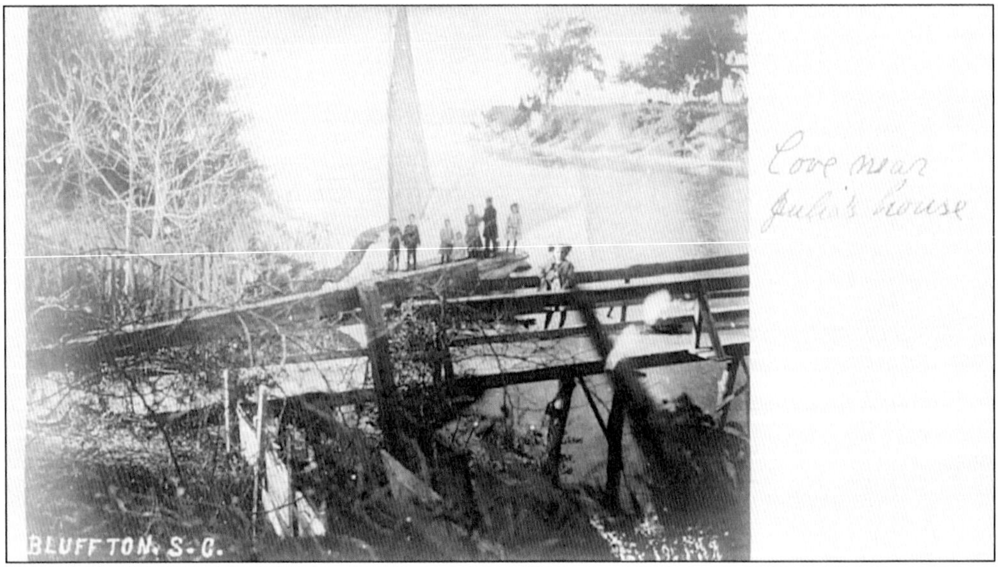


**Cove near Julia's House, Bluffton, S.C.** (Photoprint, 3 1/2" x 5 1/2"; *c.* 1907.) One account of Bluffton describes it as a place of "rare attractions . . . running up from May River a half mile into the pine barren" (the *Beaufort Gazette*, August 16, 1912). The town was intersected by four deep coves, headed by springs, which drained off the stagnant water conducive to malaria. Here on the "cove near Julia's house" can be seen not only "Hubert and Royal Snyders sail boat," but also one of the wooden "skids," or private footbridges, which in spanning the coves linked the residential parts of the village and shortened the distance to town.

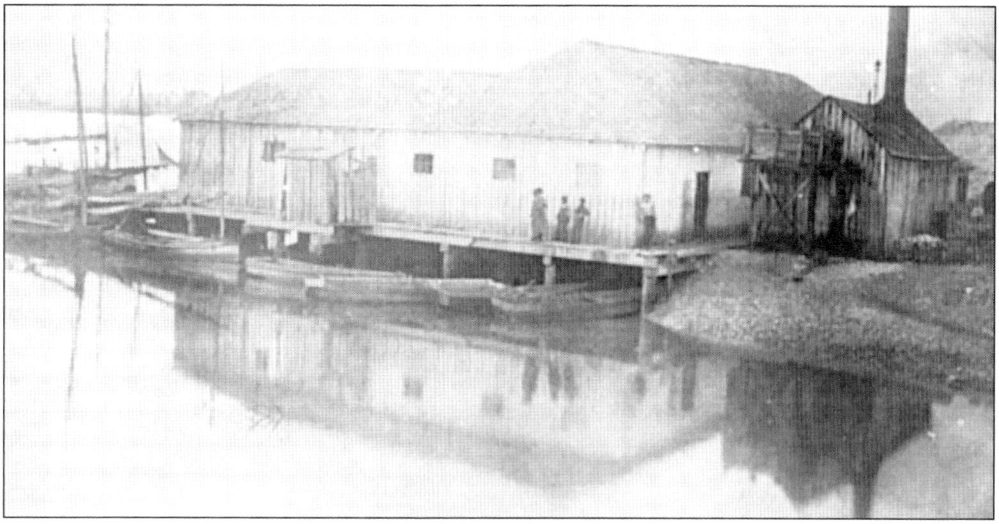

**Oyster Factory, Bluffton, S.C.** (Photoprint, 3 1/2" x 5 1/2"; *c.* 1907.) Much of the economy of Bluffton, like that of Beaufort, has traditionally been associated with the river or the nearby ocean. This photograph of an oyster processing plant signifies the village's beneficial relationship to the area's once-thriving oyster fleet. In 1910 Bluffton had a population of 350 persons. This set of one-of-a-kind amateur photocards may have been made by a hobbyist, who had purchased the film and a kit of processing supplies and instructions to produce his own pictures.

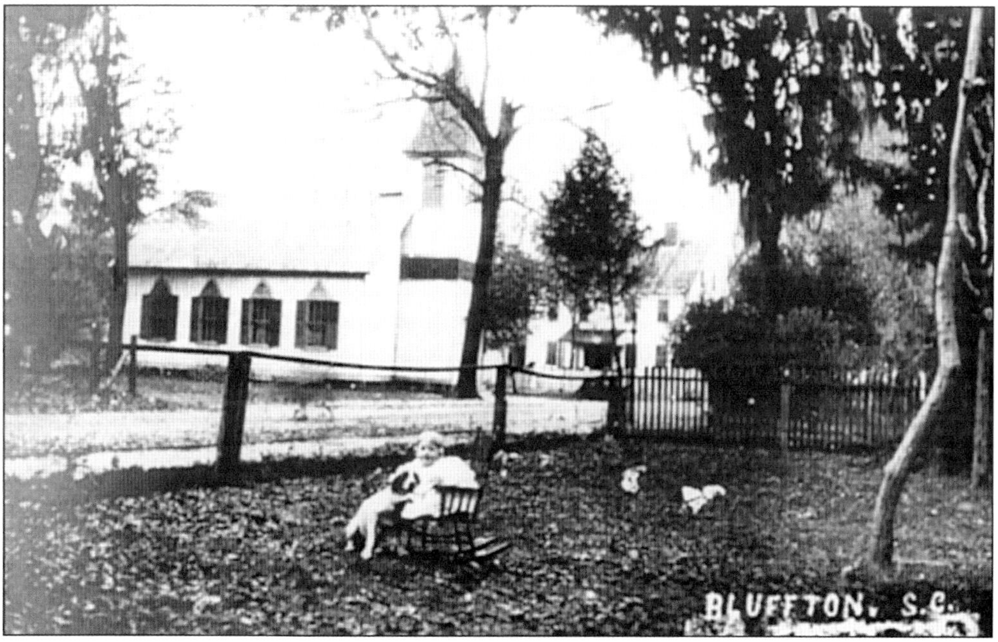


**Methodist Episcopal Church, Bluffton, S.C.** (Photoprint, 3 1/2" x 5 1/2"; *c.* 1907.) Visible beyond the child and the animals in this yard on Boundary Street is the Methodist Episcopal Church, now the Campbell Chapel African Methodist Episcopal Church. The Greek Revival-style sanctuary, which had been built in 1853 and featured board-and-batten siding, was damaged in the 1863 Federal burning of Bluffton. Purchased by the African Methodists in 1874, it underwent some alterations and additions in 1969.

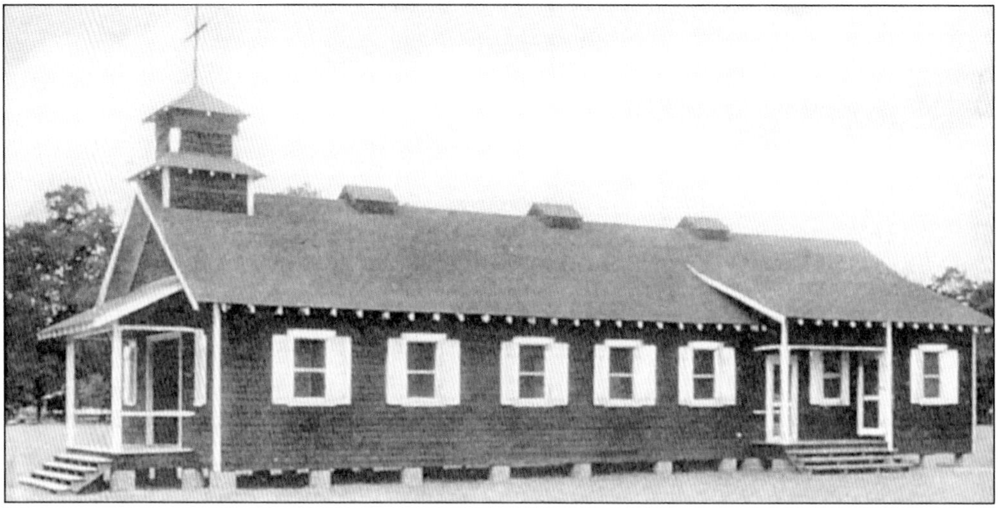

**St. Saviour's Chapel, Camp St. Mary's, Chelsea, S.C.** (Photoprint, 3 1/2" x 5 1/2"; Foltz Studio, Savannah, GA; *c.* 1937.) The long, low, natural cypress-sided St. Saviour's Chapel served as the worship center for the "new" Camp St. Mary's, the vacation school camp established on property purchased by the Roman Catholic Diocese of Charleston in 1935 on the northern side of the Okatie River near Chelsea on the western edge of Beaufort County. Dedicated by Bishop Emmet M. Walsh on July 9, 1937, the chapel survives, in a much-altered state, on the property which was sold to Beaufort County in 1997 for use as a park.

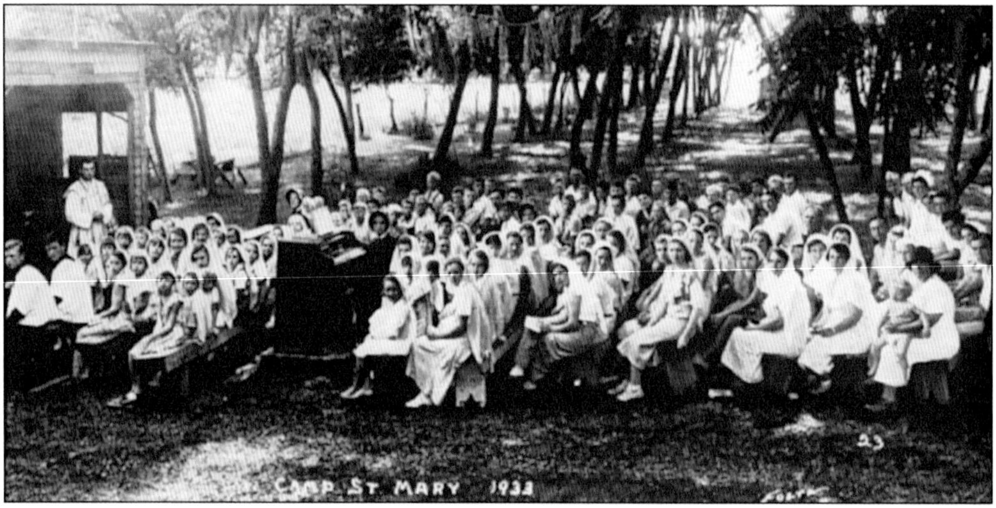


**Camp St. Mary, Chelsea, S.C.** (Photoprint, 3 1/2" x 5 1/2"; Foltz Studio, Savannah, GA; 1933.) The establishment of Camp St. Mary's, with its three-weeks' residential period of instruction, grew out of Bishop Walsh's desire to bring Catholic education to children living in the isolated rural areas of his diocese. The camp's original site, from 1930 to 1934, was the front yard of the home of Mr. and Mrs. William E. Pinckney on their large farm at Guerard's Point on the south bluff of the Okatie River. Mary Pinckney Powell recalls that tents were set up under the grove of oaks and that Mrs. Ella Pinckney "graciously opened her big home to the ladies and girls and to accommodate the Sisters of Our Lady of Mercy from Charleston" and that "campers were bedded down in every corner, even on the front porch" (*Back Over Home*, 1996). This 1933 picture shows campers and staff at an outdoor mass, with the farm's commercial locust trees in the background.

# *Two*

# JASPER COUNTY

Jasper County, located at the southern tip of South Carolina, was established in 1912, the state's third youngest county. According to local historian Grace Fox Perry, the county came into being as the result of an idea which emerged from conversations between Ridgeland men who were tired of dealing with the problems caused by living in a town which was split between two counties—Hampton and Beaufort—by the railroad track. Chief among these were merchant C.E. Perry and a new young school principal named Richard M. Jefferies, who had come to town in 1910—and who later became governor of South Carolina. They called the new county "Jasper" after the Revolutionary war hero of that name. Many of the cards from this area were made before Jasper became a county.

Hardeeville, the largest town in the county's southwest sector, did not become wholly part of Jasper County until 1950, when the old 92-square-mile Yemassee township tract was transferred to Jasper. Up to that time, the town had literally been divided between the counties of Jasper and Beaufort by the railroad tracks of the Atlantic Coast Line. The three Hardeeville cards are from the period when it was in Beaufort County.

The Jasper County postcards of this era, like those from the other counties that comprise Southern Carolina, reflect the strong, quiet, self-contained, family-centered existence typical of rural and small-town life in the "back country tradition" of what had been Old Beaufort District. The images reveal many of the routine ways and much of the grace—along with some of the hardships and limitations and disasters—of a people who largely lived by modest means in relative isolation.

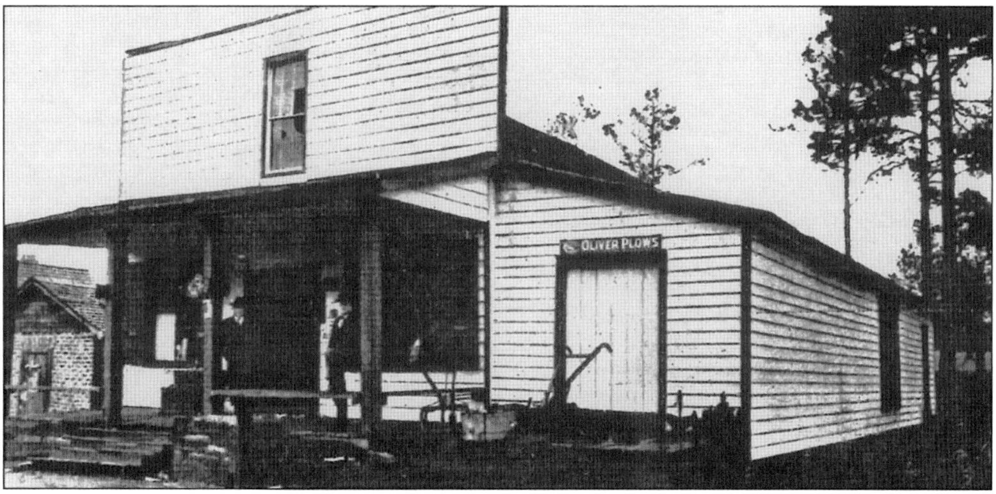


**C.M. McTEER'S GENERAL MDSC [MERCHANDISE] STORE, HARDEEVILLE, S.C.** (Halftone, 3 1/2" x 5 1/2", [C.U. Williams, #18464, Bloomington, IL]; *c.* 1914.) C.M. McTeer, whose family settled in Hardeeville about 1820, graduated from Wofford College in 1898 and opened his general merchandise store in 1900 on the northwest corner of Main Street, which later became Highway 17. These mail-order postcards, using amateur photographs and printed in small quantities, have all but disappeared from public circulation.

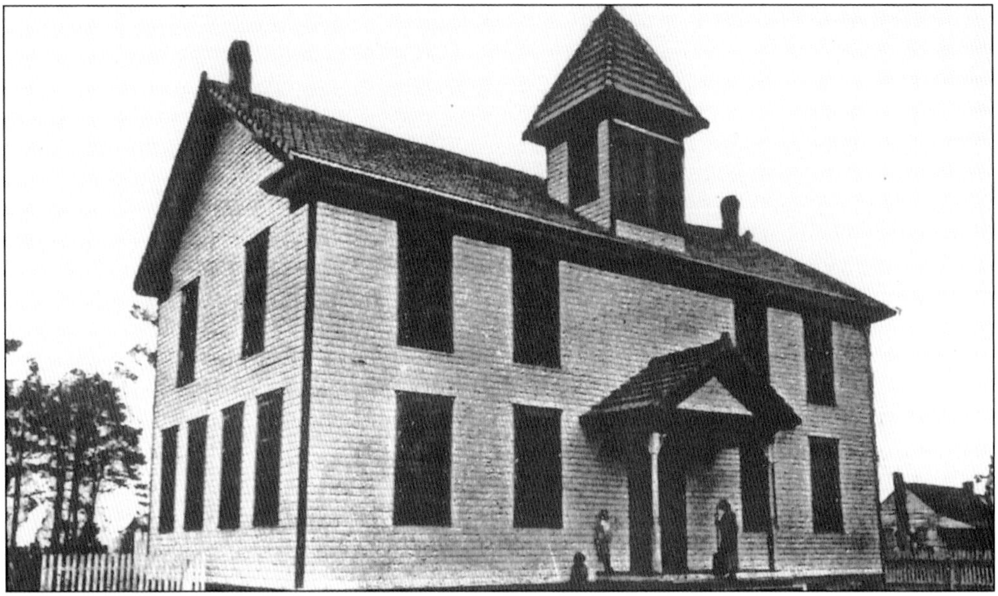

**Public School, Hardeeville, S.C.** (Halftone, 3 1/2" x 5 1/2", [C.U. Williams, #18463, Bloomington, IL]; *c.* 1914.) "The modern and well-appointed school building, recently completed for the town of Hardeeville," wrote Beaufort County superintendent of education B.H. Boyd in his report submitted on December 10, 1914, "is an illustration of our efforts to improve the school plants." The combined value of this three-classroom wooden school building and grounds was estimated at $3,700. The elementary school used this structure until the new brick building was erected on Main Street in 1928. It then became an African-American children's school until it burned down in the early 1930s.

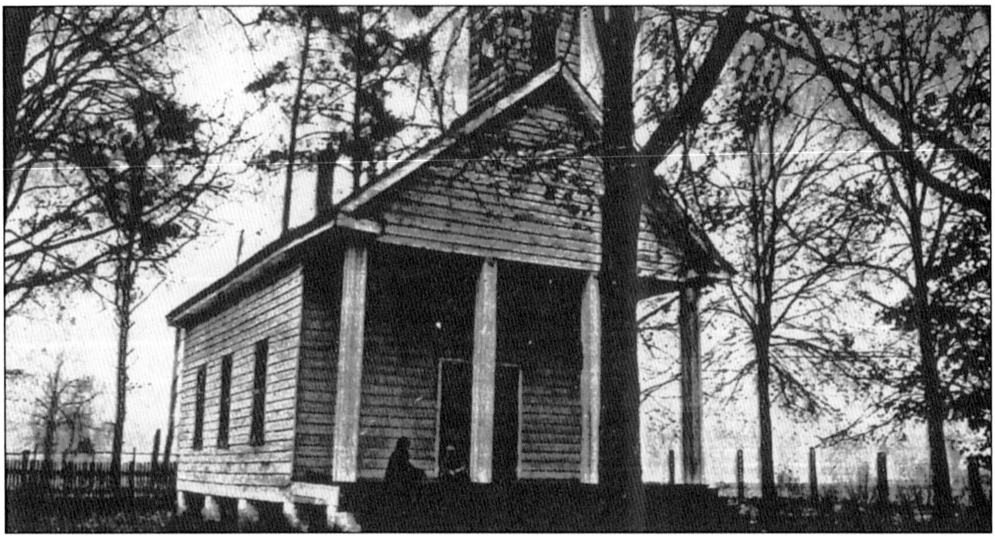

**Baptist Church, Hardeeville, S.C.** (Halftone, 3 1/2" x 5 1/2", [C.U. Williams, #18465, Bloomington, IL]; *c.* 1914.) A congregation of some 41 Hardeeville Baptist men and women built this simple frame sanctuary in 1876, slightly more than a decade after their first one was destroyed during Sherman's march through South Carolina. In 1915, the Federal government compensated the church in the amount of $1,500 for its destruction near the end of the Civil War. This house of worship was replaced by a new one in 1956.

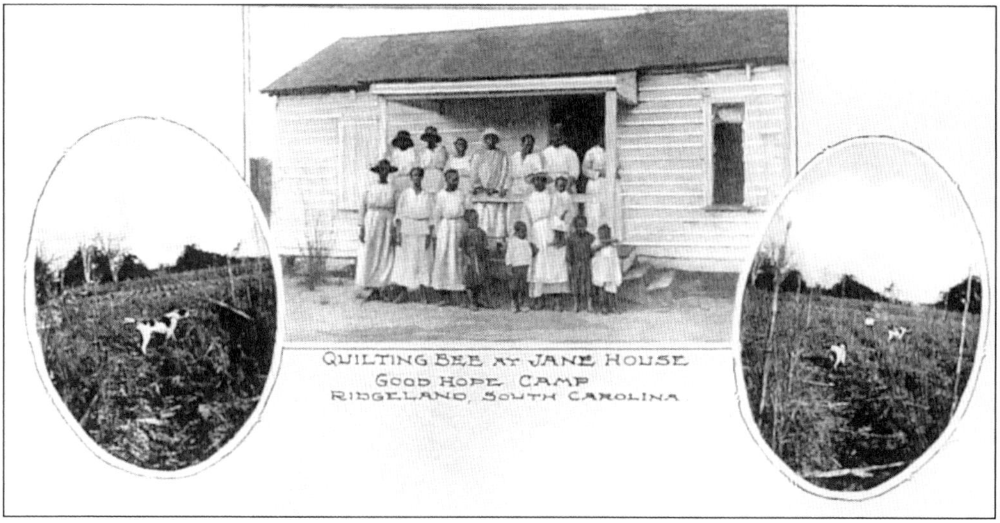


**QUILTING BEE AT JANE HOUSE, GOOD HOPE CAMP, RIDGELAND, SOUTH CAROLINA.** (Collotype, 3 3/10" x 5 1/2", Albertype Co., Brooklyn, NY; *c.* 1930.) "Picturesquely beautiful and uniquely rich in historic and cultural background is the region of Jasper County that lies in the neighborhood of Ridgeland," B.M. Gibson wrote in the *Greenville News*, September 30, 1934. Among the area's unique traditions were the quilting bees held in Jane House at Good Hope Camp, located about 6 miles east of Ridgeland. The two cameo shots here, providing other views of the place, focus upon what would have been one of the camp's chief inhabitants: the hunting dog.

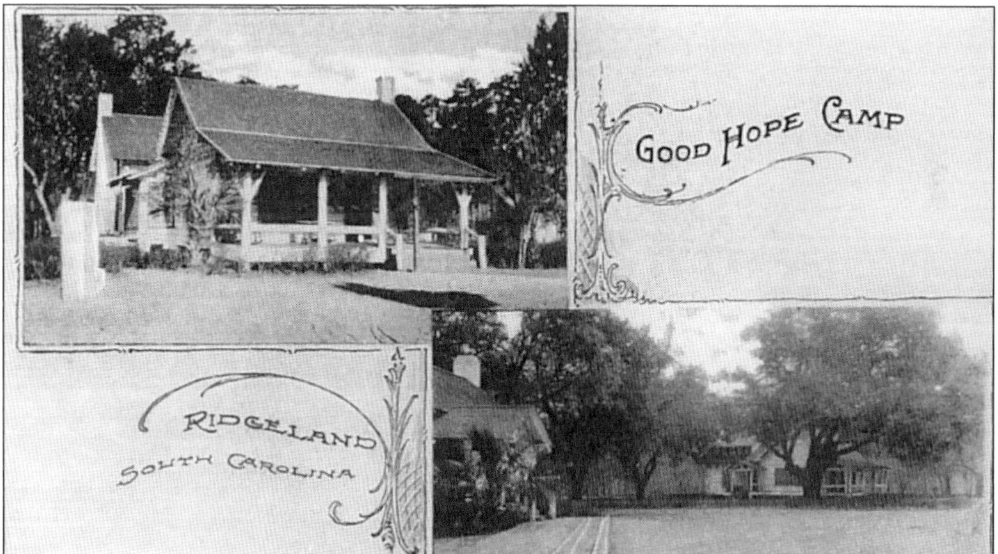


**GOOD HOPE CAMP, RIDGELAND, S.C.** (Collotype, 3 3/10" x 5 1/2", Albertype Co., Brooklyn, NY; *c.* 1930.) Grace Fox Perry, in *Moving Finger of Jasper* (1962), describes Good Hope Camp's hunting lodge as consisting of five white buildings of a log-cabin-type construction connected by brick walkways. The 19,000-acre estate was purchased from Heyward heirs in the 1890s and was eventually owned by the late Standard Oil executive Herbert L. Pratt and his descendants. The Chase family of New York later became part owner of the camp, according to Lynda S. Alsup (see *Names in South Carolina*, Winter 1977).

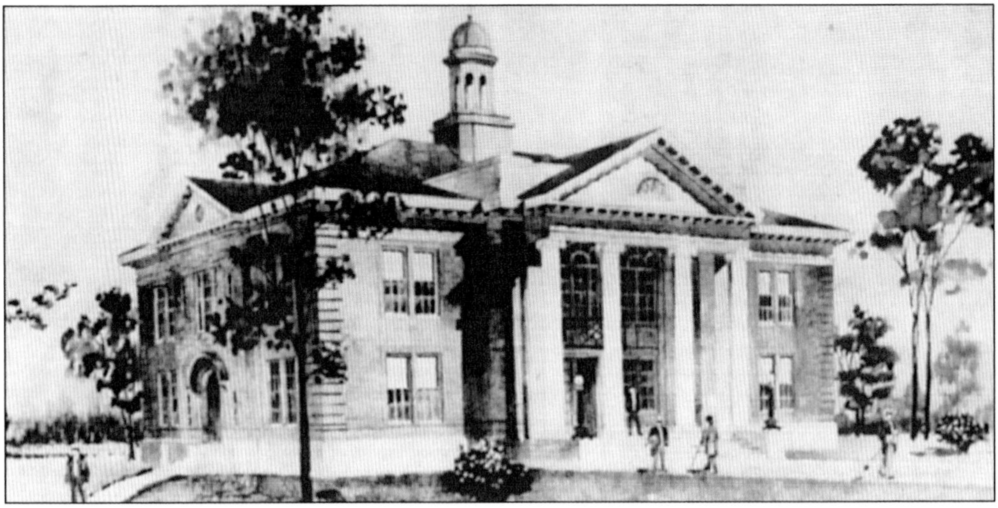

**PROPOSED COURT HOUSE—JASPER COUNTY, RIDGELAND, S.C.** (Photoprint, 3 3/10" x 5 3/10"; *c.* 1912.) A rare reproduction in postcard form of an architect's rendering, this novelty card depicts the courthouse proposed for Jasper County. Built in 1915, it stands at the corner of Russell Street and Third Avenue. The architect was William A. Edwards of Atlanta. The courthouse lacks the cupola seen in the original design here.

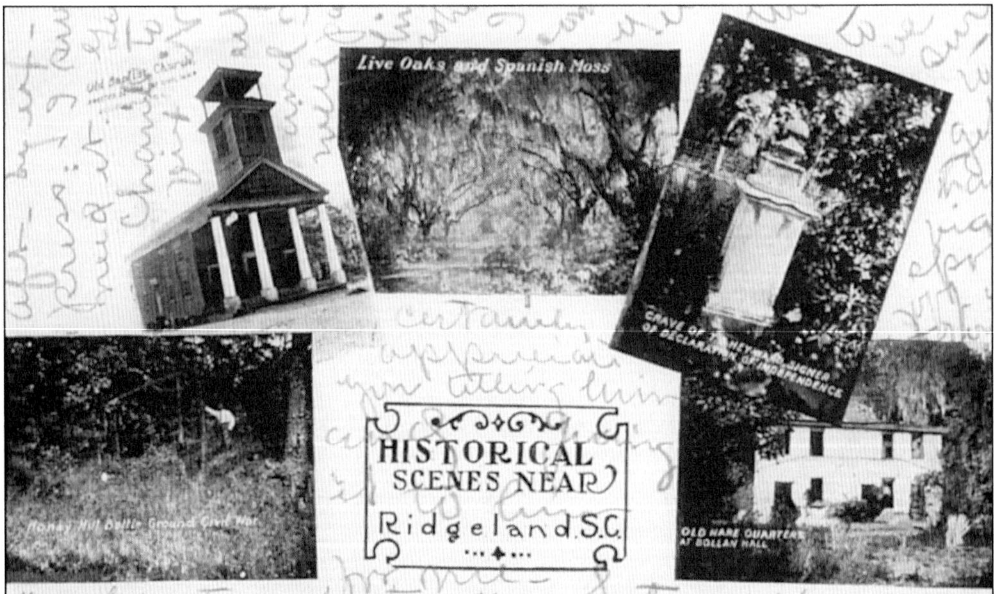


**HISTORIC SCENES, GREETING FROM RIDGELAND, S.C.** (Halftone, 3 3/8" x 5 1/2", [Kraus Mfg. Co., New York, NY]; Jefferies-Howell Co., sponsor; 1912.) This montage presents five of the sites and scenes which were considered the chief ones to be promoted and remembered in Jasper County in 1912, the year in which it was created and this card was mailed: the Honey Hill Battle Ground (a Civil War site located a few miles east of Ridgeland); the Old Baptist Church at Gillisonville (north of Ridgeland); Live Oaks and Spanish Moss; the Grave of Thomas Heyward, signer of the Declaration of Independence (east of Ridgeland at Old House); and the Old Hare Quarters at Bollan Hall.

[PORTRAIT OF QUITMAN AND MABEL NETTLES, RIDGELAND, S.C.] (Photoprint, 5 1/2" x 3 1/4"; *c.* 1915.) Quitman and Mabel Nettles, shown here in an outdoor portrait taken by an unidentified photographer, lived near Ridgeland, where they had a farm. Nettles had at one time been a railroad man and was among the young county's first commissioners. He was a Mason and a churchman: Nettles and his wife were members of the Great Swamp Baptist Church, located about 3 miles west of Ridgeland.

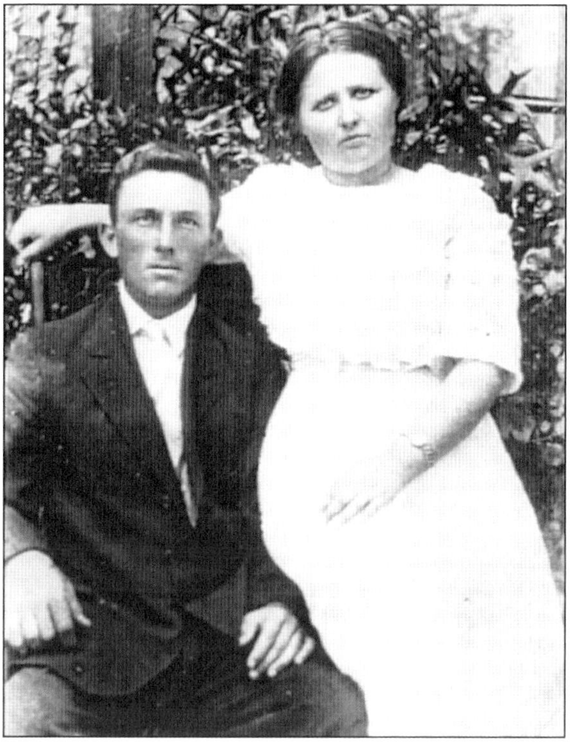

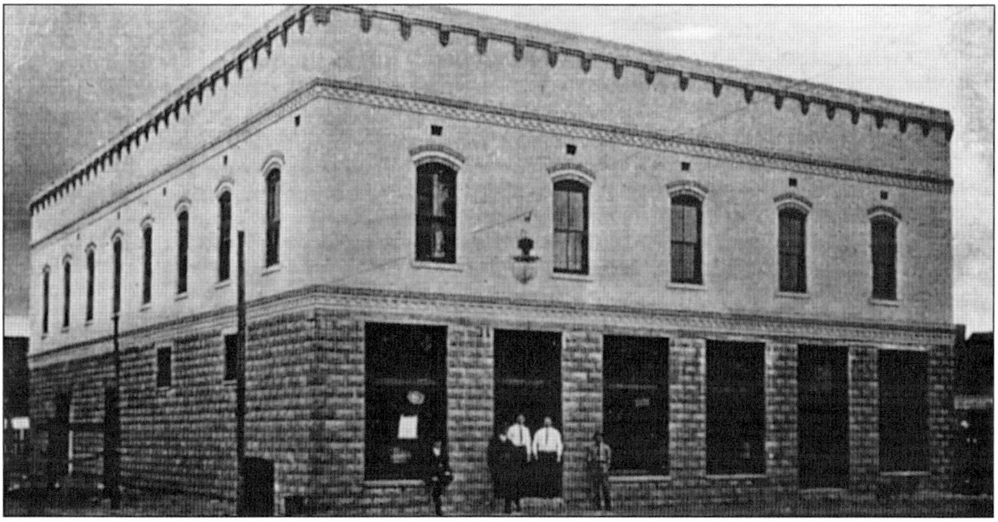

**PERRY DEPARTMENT STORE, RIDGELAND, S.C.** (Halftone, 3 3/8" x 5 1/2", [Kraus Mfg. Co., New York, NY]; Jefferies-Howell Co., sponsor; 1912.) Charles E. Perry (1862–1932) was a leading Ridgeland entrepreneur who was instrumental in the establishment of Jasper County. Grace Fox Perry reveals that the first court sessions held after the formation of the county in 1912 took place in his mercantile building. This picture of the Perry Department Store in Ridgeland was the only photograph chosen to illustrate a special article on Jasper County which appeared in *The State* (Columbia) on February 18, 1916. Ridgeland is spoken of in the article as "a thriving town with the spirit of progress as the motto of her citizens." Ridgeland had a population of 500 persons in 1910.

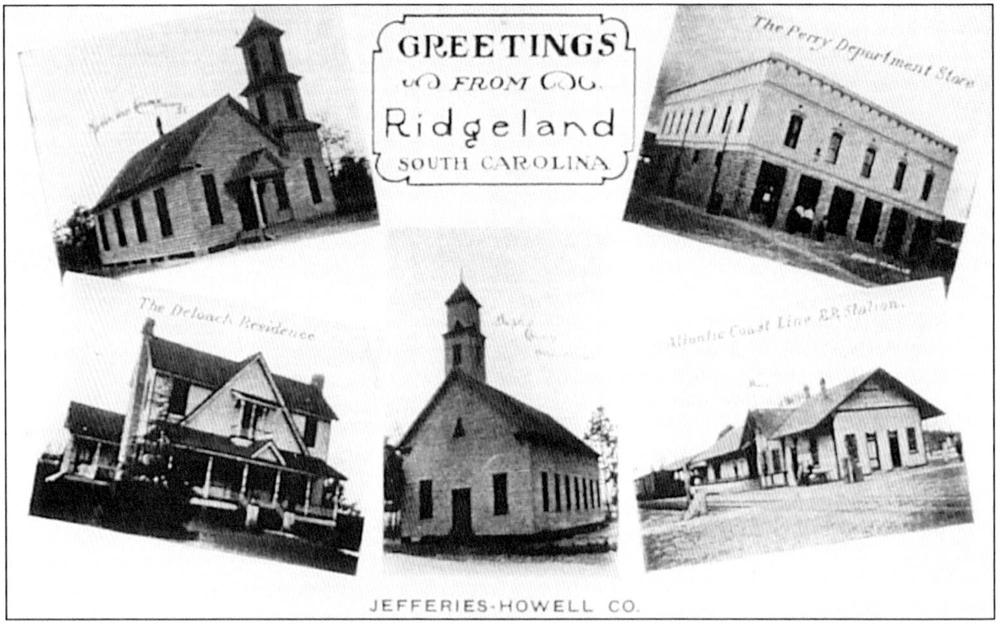


**Greetings from Ridgeland, S.C.** (Halftone, 3 3/8" x 5 1/2", [Kraus Mfg. Co., New York, NY]; Jefferies-Howell Co., sponsor; 1912.) "I . . . think that my prospects here are bright and with the coming of the new county I should be in a good position to make some money," Richard M. Jefferies (1889–1964) wrote his mother on December 29, 1910, from Ridgeland. He had come as the principal of the Ridgeland Graded School, wound up assisting in the formation of Jasper County, served as its first superintendent of education, and eventually became governor of South Carolina. By 1910, Jefferies had founded and was editing the weekly *Jasper Herald*. Four of the postcards used here, including this montage of five local landmarks, were published by the Jefferies-Howell Company.

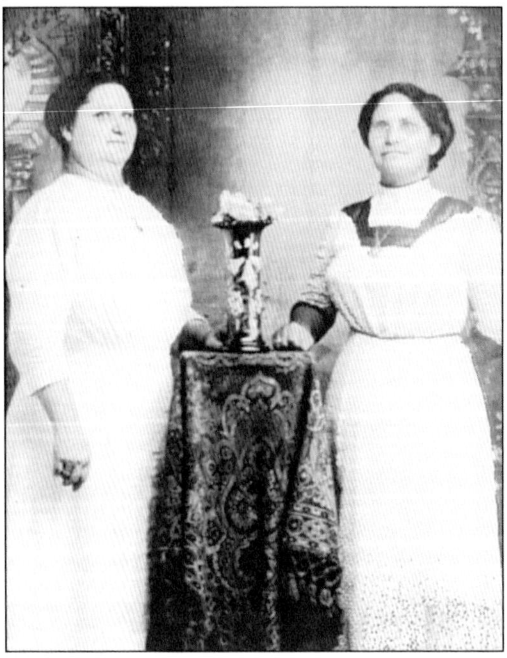

**[Portrait of the Farris Sisters, Ridgeland, S.C.]** (Photoprint, 5 3/8" x 3 1/4", *c.* 1915.) Sisters Alice Farris Frezelle and Ophelia Farris Jackson, seen here in a studio portrait which was probably made in Savannah, grew up in Ridgeland. Alice married a Savannah merchant, converted to his Catholic faith, and spent the rest of her life there as a wife and mother. Ophelia, also a Savannah homemaker and mother, became a seamstress in the city's Bethesda Boys' Home, but eventually moved back to South Carolina and spent her last years with their sister Mary Elizabeth Farris Smart ("Big Sister") in her home in Ridgeland.

**[PORTRAIT OF WILLIAM AND CURTIS SMART, RIDGELAND, S.C.]** (Photoprint, 5 4/10" x 3 5/10"; *c.* 1930.) This informal outdoor postal portrait of brothers William B. and Curtis L. Smart (b. 1922) was made in Tallahassee, Florida, about 1927. After their father's death, they came with their mother in 1933 to live with his parents on their old home place a few miles southwest of Ridgeland. Like his father, William has been a career railroad man. Curtis has retired as an officer with 30 years in the Air Force.

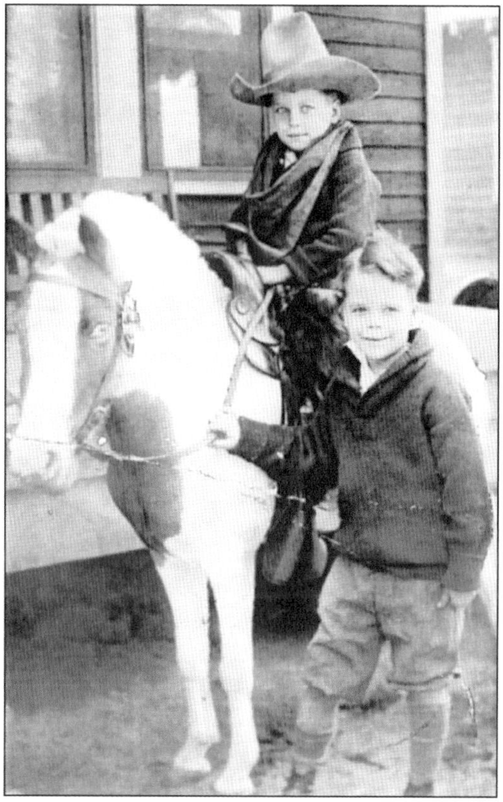

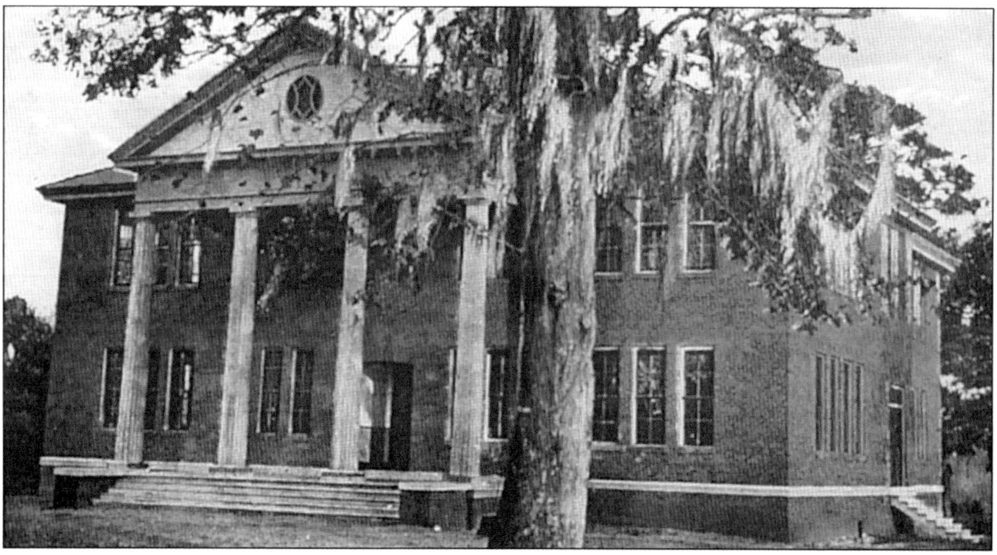

**RIDGELAND HIGH SCHOOL, RIDGELAND, S.C.** (Color lithography, 3 1/2" x 5 1/2", Curt Teich Co., #RC9210, Chicago, IL; *c.* 1916.) "Ridgeland," wrote the columnist in *The State*'s 1916 profile on the county, "takes greatest pride in her excellent public schools and the unexcelled work of her teachers." The writer goes on to reveal that "only about two months ago a new $12,000 building was turned over to the trustees, which is a very handsome building and speaks itself of Ridgeland progress."

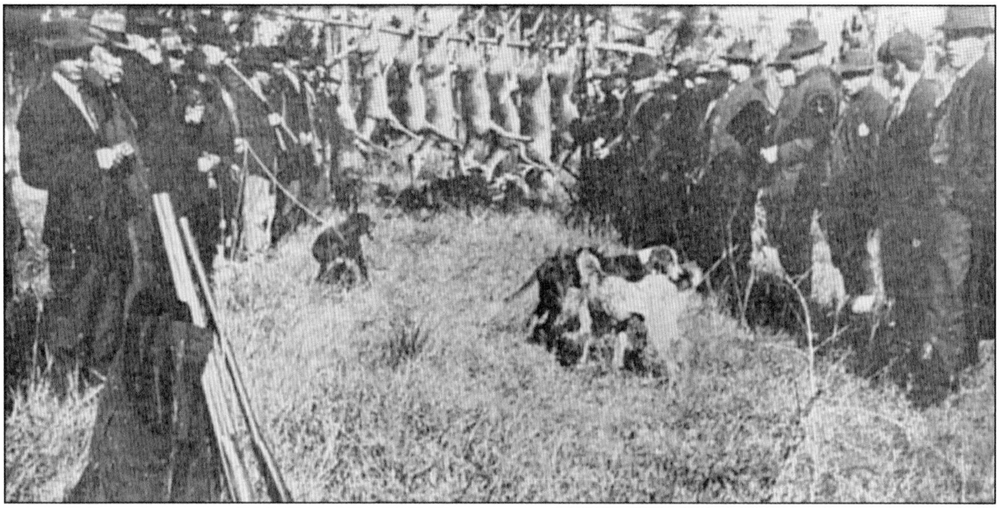

**AFTER THE CHASE, TEN DEER IN ONE DAY, NEAR RIDGELAND, S.C.** (Halftone, 3 1/2" x 5 1/2", [Kraus Mfg. Co., New York, NY]; Jefferies-Howell Co., sponsor; 1913.) "Our hunting grounds can be rented for a very small amount, thousands of acres are rented by Northern sportsmen whom we always welcome into our sunny Southland," R.B. Vance would write about Allendale County in the late 1930s. "We never hear of one violating our game laws and this is why we are glad to see them; too, it helps the farmer to pay his taxes on his outlying land." This could have been said of the entire region during the two preceding decades as well.

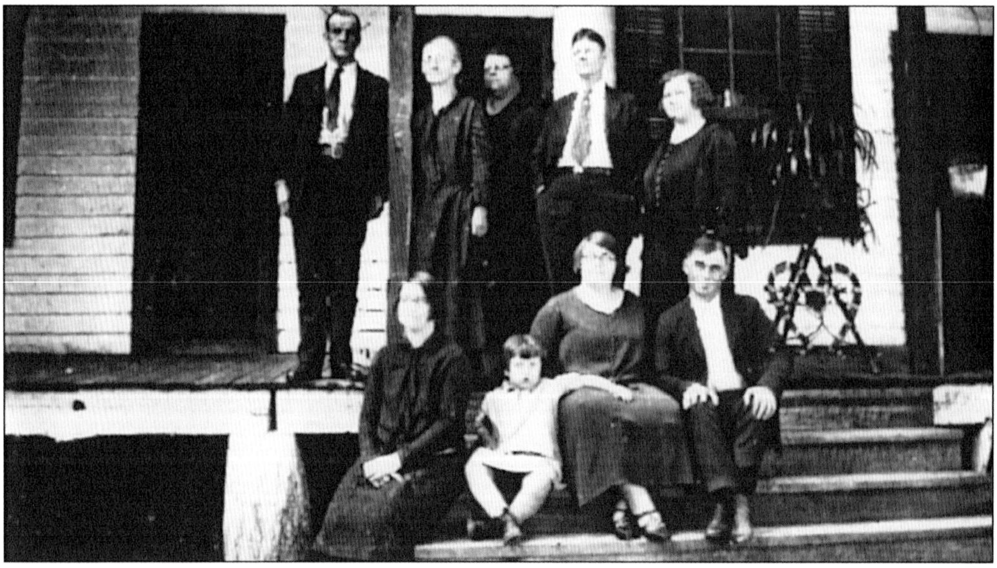

**[PORTRAIT OF THE LANGFORD FAMILY, GILLISONVILLE, S.C.]** (Photoprint, 3 1/2" x 5 1/2"; *c.* 1930.) Seen here gathered on the front porch of their home—perhaps on the occasion of a funeral—is the Langford family of the vicinity of Gillisonville, the historic old town a few miles northwest of Ridgeland which between 1840 and 1868 had served as the seat of government for Beaufort District. The family members are, left to right, as follows: (standing) John Langford, a farmer who served as an early supervisor of roads in Jasper County; his wife, Fanny Ulmer Langford; their daughter Bessie L. Roberts, who would later succeed her husband as postmaster of Coosawhatchie; son-in-law W.J. Ellis; and Mrs. (Ivy Annie Langford) Ellis; (seated) Bessie's daughters, Helen and Nancy; and the Langfords' children Ruby Ernestine and John Wesley.

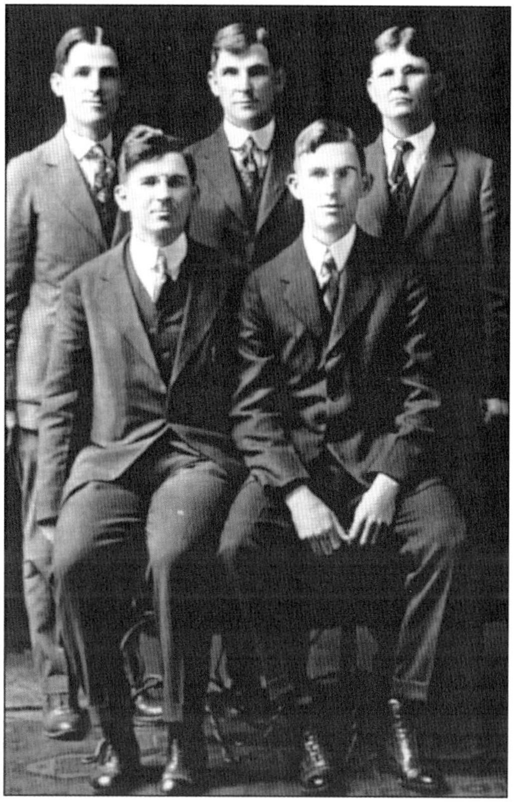

**[Portrait of the Ellis Brothers, Gillisonville, S.C.]** (Photoprint, 5 1/2" x 3 1/2", Harvey's Studio, Savannah, GA, photographer; *c.* 1928.) Harvey's Studio in Savannah made this portrait of the Ellis brothers, who were reared at "Stock Farm," located halfway between Gillisonville and Coosawhatchie. Pictured here are the following: (seated) Nathan and Earl; (standing) Dan, Junius, and William. William Jefferson Ellis made money in the timber business and served in the state senate. Junius Gather Ellis (1882–1946), farmer and turpentine operator, was married to Mary Gordon, who became South Carolina's first female state senator (1929–1932). They met when she came to the Gillisonville School as a teaching principal in 1913. Junius and W.J. acquired property in Savannah and built their mother a home there.

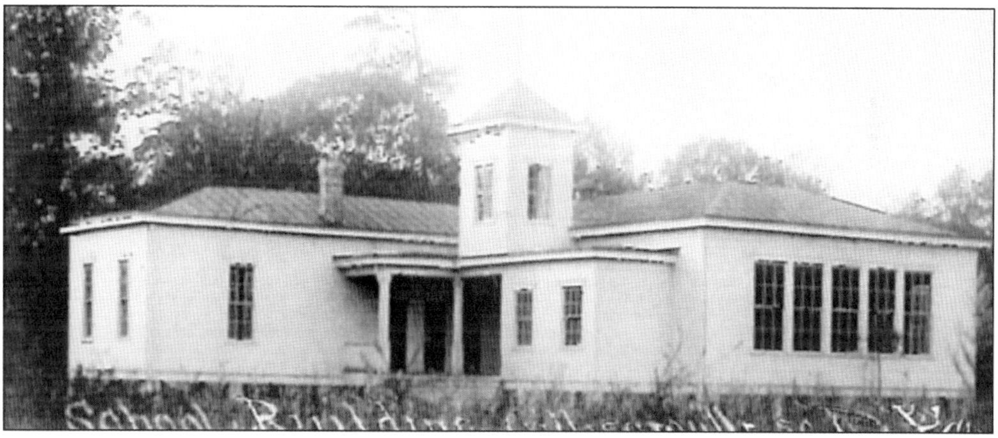

**Schoolhouse, Gillisonville, S.C.** (Photoprint, 3 1/2" x 5 4/10", R.L. Cleland, Hampton, SC, photographer; *c.* 1912.) The three-room wooden structure at Gillisonville was one of many new schoolhouses opened for use by Jasper County in the fall of 1912, according to that year's October issue of *Southern School News*, which went on to say that it was among the most beautiful of such schoolhouses in the state and that excellent work was being done there. The 1913 annual report of the state superintendent of education lists the total value of the school and its 7 acres of grounds at $3,000. Presumably, this was the school to which Mary Gordon came as a teacher-principal that year. Because a small community like Gillisonville probably could not have supported the sales of import or mail-order cards, Cleland's limited issue would have suited the need for a picture of the school.

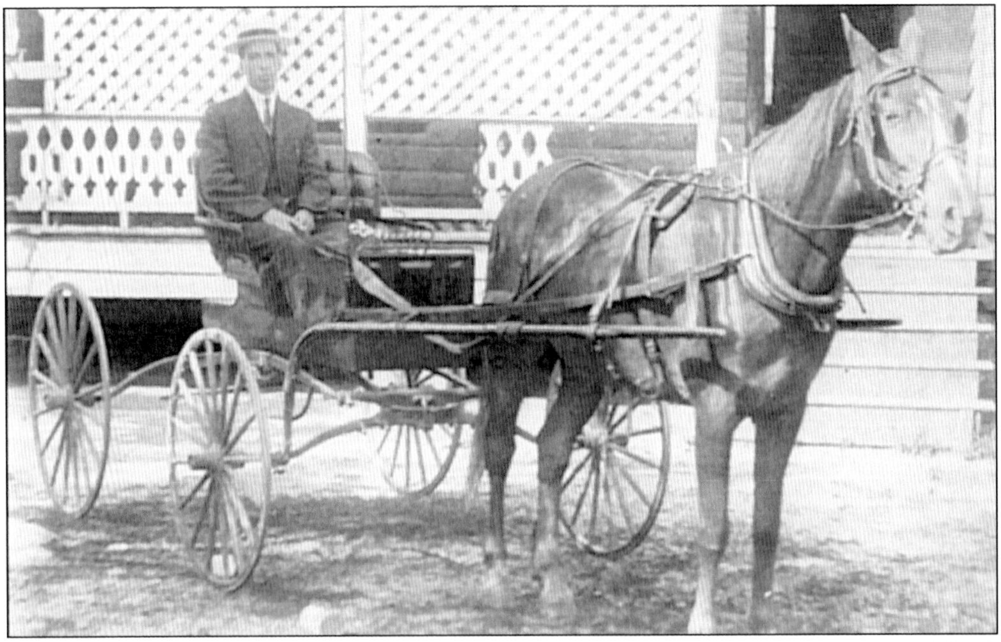

**[Portrait of Homer Phillips, Grays, S.C.]** (Photoprint, 3 3/8" x 5 3/8", R.L. Cleland, Hampton, SC, photographer; *c.* 1914.) Homer Phillips, shown here with his horse and buggy, was a member of a large and well-known farm family from the old community of Grays, located in the northernmost reaches of Jasper County and once a part of Hampton County. He later moved to Smoaks. This picture is believed to have been taken by his brother-in-law, photographer Robert Lee Cleland, who lived in Hampton.

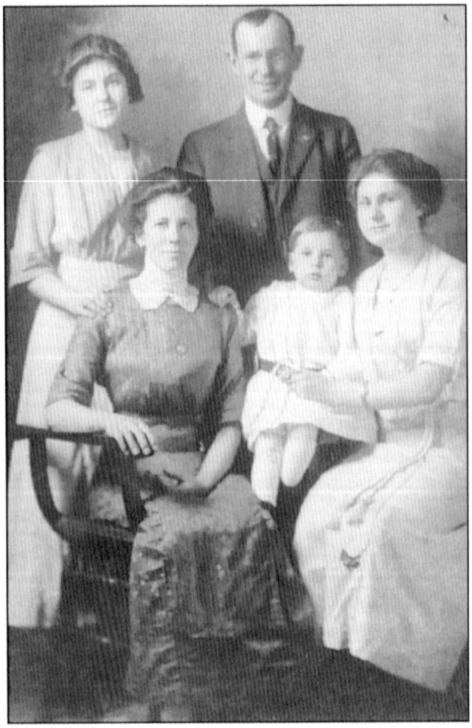

**[Portrait of the Wilson Family, Grays, S.C.]** (Photoprint, 5 3/8" x 3 3/8", Foltz Studio, Savannah, GA, photographer; *c.* 1920.) Another member of the prominent Phillips family of Grays, Cynthia Phillips Wilson (1884–1968), is shown seated here in a formal portrait along with her husband, Theodore (1871–1936), her stepdaughters Annis (left) and Margaret (right), and their son, Theodore Jr. They lived in Savannah and later in Charleston, where Wilson was engaged in the furniture business. This card, produced by Foltz Photographic Postals of Savannah, further documents the close ties between the Georgia city and Southern Carolina.

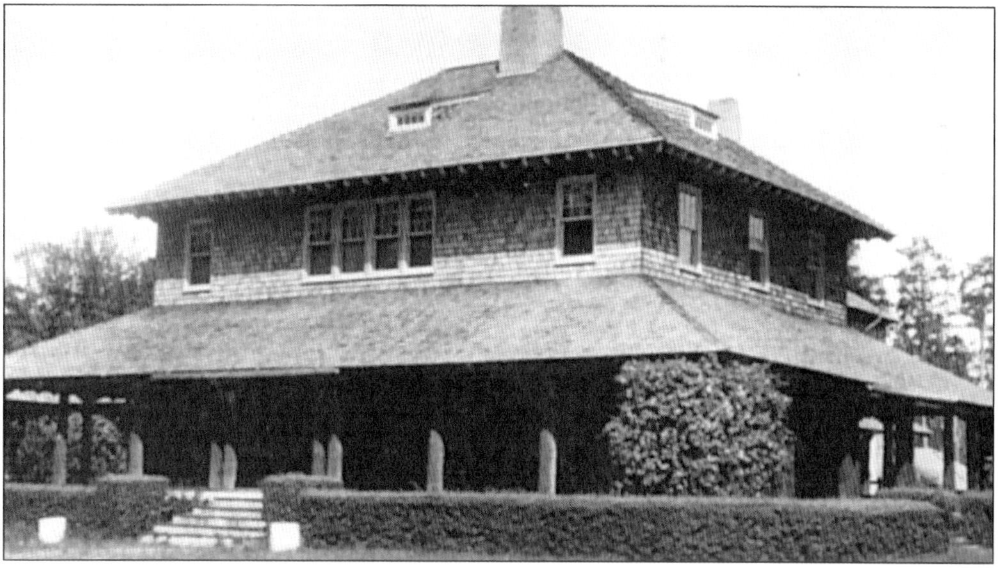

**[Pineland Hunting Club, Robertville, S.C.]** (Photoprint, 3 1/2" x 5 1/2"; *c.* 1912.) Pineland Hunting Club, located near Robertville in the northwestern section of Jasper County, was built between 1870 and 1872 on land purchased from the J.W. Lawton family by seven prominent New England industrialists, assisted by railroad director John King Garnett, in 1867. It was chartered that year as South Carolina's first organized hunt club. Constructed entirely of heart of pine harvested from the surrounding land, it featured a cedar shake roof and exterior siding of Vale Royal Eastern White Cedar shingles shipped down from Massachusetts. The structure was carefully restored and remodeled over a three-year period by the David Bormes family, who purchased this "mother" of Lowcountry South Carolina's hunting clubs in 1977.

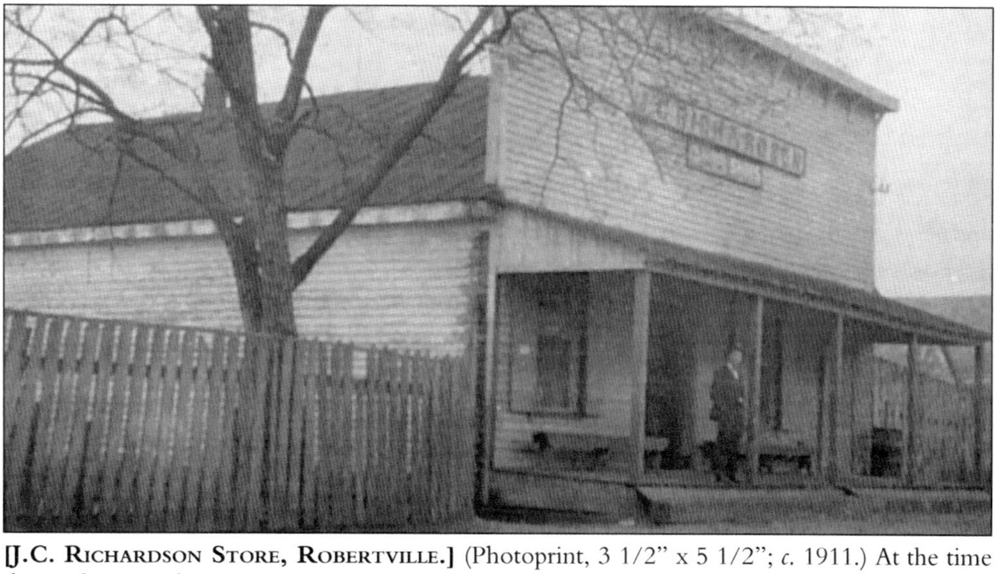

**[J.C. Richardson Store, Robertville.]** (Photoprint, 3 1/2" x 5 1/2"; *c.* 1911.) At the time this card was made, J.C. Richardson's store would have been an essential part of the small village of Robertville, which in 1910 had a population of 90. Located 9 miles northwest of Ridgeland in the Black Swamp section of the county, the town was named for descendants of Huguenot minister Pierre Robert, and it was the birthplace of General Henry Martyn Robert, author of *Robert's Rules of Order*. The original town was burned by Sherman's army in 1865.

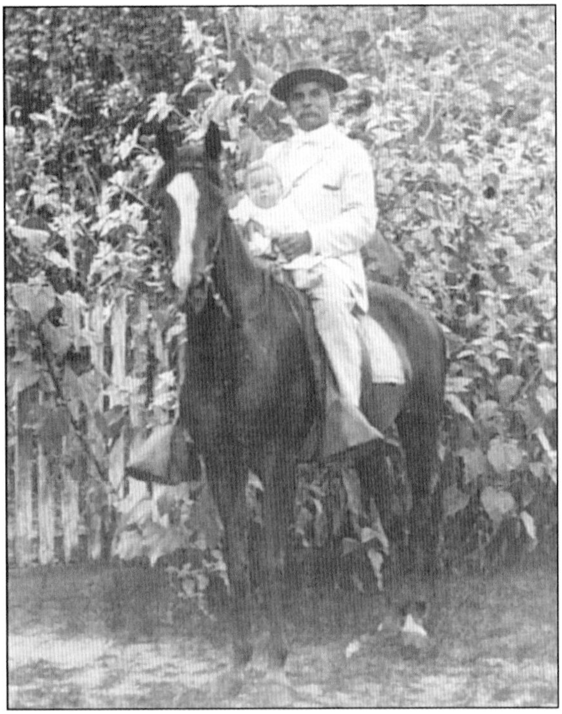

**[James Clarence Richardson Sr. and Jesse Causey Jr., Robertville, S.C.]** (Photoprint, 5 3/8" x 3 3/8"; *c.* 1912.) Robertville retail merchant and planter James Clarence Richardson (1852–1931), pictured on horseback with his grandchild Jesse Franklin Causey Jr. (b. 1912), was Jasper County's first state senator. He was elected as a Democrat for the two consecutive terms between 1913 and 1916. Sometime after 1925, he moved to Garnett, some 6 miles to the northwest, and is buried in nearby Black Swamp Methodist Cemetery.

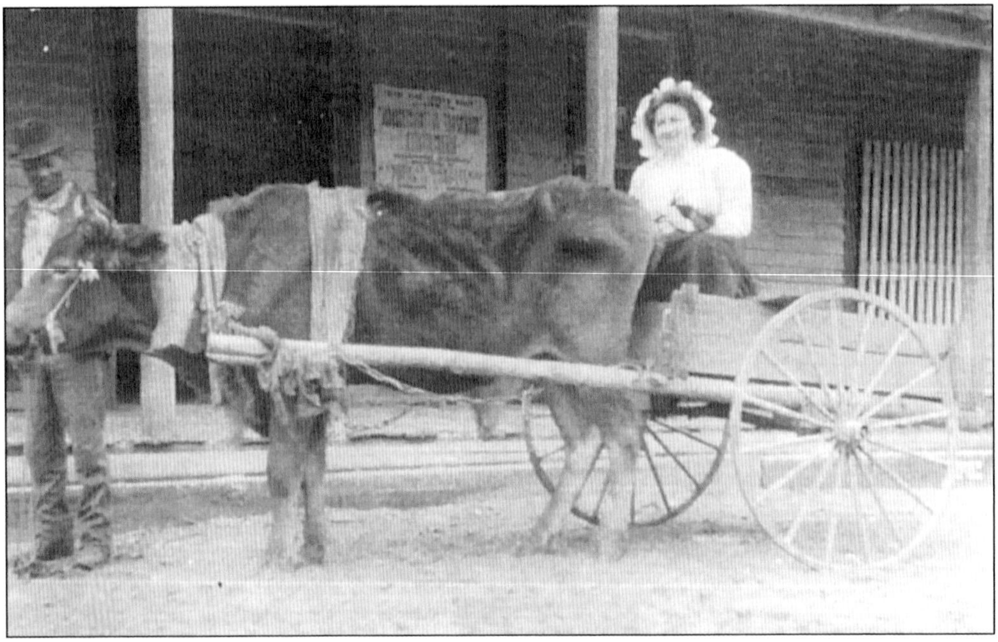

**[Portrait of a Woman in an Oxcart, Robertville, S.C.]** (Photoprint, 3 3/8" x 5 3/8"; *c.* 1912.) Jasper County's traditional agrarian economy and the make-up of its population are reflected in this spontaneous outdoor portrait probably taken by a family member. Behind the ox, placarded on the wall of J.C. Richardson's store, is a large advertisement for fertilizer manufactured by the American Agricultural Chemical Company of Savannah. The woman in the cart may be Maud C. Richardson Hopkins, one of the senator's three daughters.

# *Three*

# Hampton County

The creation of Hampton County in 1878 from the upper part of old Beaufort District arose chiefly out of economic and political differences between that section and the coastal area.

Consisting of 513 square miles lying in the Coastal Plains, the county had a predominately rural (80%) population of 19,696 residents in the mid-1920s. Abounding in woods and waters—it is bordered on the west by the Savannah River, on the east by the Salkehatchie and Combahee, with the Coosawhatchie flowing through its middle—Hampton County early on became known as a sportsman's paradise.

Because it is a county literally divided by a swamp, its history has also been one of division—between the communities on each side whose stories are told in the book *Both Sides of the Swamp* (1970). If it is a real division defined by sectional pride, rivalry, and competition, however, it is also one "based on mutual admiration," writes Mary McDonald Harper in her foreword to that book. Ultimately, she says, "we are one for all and all for Hampton County."

"Southern Carolina is the best place to live," remarked the editor of the *Hampton County Guardian* on June 14, 1916, "and Hampton County is the best part of Southern Carolina."

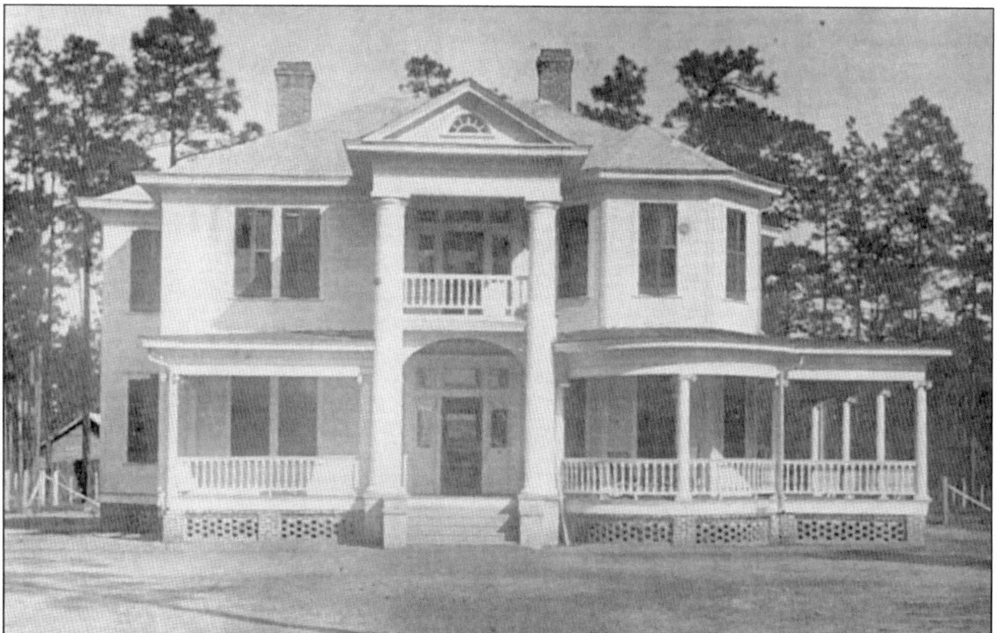

**[J.W. Chisolm House, Garnett.]** (Photoprint, 3 1/2" x 5 1/4"; *c.* 1915.) The J.W. Chisolm House, one block north of S.C. Road 20 in Garnett, was built in 1915 by the transplanted French architect and contractor Vincent Joseph Fontaine, who constructed similar homes in the Neo-classical Revival style in Estill, Brunson, and other communities in the area. J.W. Chisolm was a stockholder in the Richardson & Chisolm Store in Garnett, which in 1910 had a population of 100.

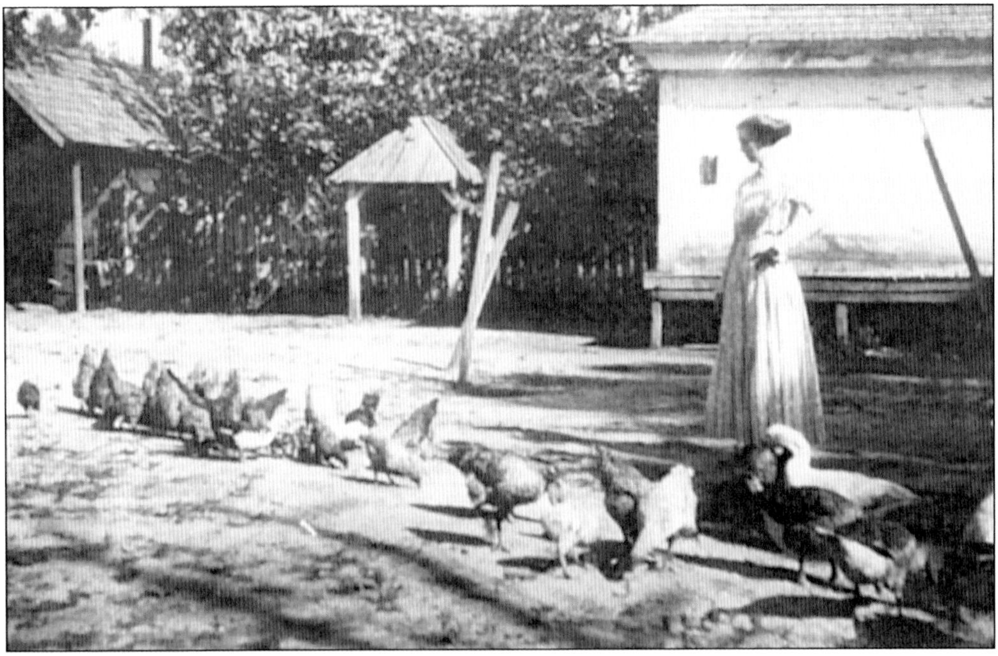

**[Scene in the Backyard of the Richardson Home, Garnett, S.C.]** (Photoprint, 3 7/16" x 5 1/2"; *c.* 1912.) This picture of one of the women in the J.C. Richardson household feeding chickens in the yard shows an activity typical of the time and place. The specific portrayal of it, however, is seldom found. Photography as a hobby had been expanding during the period. This amateur series may have followed the practice of buying by mail Kodak pre-loaded box-camera packets, which—once the images were taken—were sent back to the factory for processing, with the finished pictures then being returned to the customer.

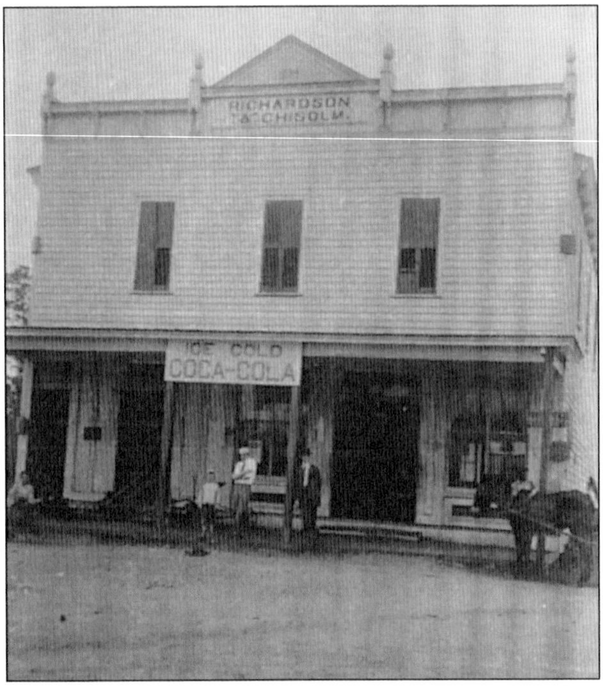


**[Richardson & Chisolm Store, Garnett, S.C.]** (Photoprint, 5 1/2" x 3 1/2"; *c.* 1912.) The Richardson and Chisolm Store, which once stood across the railroad tracks in Garnett on the north side of Highway 20 (Augusta Stagecoach Road) just west of its intersection with Highway 321, was the commercial center of this rural community at the southern tip of Hampton County. Garnett was named for Georgia native John K. Garnett, who came into the area "to develop and organize hunting clubs" (*Both Sides of the Swamp*), for which the region of Southern Carolina would become famous. This warm-weather shot features an enticement for "Ice Cold Coca-Cola."

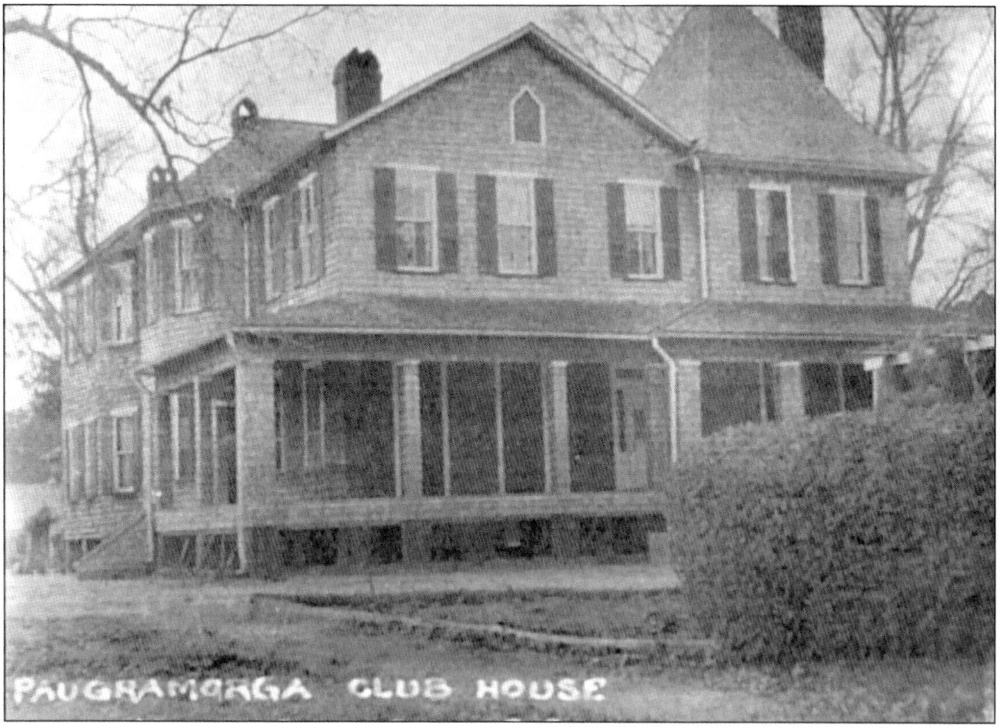


**PAUGRAMORGA [?] CLUB HOUSE, GARNETT, S.C.** (Photoprint, 3 7/16" x 5 3/8"; 1911.) The clubhouse seen here on its east side is actually the Belmont Lodge pictured long before its 1989 renovation as part of the state-owned James W. Webb Wildlife Center, located off Highway 20 a few miles west of Garnett. Reportedly begun by John K. Garnett after his acquisition of the old Tison Plantation in 1882, it was completed before 1921 by August Belmont (of the New York family of bankers and horse-racing enthusiasts), who bought the property in 1890. The name of uncertain spelling and origin is believed to have been attached to the place by the timber company which purchased it in the early 1920s.

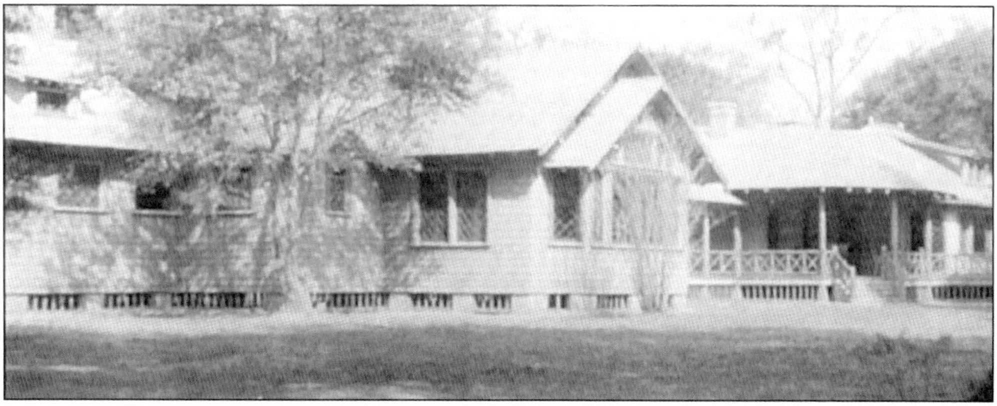

**THE HUNTINGTON RESIDENCE NEAR GARNETT, S.C.** (Photoprint, 3 7/16" x 5 7/16"; *c.* 1912.) A landmark which survives as one of the region's emblems of the post–Civil War investment of Northern capital in Southern Carolina for recreational purposes, the hunting lodge identified here as the Huntington Residence was built by this prominent New York family between 1903 and 1906. Also known as Gravel Hill, the property is located 5.5 miles west of Garnett on the north side of Highway 20 and is currently owned by the J.W. Yonce family.

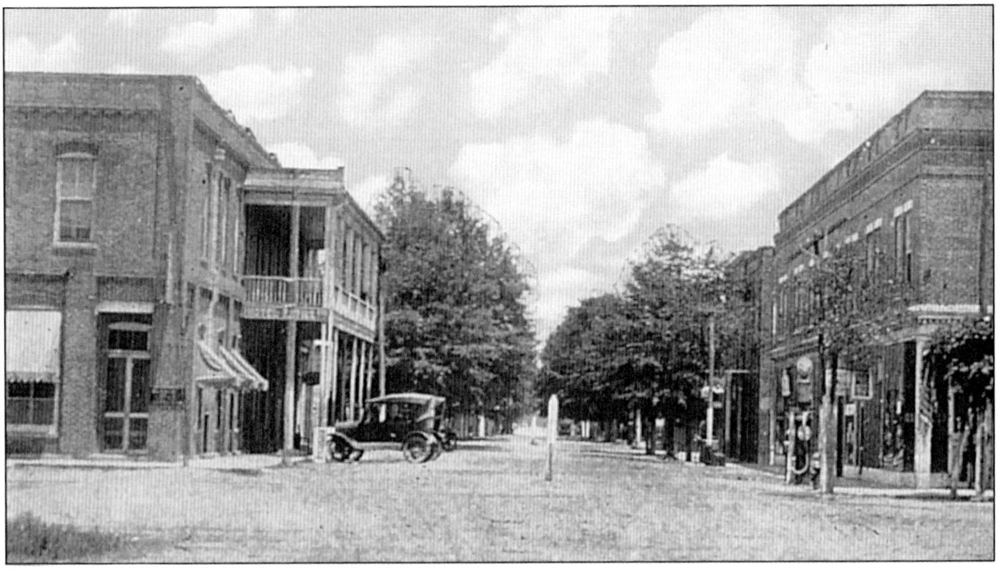

**Main Street Looking East, Estill, S.C.** (Halftone with Blue Sky, 3 1/2" x 5 1/2", [Curt Teich Co., Chicago, IL]; Asheville Post Card Co., #59848, Asheville, NC; *c.* 1926.) This view of Estill looking east at the intersection of Main Street and Third Avenue, or Highways 321 and 3, shows the old Hotel Estill, with its covered second-story porch, to the left. It no longer exists. Estill had a population of 475 in 1910.

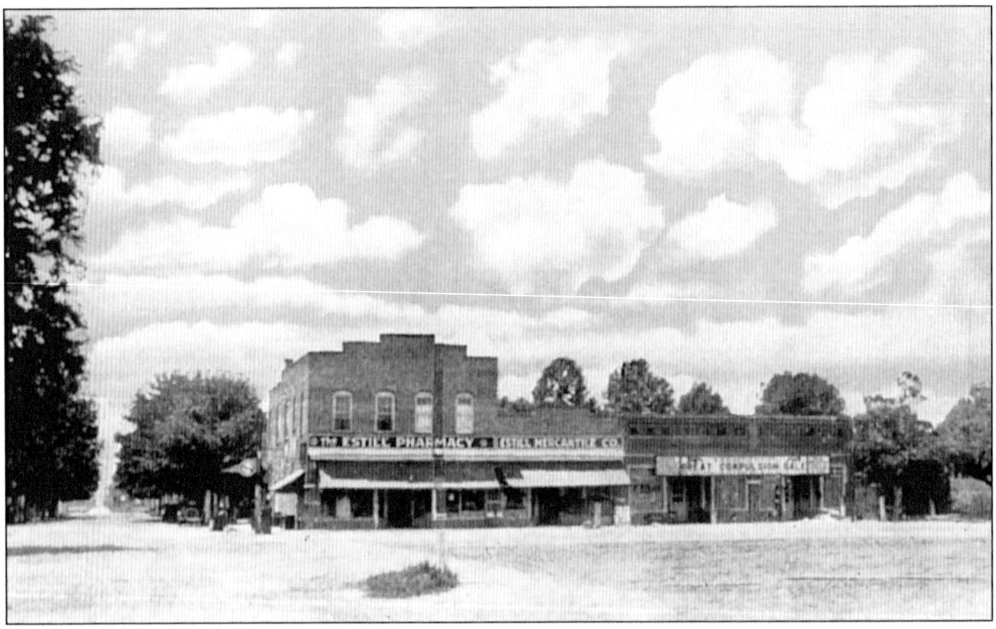


**Business Block, Estill, S.C.** (Halftone with Blue Sky, 3 1/2" x 5 1/2", [Curt Teich Co., Chicago, IL]; Asheville Post Card Co., #59844, Asheville, NC; *c.* 1926.) Modern units now stand in downtown Estill at the corner of Third and West Railroad Avenues in place of the old two-story building which housed the Estill Pharmacy. To the right of the Estill Mercantile Company was a bakery whose banner read, "Great Compulsions Sale." Situated on "the other side of the swamp" in one of the leading agricultural sections of Hampton County, Estill was its largest town, with 1,393 inhabitants by the mid-1920s.

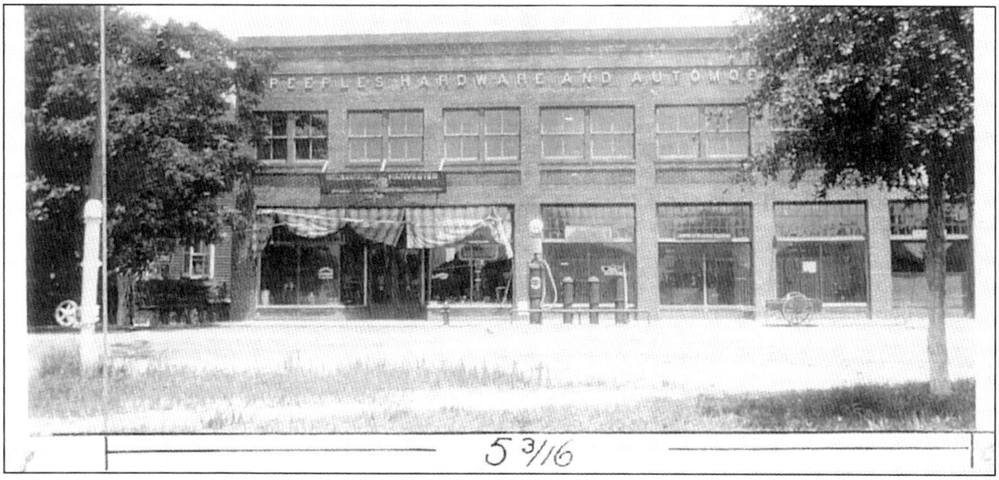


**Peeples' Hardware Store, Estill, S.C.** (Master Photoprint, Halftone, 3 1/2 " x 5 1/2", [Curt Teich Co., Chicago, IL]; Asheville Post Card Co., Asheville, NC; *c.* 1929.) This thick-walled brick commercial structure, still serving an active hardware business in Estill, was erected in the middle of the block just north of the Estill Hotel in 1920 by William and Ben Peeples. In 1924, a Ford dealership was added to the business. Gasoline pumps can be seen in front of the store and at right the cart which was used to distribute goods and haul them from the depot across the street. This marked, uncut view-card picture bears the original cropping lines made by the editor at the Asheville Post Card Company, which solicited photographs and then forwarded them to Curt Teich to be printed as postcards.

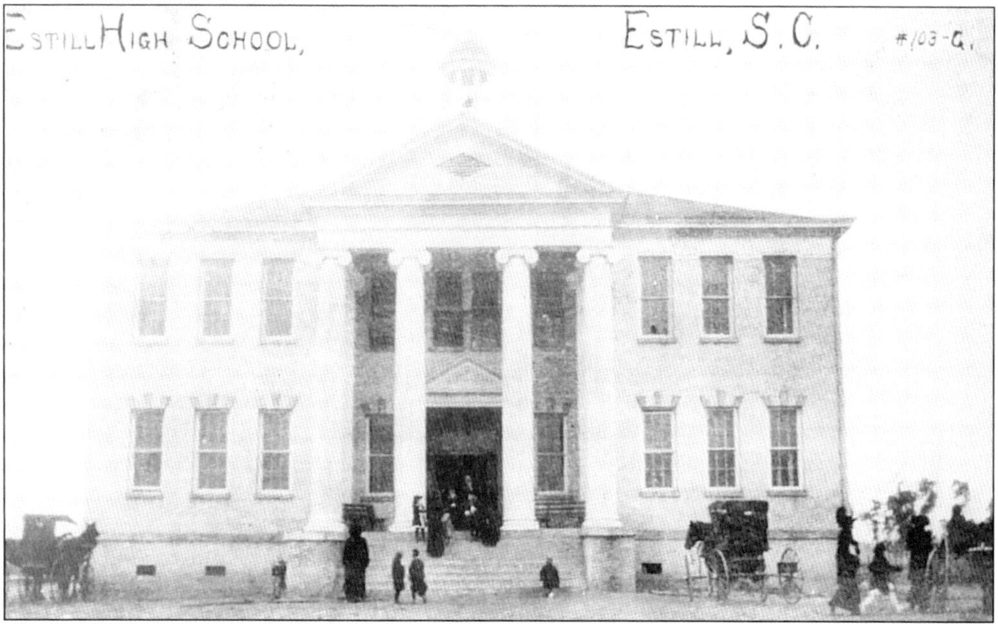


**Estill High School, Estill, S.C.** (Photoprint, 3 3/8" x 5 3/8", #103-6; *c.* 1913.) The two-story brick Neoclassic-style Estill High School, built on Fourth Street in 1911, was almost identical to the Varnville School also erected that year. The school and grounds had a combined estimated value of $10,000 in 1913. This building was replaced in the 1930s by a new elementary school. The card is postmarked June 28, 1916. This professional photoprint, perhaps made by an area photographer for the county public schools, carries his image coding system.

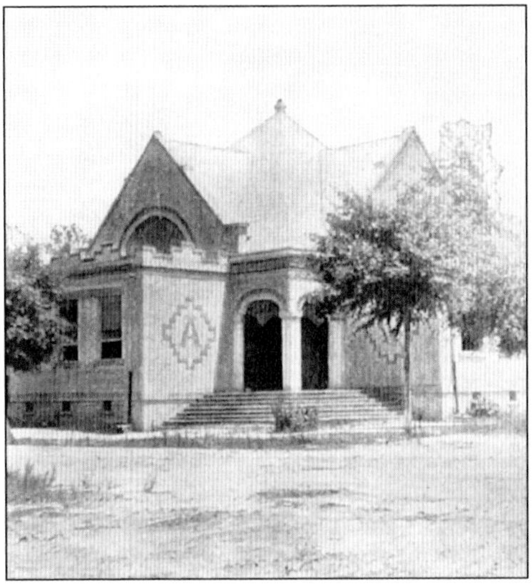

**Lawtonville Baptist Church, Estill, S.C.** (Halftone & Blue Sky, 3 1/2" x 5 1/2", [Curt Teich Co., Chicago, IL]; Asheville Post Card Co., #59845, Asheville, NC; *c.* 1926.) The Lawtonville Baptist Church was originally constituted as the Savannah River, Carolina, Church in 1775, and later became known as the Pipe Creek Church of Regular Baptists. The congregation moved to Lawtonville in 1826 and in 1884 took the community's name. The new sanctuary shown here was built for about $10,000 in 1911 to a design by Savannah architect J. DeBruyn Kops. It was dedicated on May 4, 1912.

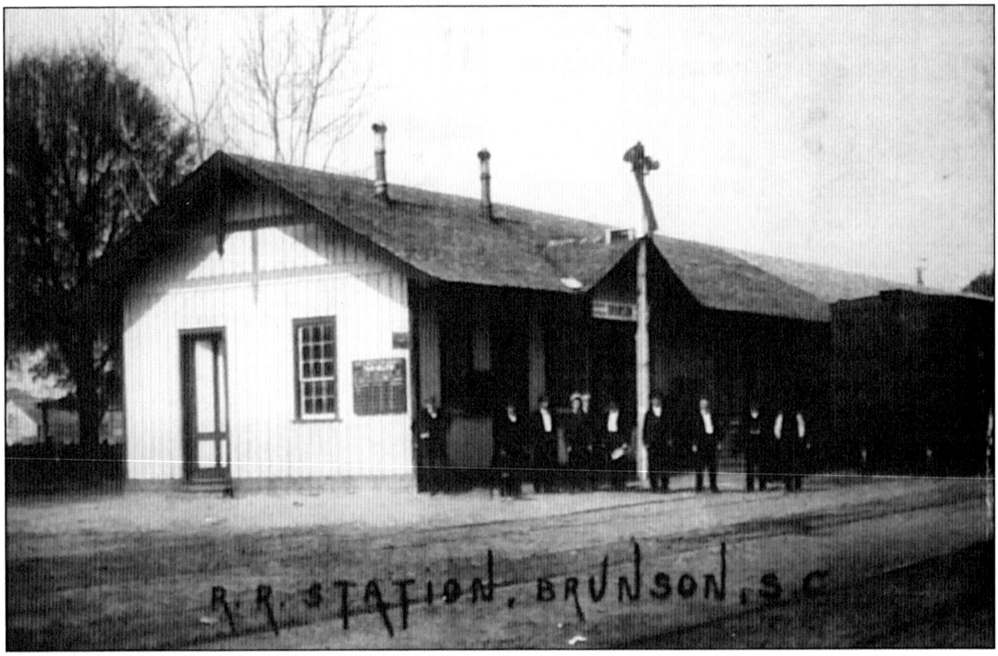


**R.R. Station, Brunson, S.C.** (Photoprint, 3 1/2" x 5 1/2"; 1908.) The Charleston & Western Carolina Railroad station at Brunson was very similar to the one at Varnville (see page 86), in its construction and the presence of the "train bulletin" board next to the multi-paneled window at left and the Western Union office sign above it. Mileage indicators to Augusta and Port Royal no doubt appear on either side of the name "Brunson" on the depot's main sign seen here above the group of townsmen and station personnel. The structure has been moved about a block from its original location and stands next to an old cotton gin. Because of this unique series of postcards, Brunson is visually one of the best-documented small towns in South Carolina. The stylized handwritten captions on these photoprint cards may be the distinguishing mark of some itinerant photographer who traveled the Charleston & Western Carolina Railroad taking view-card pictures in such towns as Brunson, Hampton, and Varnville.

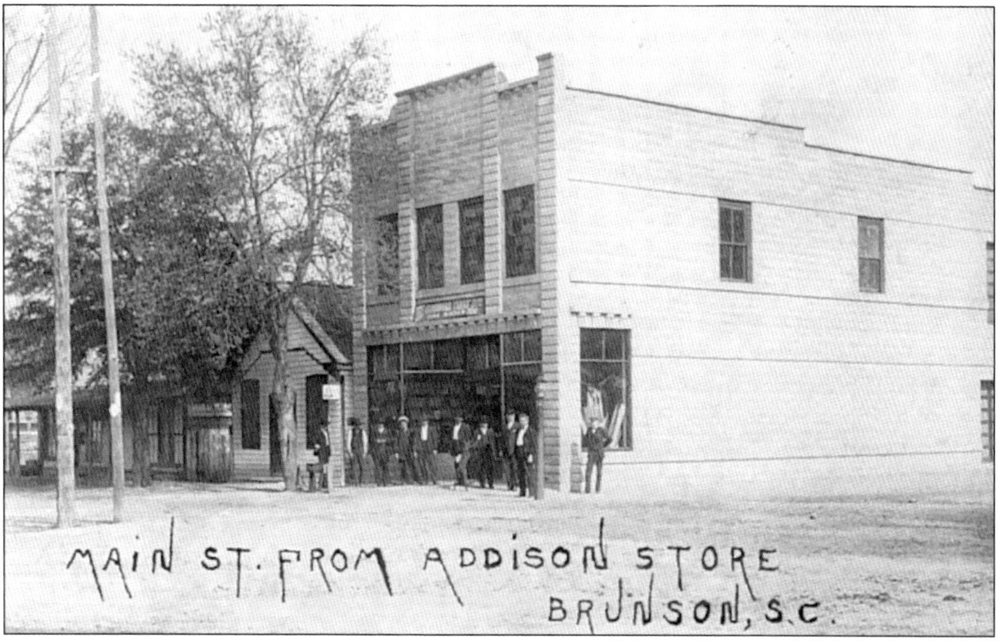


**Main Street from Addison Store, Brunson, S.C.** (Photoprint, 3 1/2" x 5 1/2"; 1908.) The Addison Store is at the center of this view of the main business section of Brunson, which had its beginnings on the site of the post office donated by William E. Brunson. Chartered in 1874, the town had a population of 500 by 1910.

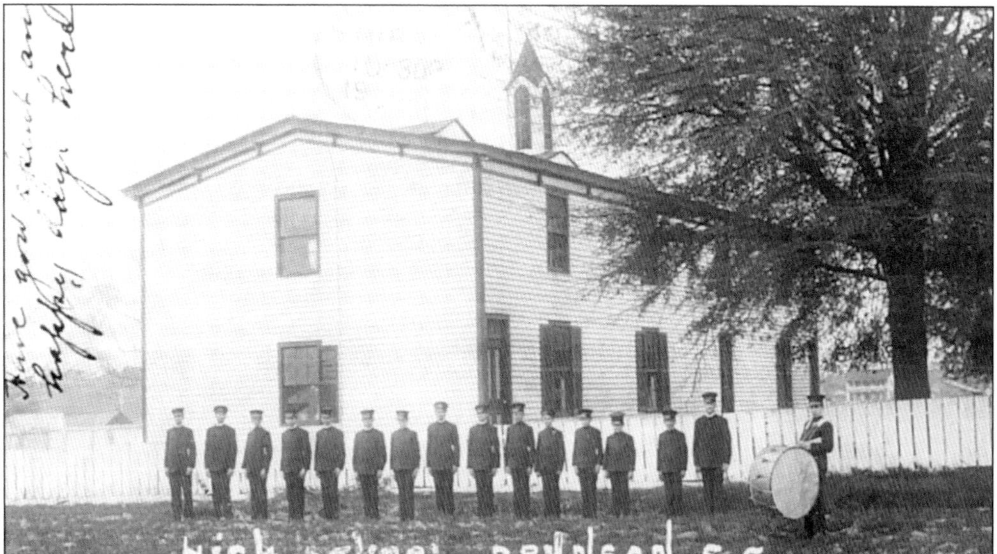


**High School, Brunson, S.C.** (Photoprint, 3 1/2" x 5 1/2"; 1908.) Education seems to have been among the chief concerns of the settlers of Brunson, which had at its center the Pineville Academy—later known successively as Brunson Academy, Brunson Collegiate Institute, and Brunson Military Academy. After its initial establishment in a log building, it came to be housed in a two-story structure whose second floor functioned as a dormitory. Brunson High School was organized in 1905, and in 1908 a brick school building was erected—"the first for any small town in this area" (*Both Sides of the Swamp*).

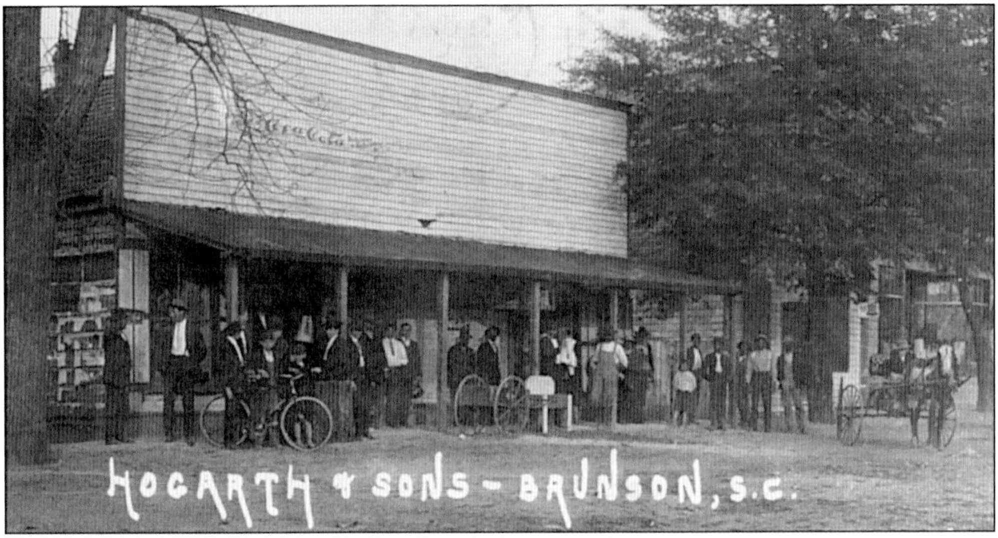


**HOGARTH & SONS, BRUNSON, S.C.** (Photoprint, 3 1/2" x 5 1/2"; 1908.) The citizens of Brunson, "by a little co-operating," could make theirs "the best town between Augusta and Charleston," reads a merchant's ad in the *Hampton County Guardian*, June 10, 1914. "Let every man, woman and child buy their goods at home and success is ours." Although much changed, the basic commercial structure here on North Railroad Avenue remains and still houses a business operated by a descendant of the Hogarth family.

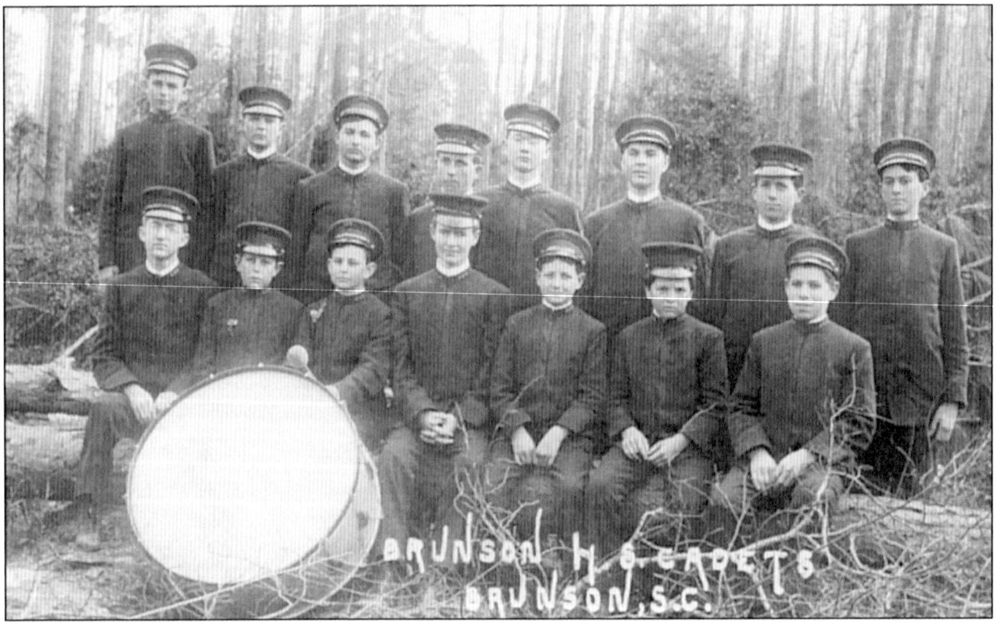


**BRUNSON H.S. CADETS, BRUNSON, S.C.** (Photoprint, 3 1/2" x 5 1/2"; 1907.) The young men tagged here simply as Brunson H[igh] S[chool] Cadets are further identified in *Both Sides of the Swamp* as band members from the Brunson School. Pictured in this *c.* 1907 informal portrait are, from left to right, the following: (first row) Wallace Cone, Ralph Lightsey, Mack Langford, McTeer Bowers, Ellis Bowers, Forest Barnes, and Herbert Eagerton; (second row) Walter Brunson, Farnum Moore, unidentified, Edgar Bowers, Dick Addison, Charlie Miley, Frank Bowers, and Cliff Langford.

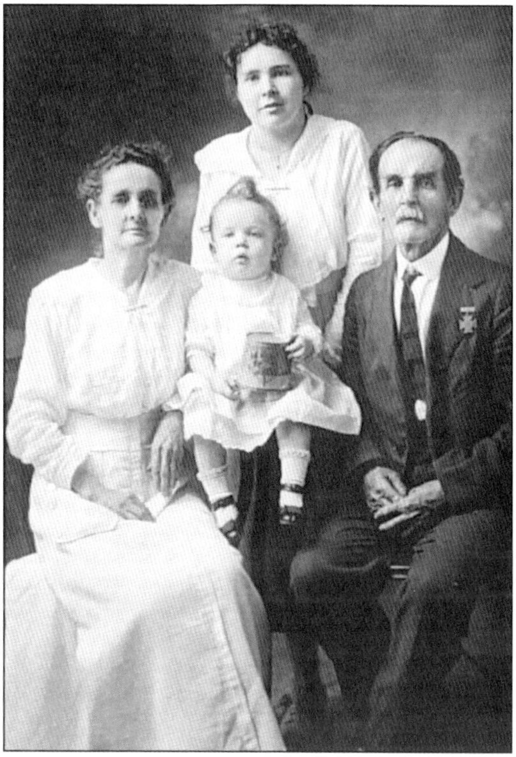

**[Portrait of the Langford Family, Brunson, S.C.]** (Photoprint, 5 1/2" x 3 1/2"; 1917.) Four generations of the Langford family of Brunson pose for a postcard portrait taken on August 27, 1917. From left to right are Rosa Ulmer, young Roland Seckinger, Edith Seckinger, and Barney H. Langford.

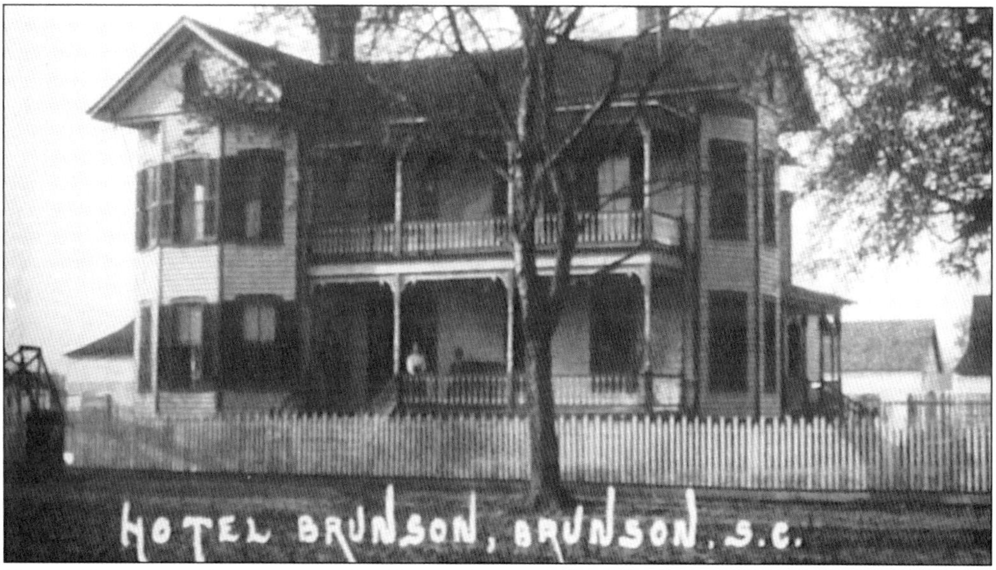


**Hotel Brunson, Brunson, S.C.** (Photoprint, 3 1/2" x 5 1/2"; 1908.) Brunson was a stop on the Charleston & Western Carolina Rail Road and was the location of the annual county fair. As a market for cotton, watermelons, and truck-farm produce, Brunson would have had need for a hotel or two. Hotel Brunson was actually one of three hotels that once served the community. Penned on the verso of this card, postmarked October 28, 1908, is this message: "This Building burned last night nothing at all saved narrow escape for the people some had to climb down the post happened 3'clock a.m."

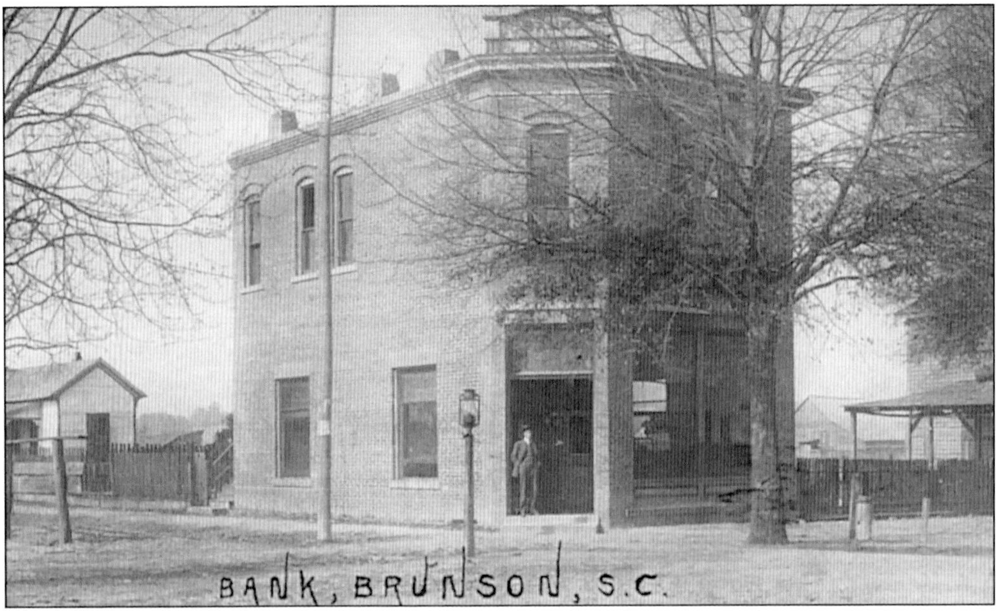


**Bank, Brunson, S.C.** (Hand-Colored Photoprint, 3 1/2" x 5 1/2"; 1908.) The Bank of Brunson, believed to have been in operation as early as 1907, was located in this two-story building at the corner of South Manker and South Railroad Streets. It later became the First National Bank. The building is remembered to have existed into the late 1960s. The corner entrance is typical of many of the bank buildings erected during this period.

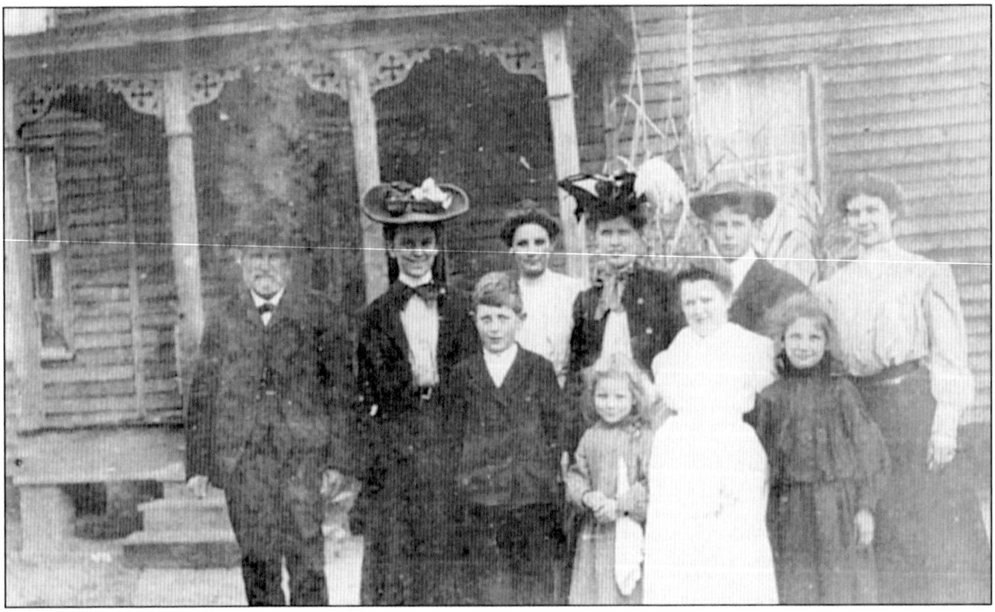

**[Portrait of the Lightsey Family, Brunson, S.C.]** (Photoprint, 3 1/4" x 5"; 1906.) Pictured in this informal postcard portrait, taken in front of the Judson H. Lightsey home at 213 Railroad Avenue in Brunson, are, from left to right, as follows: (front row) Ralph L. Lightsey, Lee Lightsey, Miss Hattie Lightsey, and Mildred Lightsey; (second row) Obie Kinard, Miss Langley, Mrs. J.H. Lightsey, Miss Theresa Lightsey, J. Merman Lightsey, and Miss Emma Lightsey. This copy was mailed on May 28, 1906.

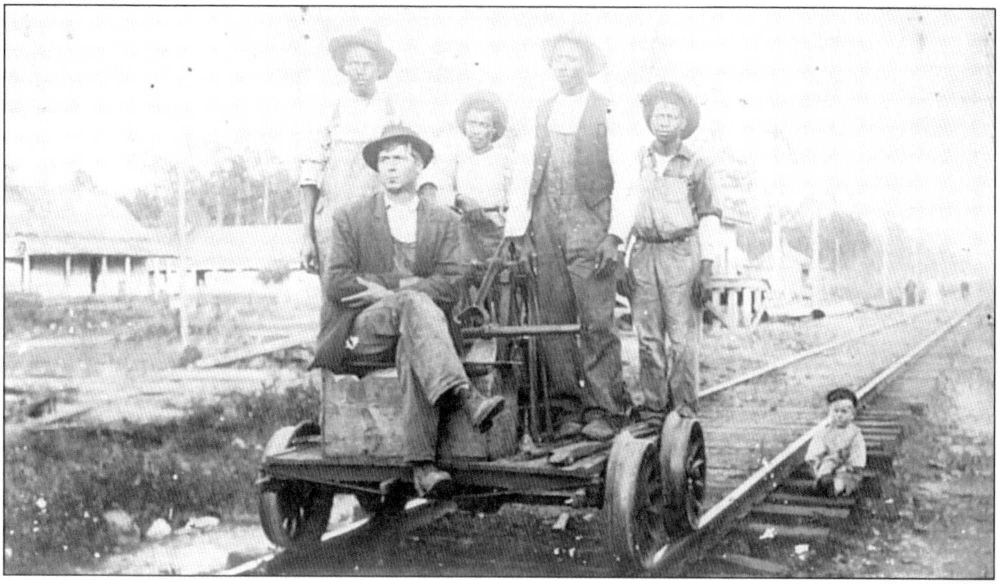

**[Picture of a Railroad Crew, Hampton County, S.C.]** (Photoprint, 3 3/8" x 5 3/8"; *c.* 1918.) Mr. Martin Elbert "Bert" Terry, a section foreman with the Charleston & Western Carolina Railroad, is shown here seated in front of his crew on a mobile service unit along a portion of tracks in the Hampton area. The child sitting on the crossties at right has not been identified. This professional looking, one-of-a-kind view taken at a railroad work site may have been made by an itinerant photographer simply wishing to capture something of the life of railroad men. Or perhaps it was taken by Terry's wife.

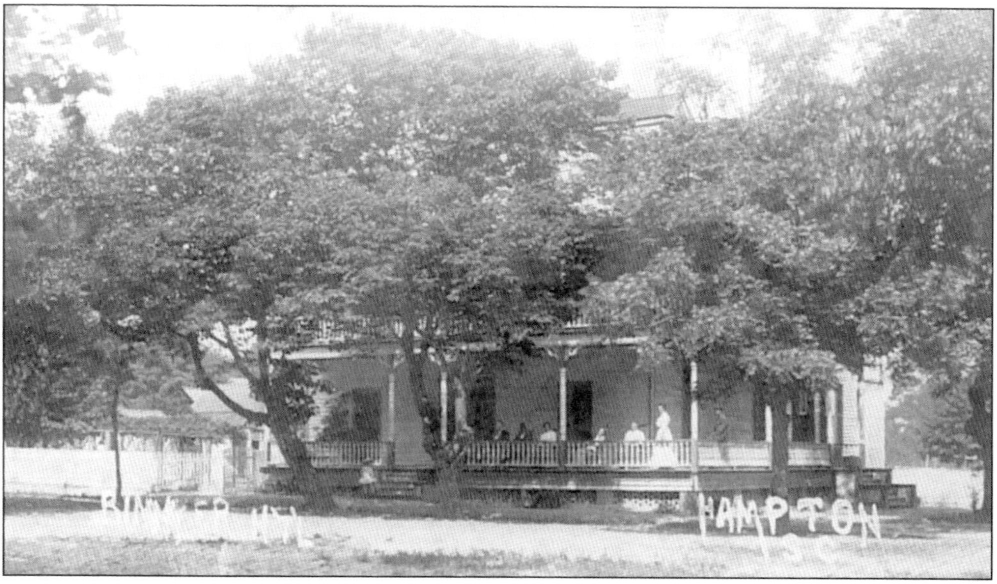


**Binnicker Hotel, Hampton, S.C.** (Photoprint, 3 1/2" x 5 3/8"; *c.* 1908.) For more than 45 years, Mrs. Susan Ellis "Tudie" Binnicker operated hotels which stood at the corner of Lee (Main) and Magnolia, across from the railroad tracks. The one above, built *c.* 1907–1908 to replace an earlier one lost to fire, had 19 bedrooms. In season and out, it became temporary home to many of the region's prominent politicians, circuit court judges, and court reporters. It was demolished in 1986. The photographer of this card also made the Brunson pictures.

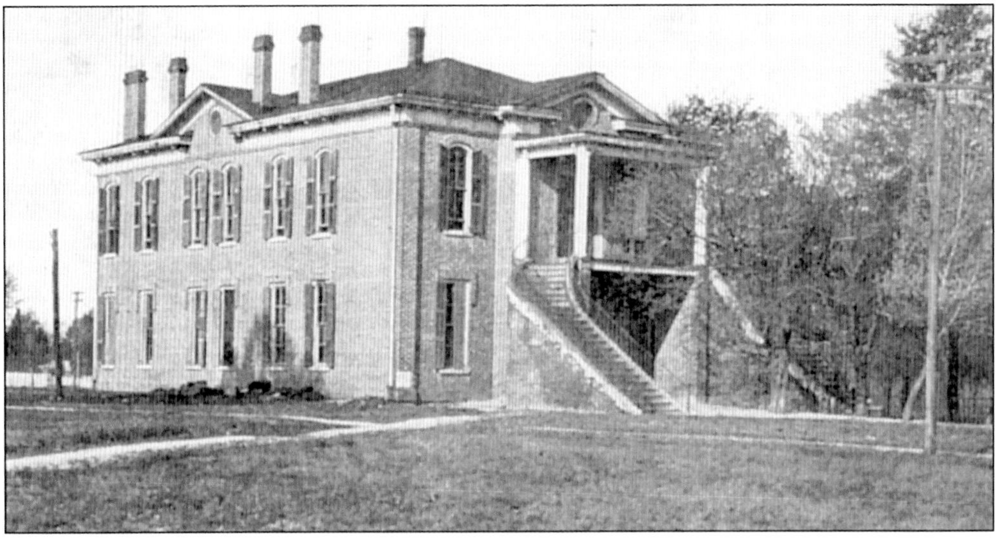

**Court House, Hampton, S.C.** (Halftone, 3 1/2" x 5 1/2", [Rich Photo-Process Co., New York, NY]; W.T. Johns, Hampton, SC, sponsor; 1908.) The cornerstone of the Hampton County Courthouse, built on land donated by Mrs. Josephine A. Hoover, was laid by General Wade Hampton on October 12, 1878, while he was governor of South Carolina. Different in appearance from any other county courthouse in the state, the brick Italianate Victorian structure, which still stands on Main Street, features a second-story arch over its front entrance. In 1925, it underwent major renovations, resulting in the removal of the double curved stairway and the eight interior chimneys.

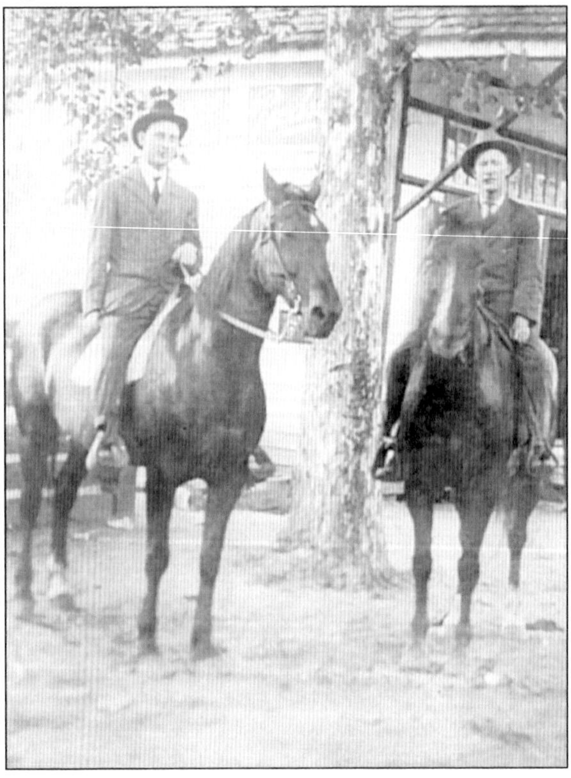

**[Portrait of J. Frank Rivers and G.T. Crews, Hampton, S.C.]** (Photoprint, 5 3/8" x 3 3/8"; 1909.) J. Frank Rivers Sr. (1889–1975), who served as mayor of Hampton from 1930 to 1948, is shown here, at left, with his friend G.T. Crews, a dealer in horses and mules. The picture is believed to have been taken in 1909 in front of the original J.H. Rivers and Son business on Lee Avenue. In 1910, Hampton had a population of 725.

**[Portrait of "Doc" Mixon and Eugene Stanley, Hampton, S.C.]** (Photoprint, 5 3/8" x 3 3/8"; *c.* 1918.) This World War I portrait of two uniformed Hampton area men is dated January 10, 1918. It may have been taken by Hampton photographer Robert Lee Cleland (see page 85).

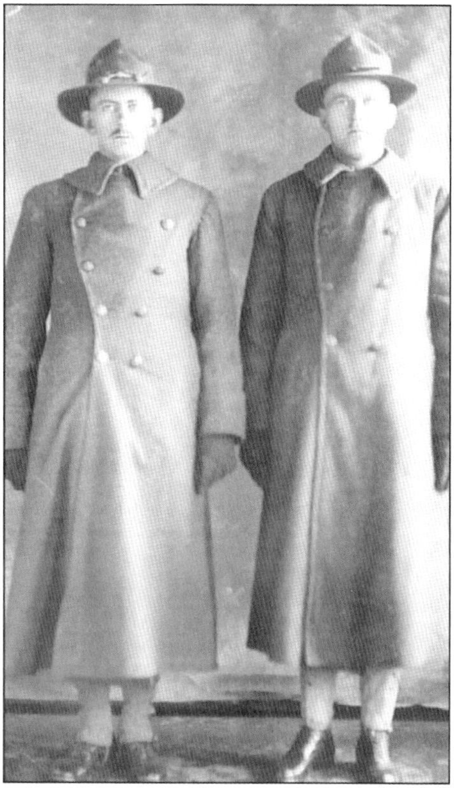

**Bank of Hampton, Hampton, S.C.** (Halftone, 3 1/2" x 5 1/2", [Rich Photo-Process Co., New York, NY]; W.T. Johns, Hampton, SC, sponsor; *c.* 1908.) This picture of the Hampton Bank, on Elm Street, is one of the three views of the town made by a mail-order company for jeweler W.T. Johns in 1908. The bank, which was established *c.* 1890–1892 and erected this building in the Italian Victorian style *c.* 1897, served the community until it was forced to declare bankruptcy in 1926. Since then, the building has been used for a multitude of purposes. It currently houses the Hampton Museum and Visitors Center.

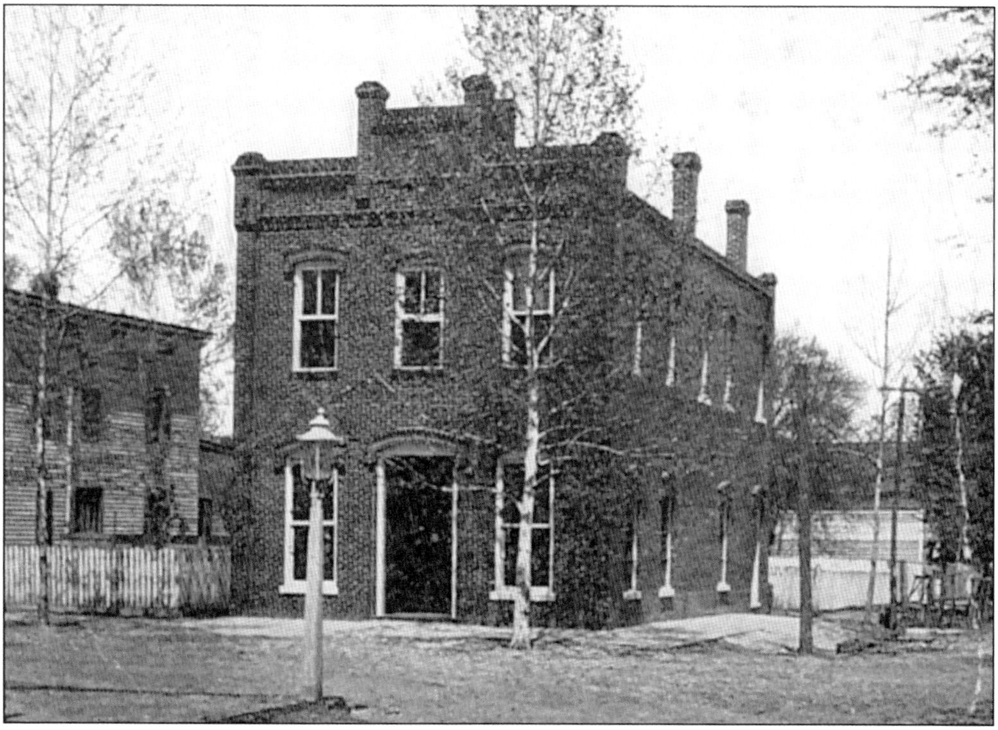

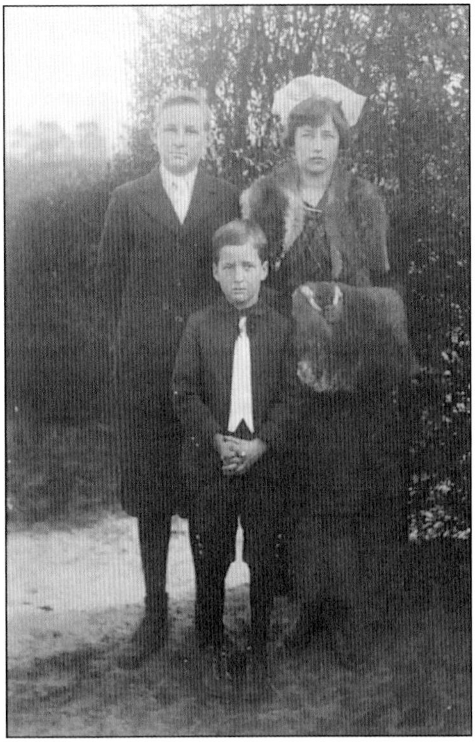

**[Portrait of the Peeples Children, Hampton, S.C.]** (Photoprint, 5 1/2" x 3 3/8"; 1914.) This postcard portrait of the three children of Eugene and Emma Johns Peeples was taken in 1914. Eugene Jr. (1901–1983), at left, moved to Texas; Earl (1908–1979) became director of Peeples' Funeral Home in Hampton; Aline (1899–1945) married Frank Ayer.

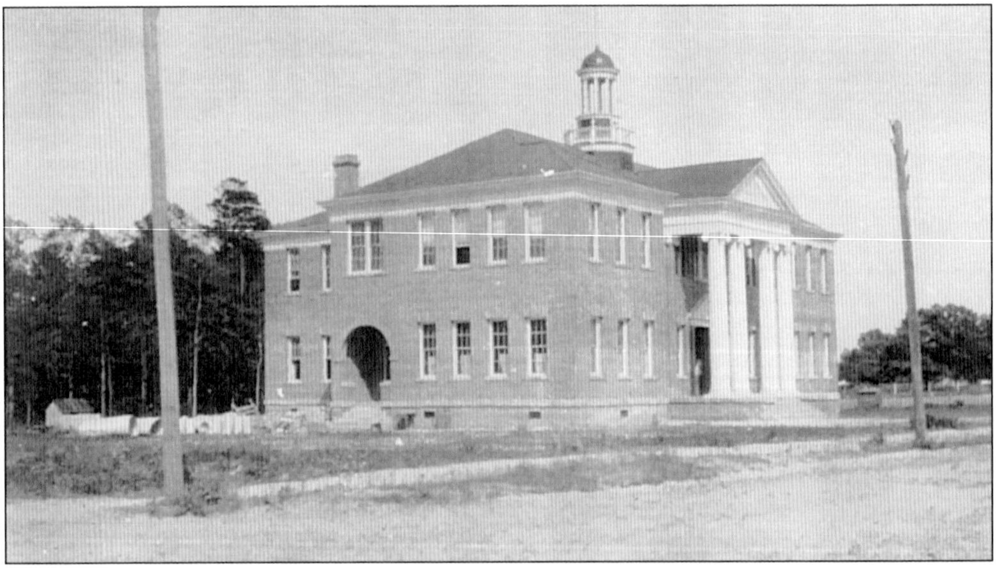

**New High School Building, Hampton, S.C.** (Photoprint, 3 3/8" x 5 3/8"; 1912.) This "new" Hampton High School, very similar to those built about the same time in the other county towns of Varnville and Estill, was dedicated on March 6, 1912. Ira B. Jones, former chief justice and the candidate for governor, was the speaker of the evening. The school was torn down when another one was erected in 1955. This card belonged to J.W. Rouse, county superintendent of education, 1910–1920, who focused especially upon the consolidation of schools and the building of schoolhouses.

**"The Guardian," Hampton, S.C.** (Photoprint, 5 3/8" x 3 3/8"; 1912.) Hampton's first newspaper, the *Hampton County Guardian*, has been published continuously since its establishment in 1879 by Miles B. McSweeney, who later became governor of South Carolina (1899–1902). The original Guardian Building, touted as downtown Hampton's only three-story structure, can still be seen at the corner of Lee Avenue and Maple Street. This photograph may have been made by Cleland or the W.H. Rentz Studio, which produced view-cards in the region.

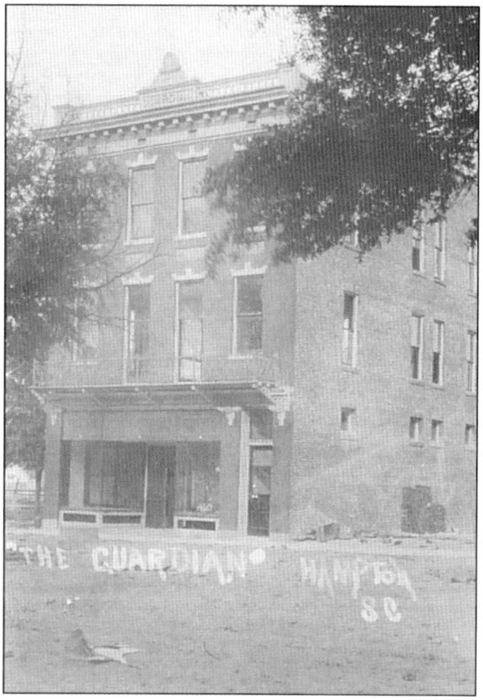


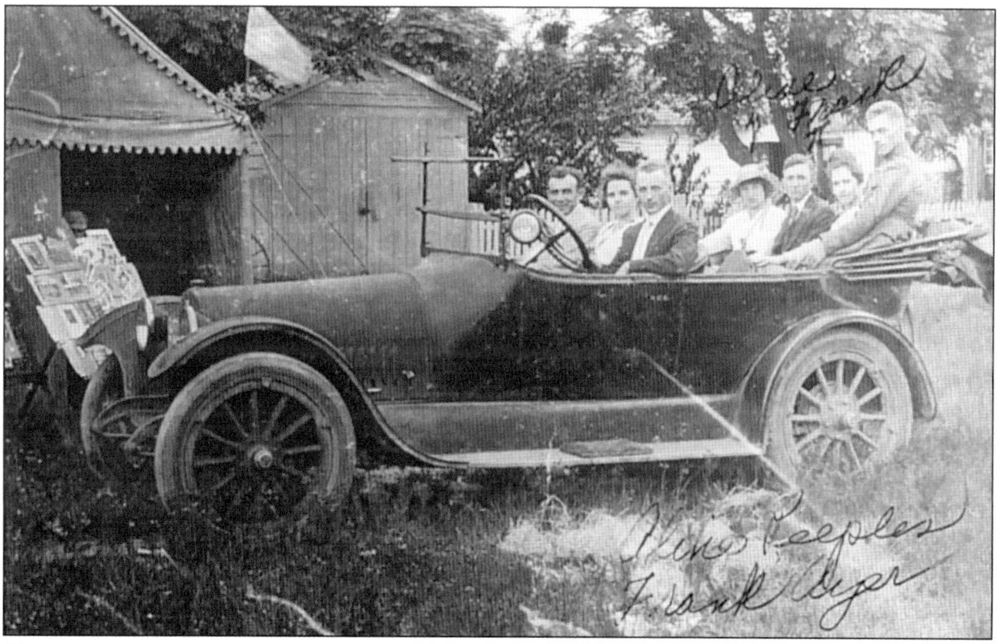


**[Portrait of the Ayers and Friends, Hampton, S.C.]** (Photoprint, 3 1/2" x 5 3/8"; *c.* 1925.) Aline Peeples Ayer (1899–1945) and Frank Ayer (1894–1963), who were married in 1924, are shown here (on the far side of the back seat), along with some unidentified friends or relations, in a touring car believed to have been parked at 1 Magnolia Avenue in Hampton. Perhaps the tent here belonged to an itinerant photographer, which this group was visiting. Ayer, from Bamberg, was a veteran's service officer.

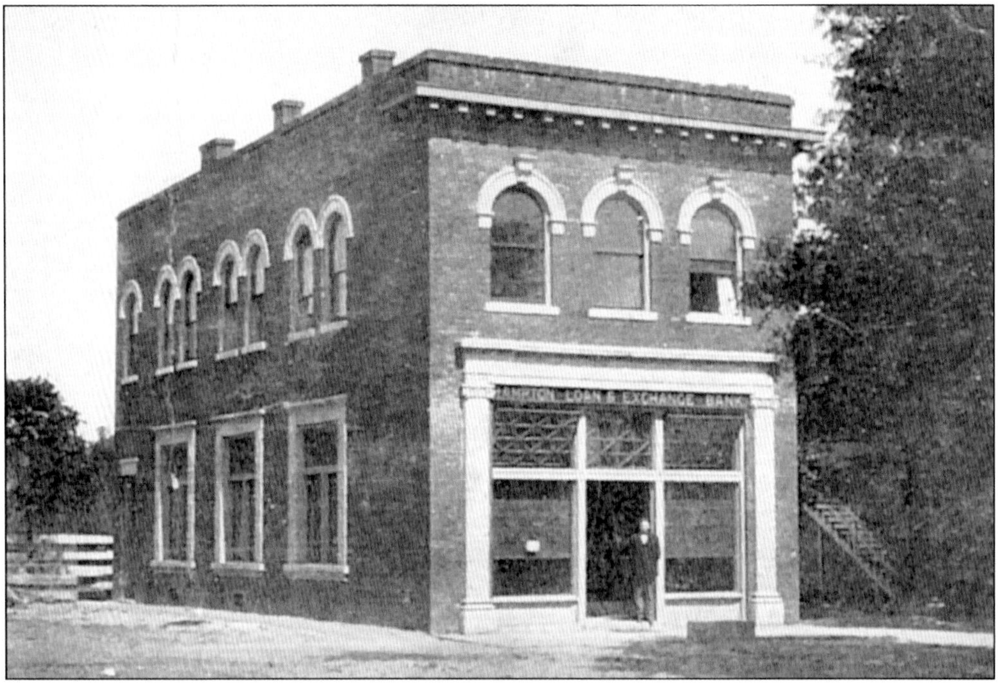


**Hampton Loan and Exchange Bank, Hampton, S.C.** (Halftone, 3 1/2" x 5 1/2", [Rich Photo-Process Co., New York, NY]; W.T. Johns, Hampton, SC, sponsor; *c.* 1908.) "Many can recall when banks were not thought of in this county," an unnamed correspondent wrote about Hampton in *The State* (Columbia), February 18, 1916. "Today," he continued, "there are seven small banking institutions, located at various points in the county, and each one seems to be doing well for itself and for the community in which it is located." This bank building, now vacant, still stands on Lee Avenue in Hampton.

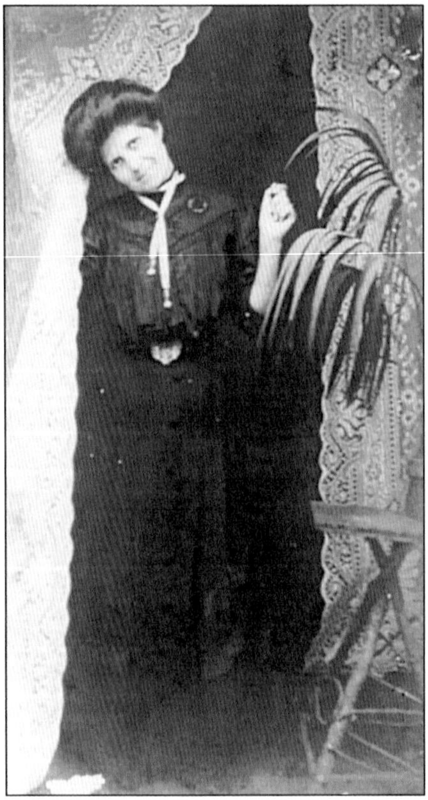

**[Portrait of Mrs. R.L. Cleland, Hampton, S.C.]** (Photoprint, 5 1/2" x 3 1/2", R.L. Cleland, Hampton, SC, photographer; 1908.) Robert Lee Cleland probably made this studio portrait of his wife, Lillian Phillips Cleland (1888–1979), around the time indicated by the date which she penned along with Christmas greetings to Miss Lena Phillips on the card's reverse: "12/22/1908." The Clelands would have been married less than one year and living in Aiken County at this time. One of their daughters, Elizabeth Cleland Peeples, would later recall that her father loved to travel and on his trips would purchase all the family's clothing.

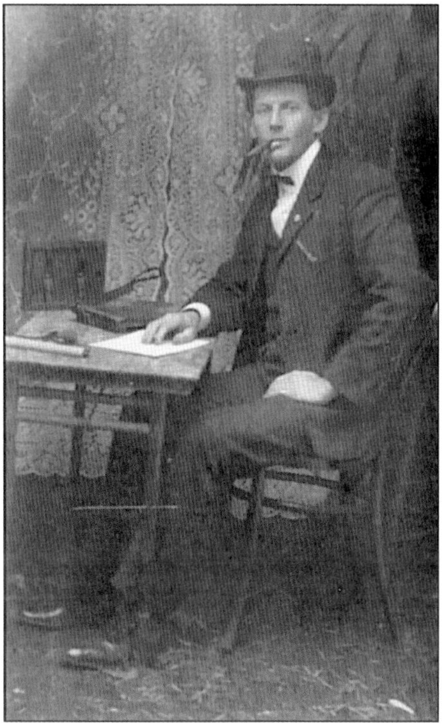

**[Portrait of R.L. Cleland, Hampton, S.C.]** (Photoprint, 5 1/2" x 3 1/2", R.L. Cleland, Hampton, SC, photographer; *c.* 1910.) Robert Lee Cleland (1874–1950), seen here in what is possibly a self-portrait, was born and reared near Grays. After his marriage in 1908 to Lillian Phillips, also of Grays, they settled in Montmorenci, Aiken County, where Cleland first established himself as a photographer. He later moved to Varnville and sometime after 1914 to Hampton, where in 1925 he became manager of the local bottling works. Cleland would have taken many of the photographs in the region during this period.

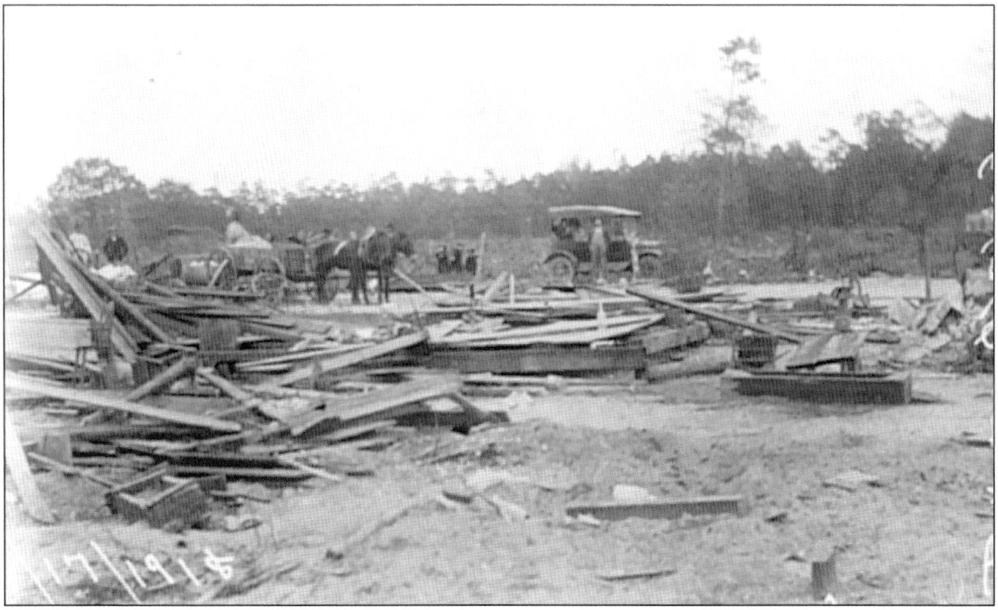

**[Picture of Cyclone Devastation, Hampton County, S.C.]** (Photoprint, 3 3/8" x 5 3/8", R.L. Cleland, Hampton, SC, photographer; *c.* 1918.) Early Sunday evening, November 17, 1918, a cyclone of terrific force passed through the western part of Hampton and touched down on the property of Mr. and Mrs. A.D. Thomas about 3 miles east of town. An eight-year-old son was killed, and their home, stables, and barns were destroyed. Hampton photographer Robert Lee Cleland made at least two postal photographs of the devastation, of which this is one.

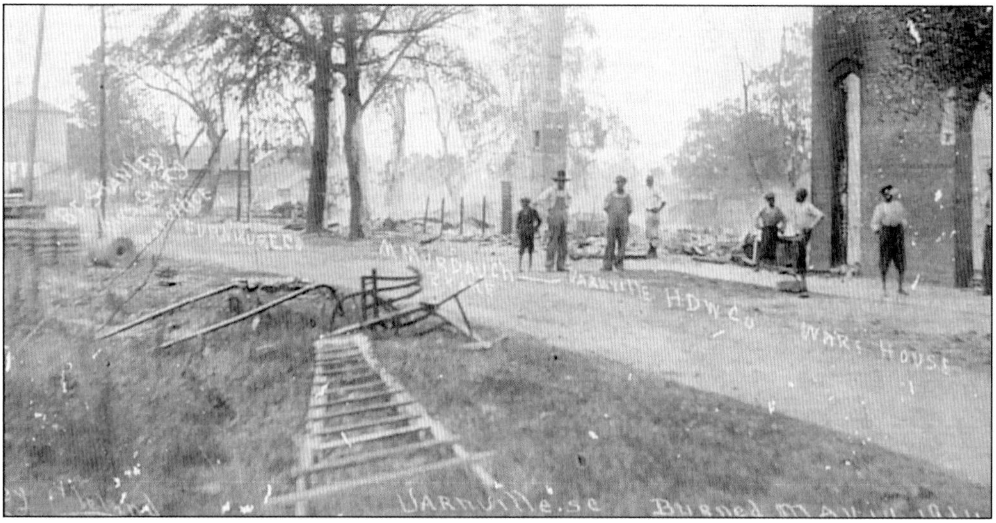


**[Fire Scene, Varnville, S.C.]** (Photoprint, 3 1/2" x 5 1/2", R.L. Cleland, Hampton, SC, photographer; 1914.) In 1925, the *Savannah Morning News* would describe Varnville as a "thriving town with a distinct business air." But not a dozen years earlier, on the morning of May 14, 1914, the town had lost its business district in "the largest fire in the history of Hampton County." Robert Cleland, who took this picture, has written on it the names of the businesses and residences destroyed by the fire, which caused an estimated $70,000 worth of damage. The *Hampton County Guardian* carried a manipulated version of this photograph on the front page of its issue for May 20.

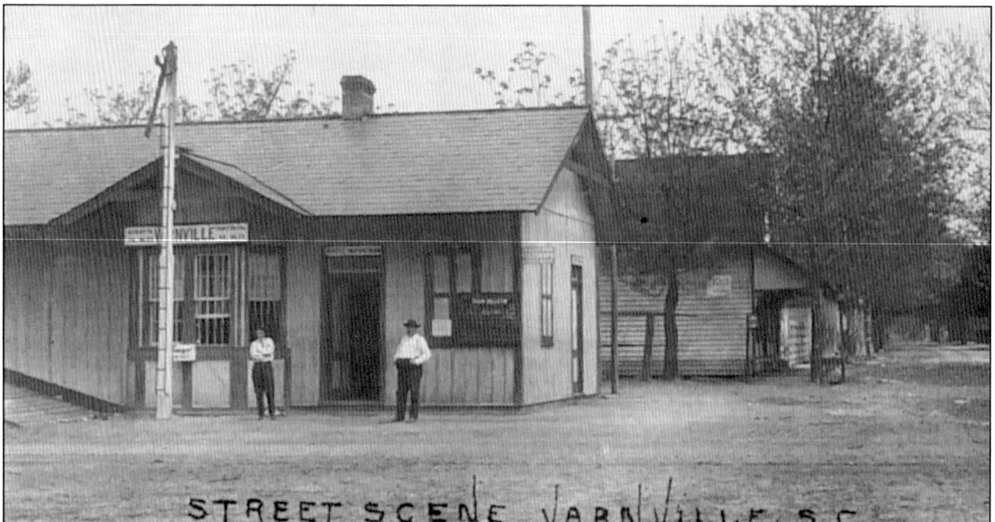


**Street Scene, Varnville, S.C.** (Photoprint, 3 1/2" x 5 1/2"; 1908.) In the book *Both Sides of the Swamp*, the two men here are identified as Frank Mears and Charles Taylor, and the structures as the Newlin-Murdaugh Dry Goods Store, Old Town Hall, and the A.R. Speaks Store. The building at left is the Charleston & Western Carolina Railroad depot, with its "train bulletin" board and Western Union office sign at right. Distances are indicated to Augusta (70 miles) and Port Royal (42 miles) on the large station sign at left. The sign over the entrance reads, "White Waiting Room." The photographer of this card also made the Brunson series.

# *Four*

# COLLETON COUNTY

Colleton County, bound on the east by the Edisto River and on the west and southwest by the Salkehatchie and Combahee Rivers, bears the name of one of the three counties created when the Province of Carolina was divided in 1682. The county was reorganized in 1798 under the new government. In 1925, it covered 1,126 square miles and had a population of 30,437.

Walterboro, named for two brothers of German descent who settled in the area in 1784, had been the county seat of Colleton District since 1817 and was officially incorporated by 1826. It lies in the center of the county almost equidistant from Charleston and Savannah.

Colleton was primarily a county of small farms, Ben E. Adams wrote in Charleston's *Sunday News*, June 24, 1923, "and this usually means a good citizenship." And a correspondent for *The State* (Columbia) remarked on February 17, 1916, that "Walterboro and Colleton County . . . with its early high standard of civilization, has always occupied an important place in the State's history." That year, *Press and Standard* editor W.W. Smoak was instrumental in organizing the Southern Carolina Association at Walterboro.

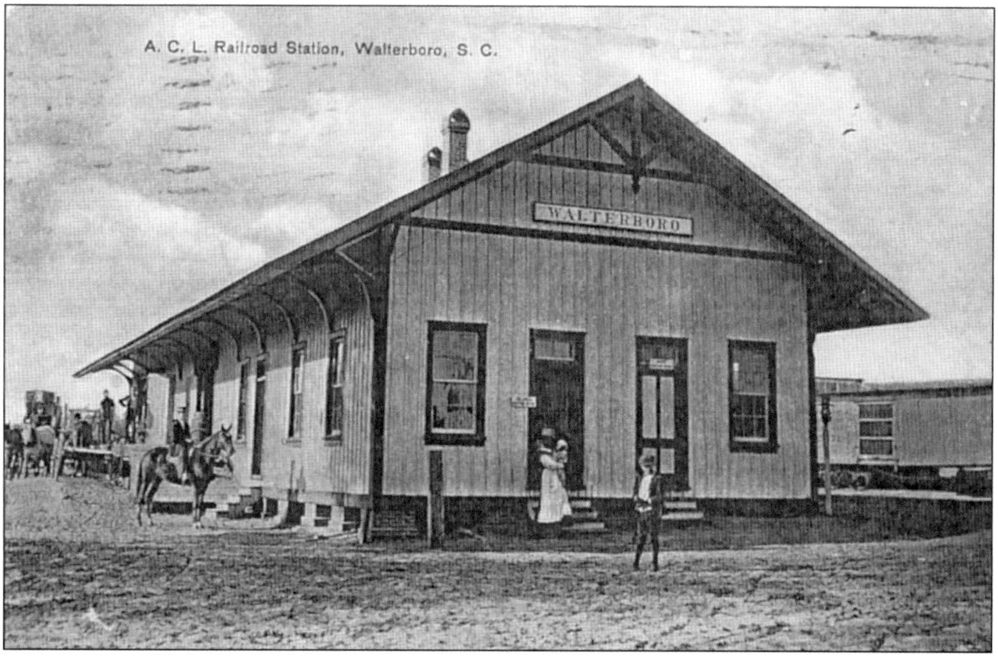


**A.C.L. RAILROAD STATION, WALTERBORO, S.C.** (Collotype, 3 1/2" x 5 1/2", [Alfred Schulze Co., Berlin, Germany]; American News Co., #B7257, New York, NY, importer; 1911.) By the mid-1890s, Walterboro boasted the largest railway station on the line between Charleston and Savannah. This view, facing west on Railroad Avenue, shows the old Atlantic Coast Line depot, now non-existent. In 1911, when this card was postmarked, Walterboro presented itself as "The City of Possibilities" (see the Trade and Industrial Edition of the *Press and Standard*, August 2, 1911). It had a population of 1,500.

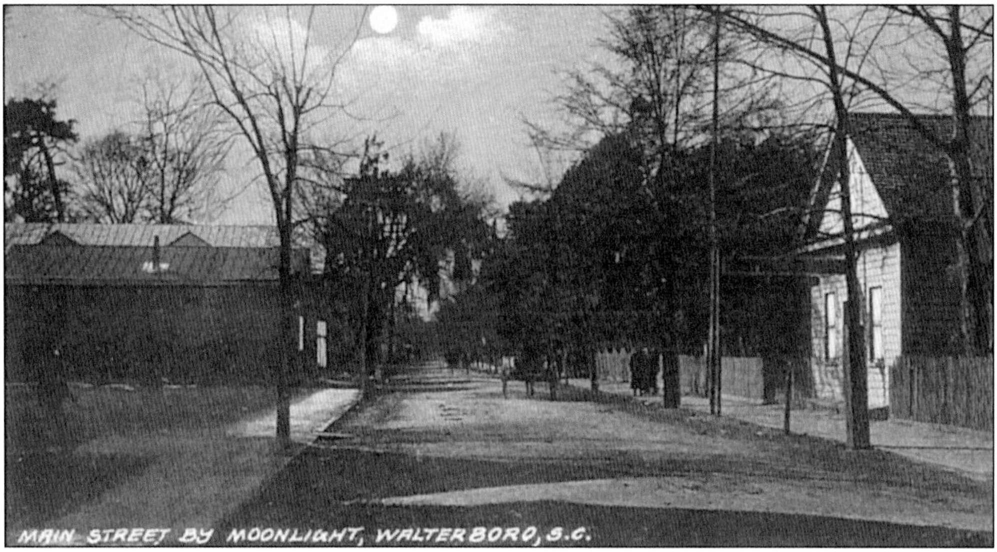


**MAIN STREET BY MOONLIGHT, WALTERBORO, S.C.** (Color Lithography, 3 1/2" x 5 1/2", [C.G. Röder, #231659, Leipzig, Germany]; American News Co., #E 632, New York, NY, importer; *c.* 1908.) In this Main Street view looking toward the courthouse, S. Finn's Jewelry Store appears to be the building to the right. This rare manipulated image changes a daylight picture—with the shadows of the trees still visible on the ground—into a moonlit version of the street scene. Published by Terry and Shaffer, these cards would have been sold in that business establishment, located just up the way on the same side of the street as Finn's store.

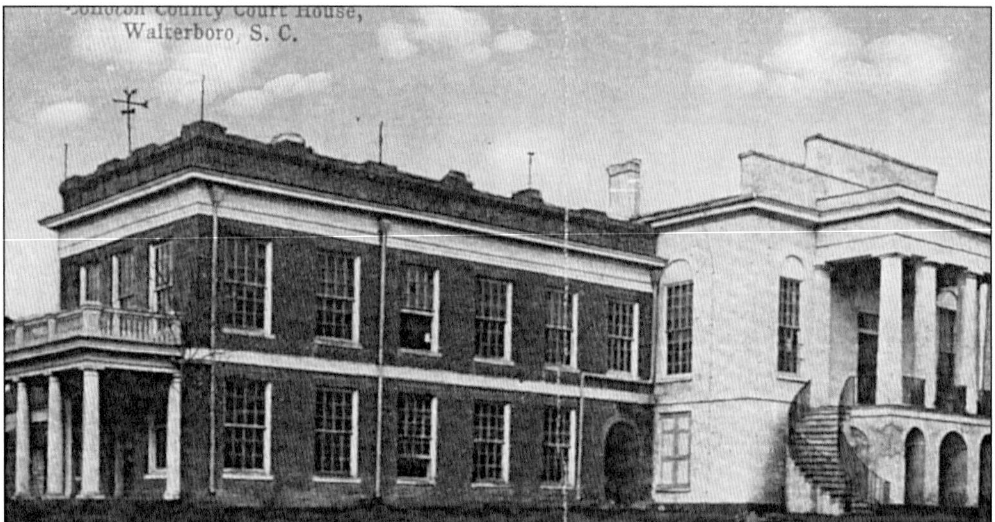


**COLLETON COUNTY COURT HOUSE, WALTERBORO, S.C.** (Halftone, 3 1/2" x 5 1/2", Auburn Post Card Mfg., Auburn, IN; 1929.) The Colleton County Courthouse, corner of Jefferies Boulevard and Hampton Street, was completed in the fall of 1822 when the first term of court was held. Noted South Carolina architect Robert Mills, as state engineer, is credited with having designed the Classic Doric portico at the front of the Greek Revival structure. Here the courthouse is shown with the first of the two large wings which have been added to the original two-story building—this one at the turn of the century. The courthouse is on the National Register of Historic Places.

**[Portrait of the Godleys, Walterboro, S.C.]** (Photoprint, 5 1/2" x 3 1/2"; *c.* 1922.) Jacob S. "Jake" Godley, portrayed here with his wife, Ida Ponds Godley, owned and operated a grocery store on the eastern outskirts of Walterboro. He was a veteran of World War I.

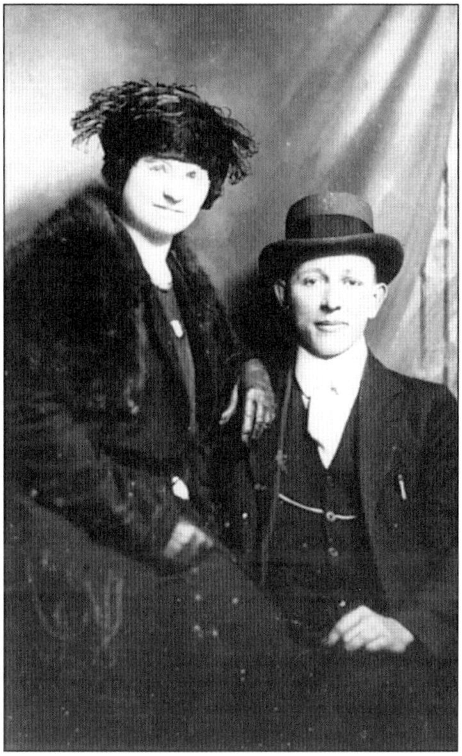

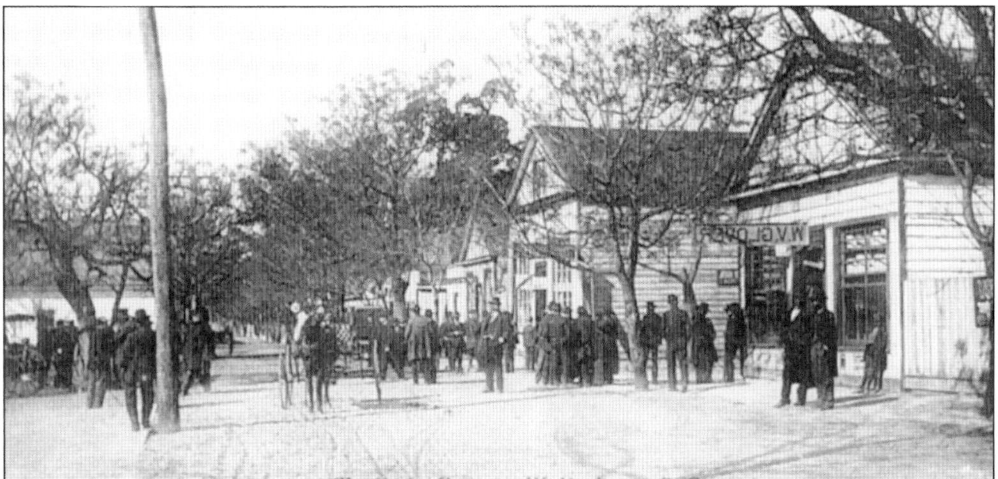


**Shaffer's Corner, Walterboro.** (Collotype, 3 1/2" x 5 1/2", unknown German printer; American News Co., #1145J, New York, NY, importer; 1914.) Shaffer's Corner, as the northeast block at the intersection of East Washington (Main) and Walter Streets used to be known, was a commercial mainstay of old "uptown" Walterboro. It took its name from the sprawling, six-building enterprise of Terry and Shaffer, founded in 1875 by John K. Terry and Captain A.C. Shaffer, and considered the town's oldest general merchandise establishment. Seen at the right, in a picture which has inadvertently been reversed in printing, is W.V. Glover's general store, established in 1906 and located across from the courthouse.

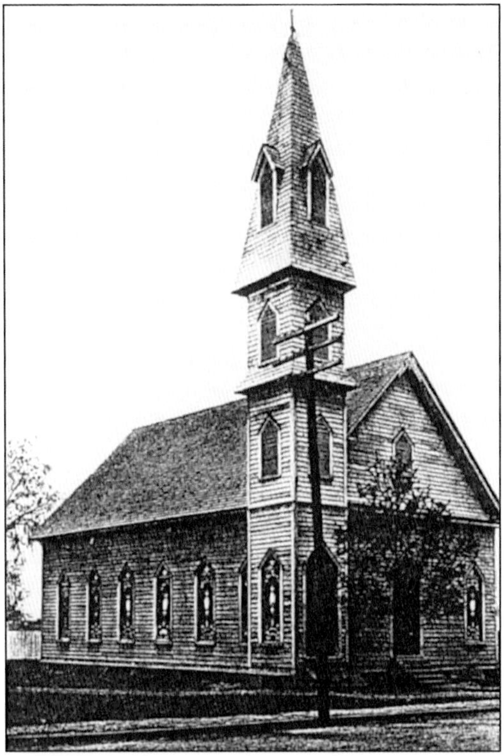

**Bethel Methodist Episcopal Church, Walterboro, S.C.** (Collotype, 3 1/2" x 3 1/2", unknown German printer; American News Co., #AA4765, New York, NY, importer; 1910.) The fourth and last sanctuary to be erected by Bethel Methodists on the original site deeded to the church by Robert Barnwell Rhett in 1828, at the corner of Washington Street and Railroad Avenue, this one was built soon after the 1902 demolition of its predecessor and served as the church's house of worship for more than 25 years. A new church on Hampton Street was dedicated on May 22, 1929.

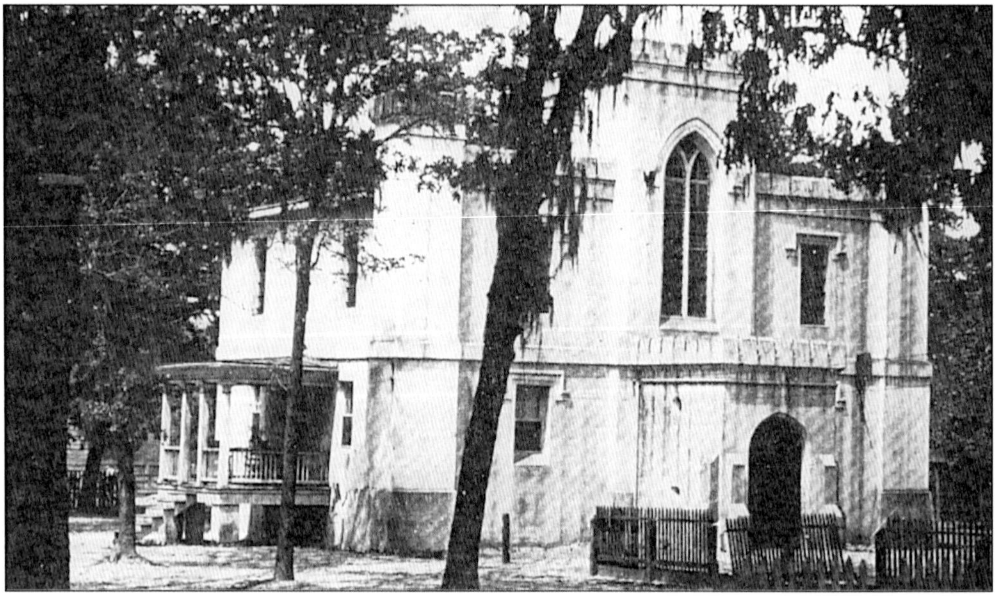

**The Jail, Walterboro, S.C.** (Halftone, 3 1/2" x 5 1/2", Auburn Post Card Mfg., Auburn, IN; 1932.) The Old Colleton Jail, 241 Jefferies Boulevard, was designed by Charleston architects Edward Jones and Francis D. Lee and constructed by Jonathan and B. Lucas in 1855–1856. Resembling a miniature fortified castle, this Neo-Gothic edifice replaced the one that had been built in 1822. Presently adapted for use as county offices, it is included on the National Register of Historic Places.

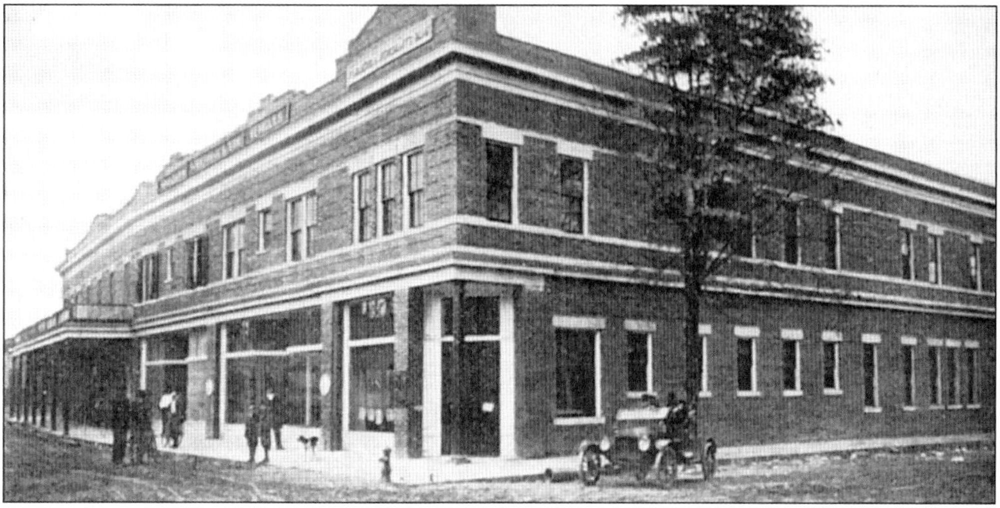

**HOTEL ALBERT, A. WICHMAN & SON, FARMERS & MERCHANTS BANK, WALTERBORO, S.C.** (Color Lithography, 3 1/2" x 5 1/2", [Tichnor Brothers Inc., Boston, MA]; 1914.) This large brick multi-purpose building, minus the extended colonnaded entrance at the left and currently adapted for use as apartments and "shoppes," still stands at the corner of Wichman and East Washington Streets. It represented the "downtown" business domain of German-born Albert Wichman (d. 1909), as distinct from the "uptown" establishment of Walterboro's other lien merchant of the period, Captain A.C. Shaffer. Wichman's Farmers & Merchants Bank, with its corner entrance visible here, was the second oldest of the county's banks (organized in 1902) and by 1916 boasted the largest capital ($50,000).

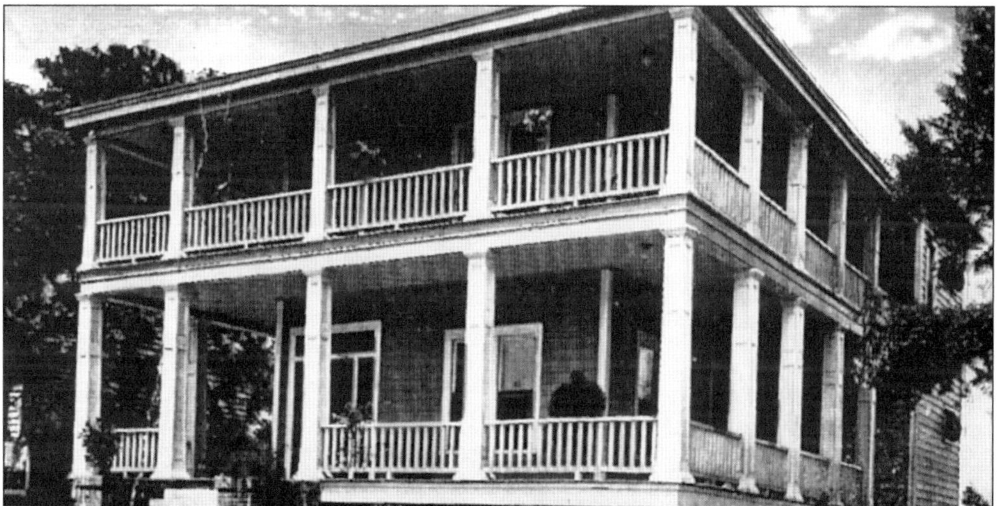

**THE CLARA ESDORN INFIRMARY, WALTERBORO, S.C.** (Color Lithography, 3 1/2" x 5 1/2", Curt Teich Co., Chicago, IL; *c.* 1918.) For many years Walterboro's only hospital, the Clara EsDorn Infirmary opened in May 1916 with founder-physician Charles H. EsDorn (1878–1923) as surgeon-in-charge. It stood next to the EsDorns' residence (barely visible at left) on the northeast corner of Webb and Witsell Streets in the old Hickory Valley section of town. Clara, who was superintendent and anesthetist, renamed it for her husband after his death. Its first class of trained nurses graduated in 1919. In its later years, much modified and used as doctors' offices, the building burned down on October 27, 1992.

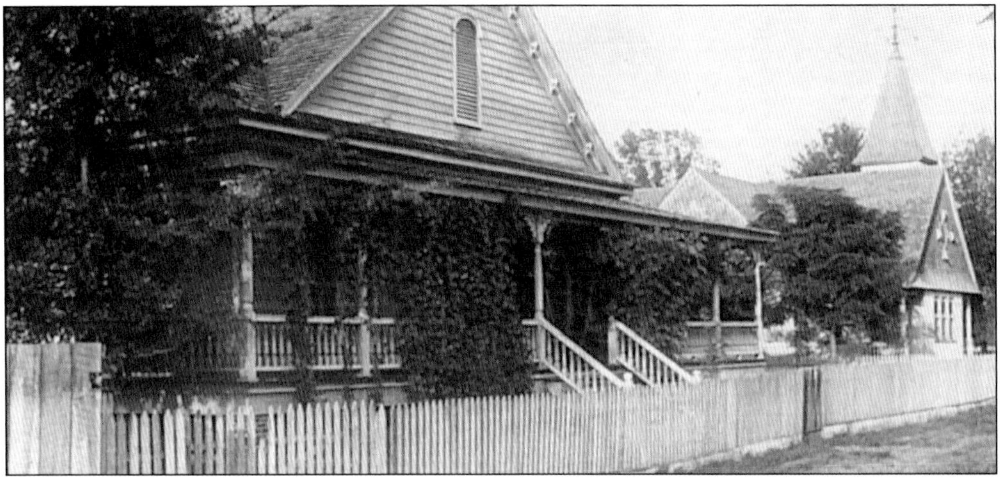

[BAPTIST CHURCH AND PARSONAGE, WALTERBORO, S.C.] (Photoprint, 3 1/2" x 5 1/2"; 1906.) The old Baptist parsonage, at left, is located at 123 Neyle Street. The church at the right, corner of Neyle and Miller, was completed in 1897 to replace an earlier structure destroyed by the storm of 1893. Dr. B.H. Padgett signed the building contract and supervised the work of Jimmy Wood, the African-American carpenter who constructed the new edifice. It served as the sanctuary for the church (known as First Baptist since 1911) until a new site was acquired in 1954. This structure, now somewhat altered, has continued to function as a house of worship. The parsonage still stands as a private residence.

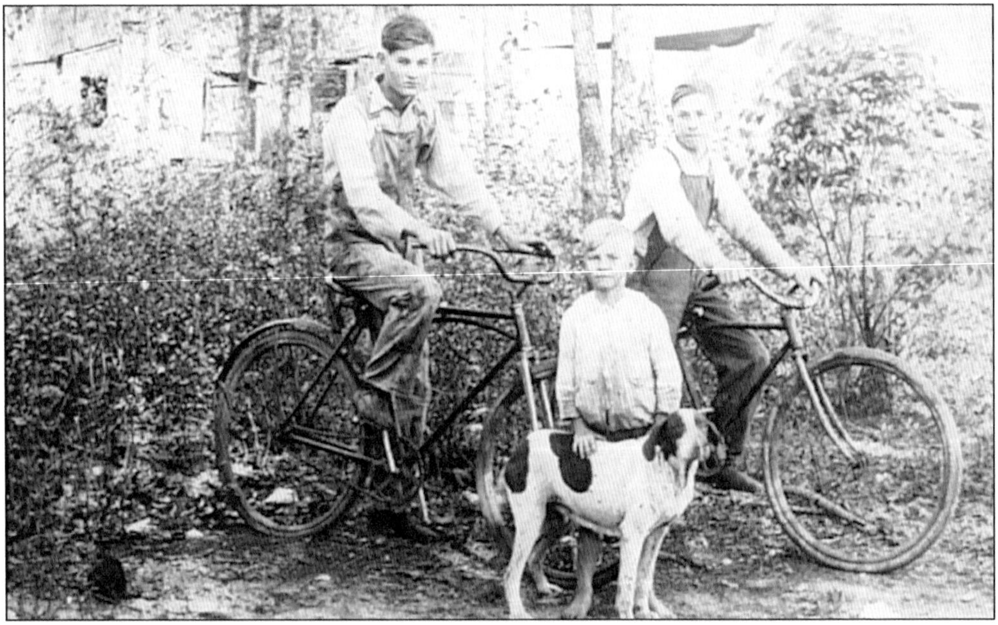

[PORTRAIT OF THREE BOYS, COLLETON COUNTY.] (Photoprint, 3 1/2" x 5 1/2", *c.* 1918–1924.) This one-of-a-kind picture of youngsters with their pets and bicycles was typical of the kind of informal portraits which families and individuals had made to mail or to hand out to friends and relations. The two boys with their bikes were the sons of Abe Ruth and Carrie-Lee Ponds Murdaugh, who lived in the western part of the county between Islandton and Ashton. Vernon, at left, died young of appendicitis; Joseph ("J.J."), at right, died in 1970. The boy with the dog was one of the homeless children Mrs. Murdaugh took in and cared for.

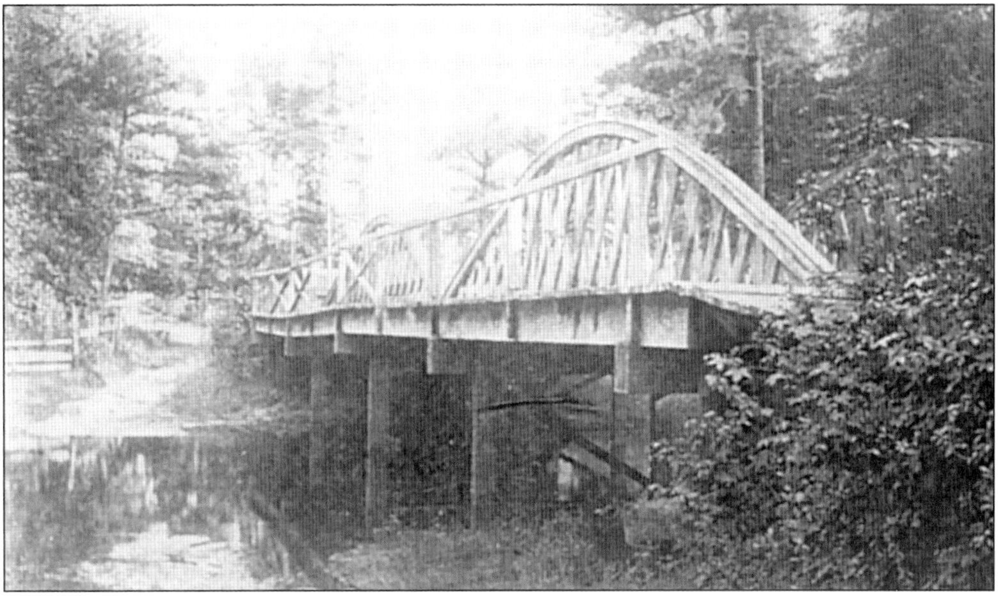

**[Bridge, Colleton County.]** (Photoprint, 3 1/2" x 5 1/2", 1907.) This old ornamental bridge, also known as the Ireland Creek Bridge, once crossed the little stream north of Walterboro near the intersection of Highways 15 and 64. In sight of the bridge, but screened by trees, was a swimming hole, which was a favorite haunt of the local boys. "There were no bathing suits," wrote M.P. Howell in one of his "Country Chairman" columns in the *Press and Standard* in the early 1940s, "and every boy was a good swimmer, expert in the art of 'ducking.' The rivalry between uptown and downtown extended even there."

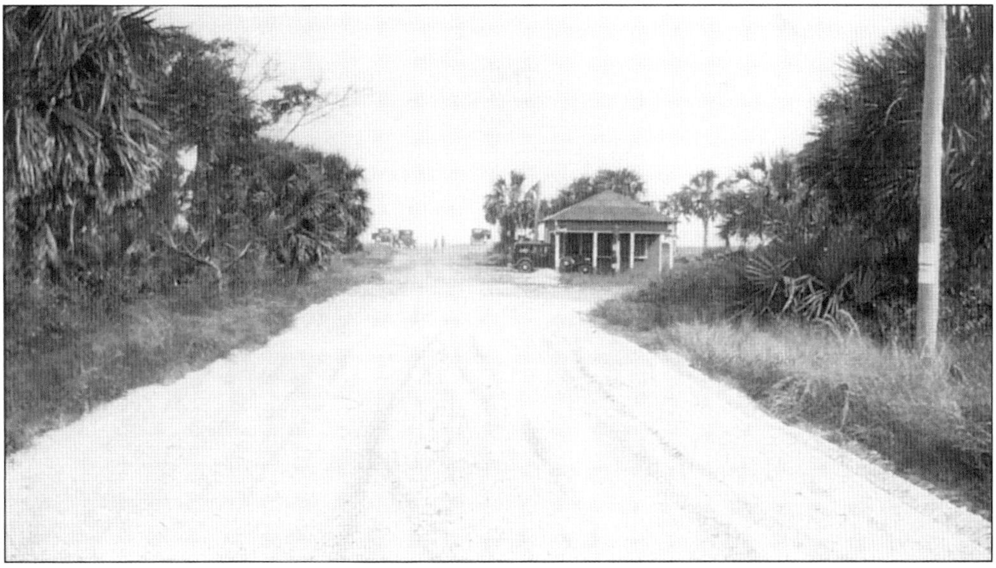

**[Entrance to Edisto Beach, Colleton, S.C.]** (Master Photograph, Halftone, 3 1/2" x 5 1/2", Asheville Postcard Co., *c.* 1927.) Edisto Beach, the easternmost sliver of Colleton, is the site which allows it to qualify as one of South Carolina's Atlantic seaside counties and testifies to its long history as a resort area. Located some 40 miles south of Charleston, Edisto Beach is accessible by land only through Edisto Island, in Charleston County, of which it was once a part.

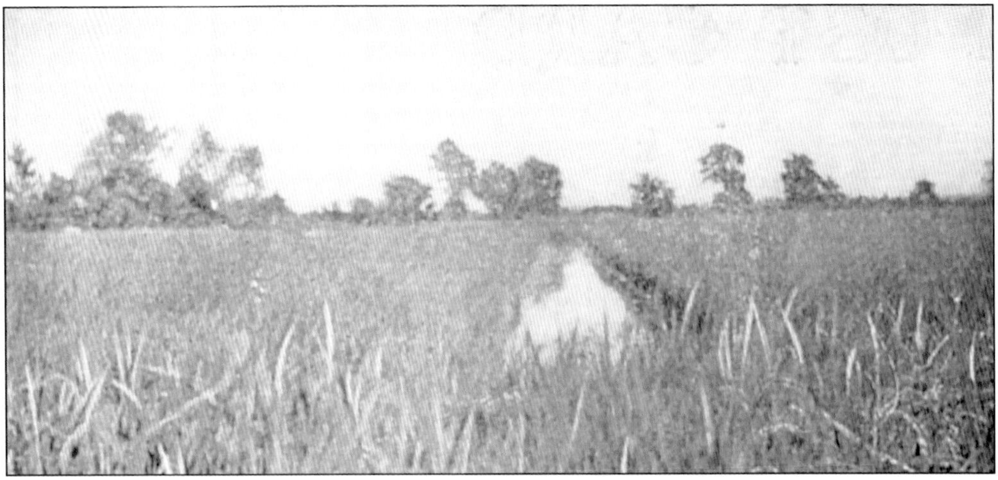

**Ricefield, Combalee [sic] Run, S.C.** (Halftone, 3 6/10" x 5 7/10", Signal Printing Co., Crowley, LA; *c.* 1906.) Formerly the seat of the Carolina rice industry, Colleton County once led the state in the production of this commodity. Shown here is a tidal canal "running" through a rice field off the Combahee River beyond the tree-lined bank in the distance. This site would have been located somewhere along the 12- to 15-mile stretch of the river in the southwest corner of the county where the old rice plantations were situated.

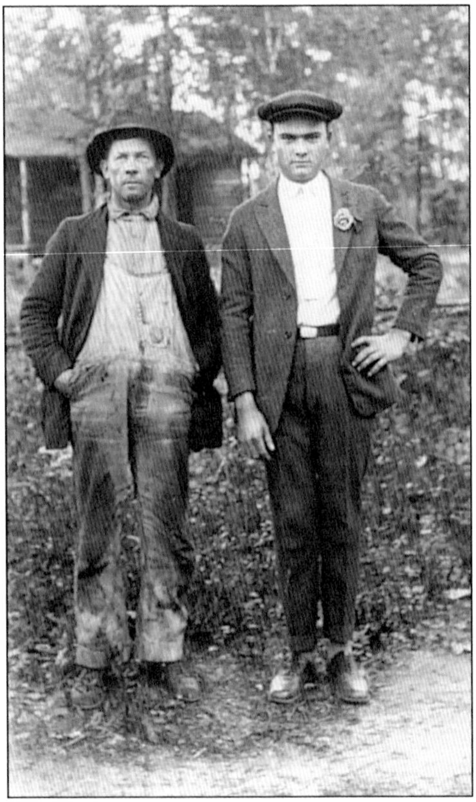

**[Portrait of Abe Murdaugh and Friend, Colleton County.]** (Photoprint, 5 1/4" x 3 1/2", *c.* 1922.) Abe Ruth Murdaugh (1883–1958), pictured here in his work clothes next to an unidentified friend, owned a sawmill and a country store across the road from his home about midway between the communities of Islandton and Ashton in the western part of Colleton County. Probably taken by a family member or acquaintance, this image would have been shot on film which then was taken to a store in town to be processed. The postcard prints would have been picked up in a few days or a week, perhaps in an order of multiple copies.

# *Five*

# Bamberg County

On August 12, 1891, the editor of the *Bamberg Herald* spoke of the "desirability of a new county to be carved from the whitening cotton fields of Barnwell and the rich pastures of Colleton, and Bamberg's charming felicity of location, which makes it the right place for the court house . . . ." Six years later Bamberg County was established from a portion of old Barnwell District and named for the family that had founded the town in its northern section, which then became its seat of government.

One of the smallest and most compact counties in South Carolina, Bamberg covers 395 square miles and in the mid-1920s had a population of 25,000. It is equidistant from the coast on the east and the Georgia line on the west, with the South Edisto River forming its boundary with Orangeburg County on the north and the Salkehatchie River forming its boundary with Allendale on the south.

Like those of the other counties in the Coastal Plains, Bamberg's fortunes were long tied to agriculture (cotton being the main crop) and the railroad (the claim being made in 1915 that its rail facilities were perhaps better than in any other part of the region). In the mid-1920s the county boasted a total of 66 miles of railroads, including those of the Southern, the Atlantic Coast Line, and the Seaboard Air Line.

A.W. Knight, in the essay on Bamberg in *Opportunities in Edisto-Savannah Territory* emphasized, along with the county's "equable climate and labor conditions," its freedom from bonded debt, its low tax rates, strong banking institutions, good highways, and a commitment to education "and other progressive ideas which make for the prosperity and happiness of its people."

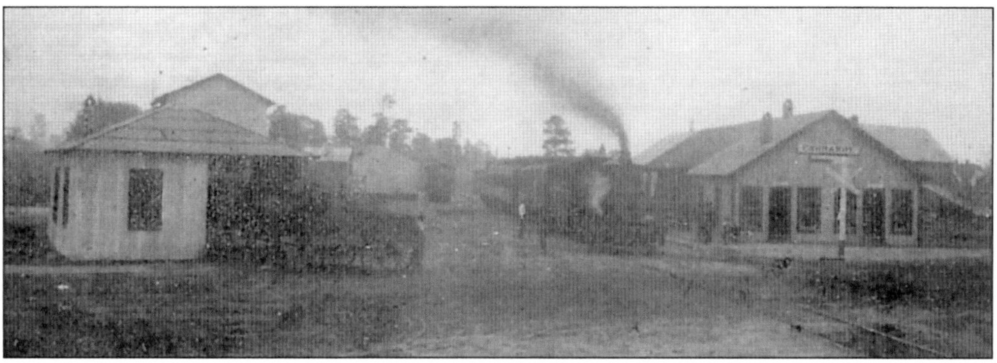

**[R.R. Station, Ehrhardt.]** (Photoprint, 3 1/2" x 5 1/2"; 1913.) Ehrhardt is the initial town the traveler encounters on entering Bamberg County from the south. Named for Conrad Ehrhardt, the native of Weiterade Kuhrhessen, Germany, who by 1852, along with other Germans, had settled in the area, the town grew and thrived in proportion to the growth and development of the railroads in the area from about 1890 to 1930. While a post office had been established at Ehrhardt in 1876, the town was not incorporated until 1898, when a branch line of the Atlantic Coast Line (ACL) Railroad was extended to it. Then, in 1915 the local Bamberg, Ehrhardt, and Walterboro (BE&W) line, built largely with Bamberg capital and leased to the ACL to operate, opened rail communication between the two county towns. The BE&W Company lasted until 1937.

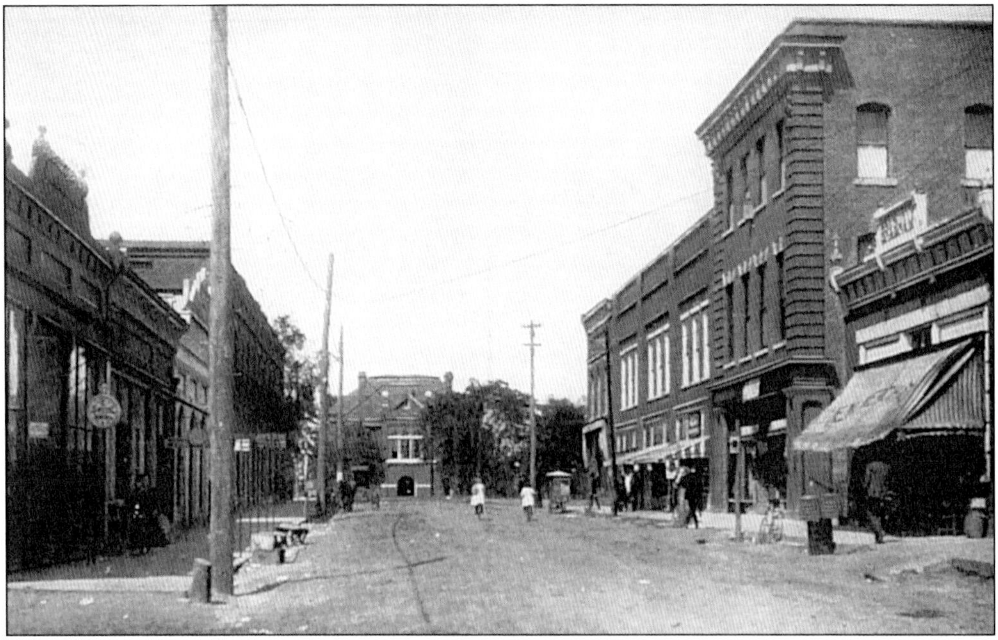

**Main Street, Bamberg, S.C.** (Color Lithograph, 3 1/2" x 5 1/2", E.C. Kropp Co., Milwaukee, WI; People's Drug Company, Bamberg, SC, sponsor; 1911.) Two girls ride their bicycles up a sparsely peopled Main Street toward the courthouse in a picture that People's Drug Company had published and distributed by 1911. The tall brick building to the right is City Hall, which in 1998 was standing empty. On the left is the store of J.D. Copeland, a dealer in general merchandise whose establishment was built in 1891 and is also still standing, but vacant. In the *Bamberg Herald* of August 12, 1891, it was advertised as "the prettiest store in town."

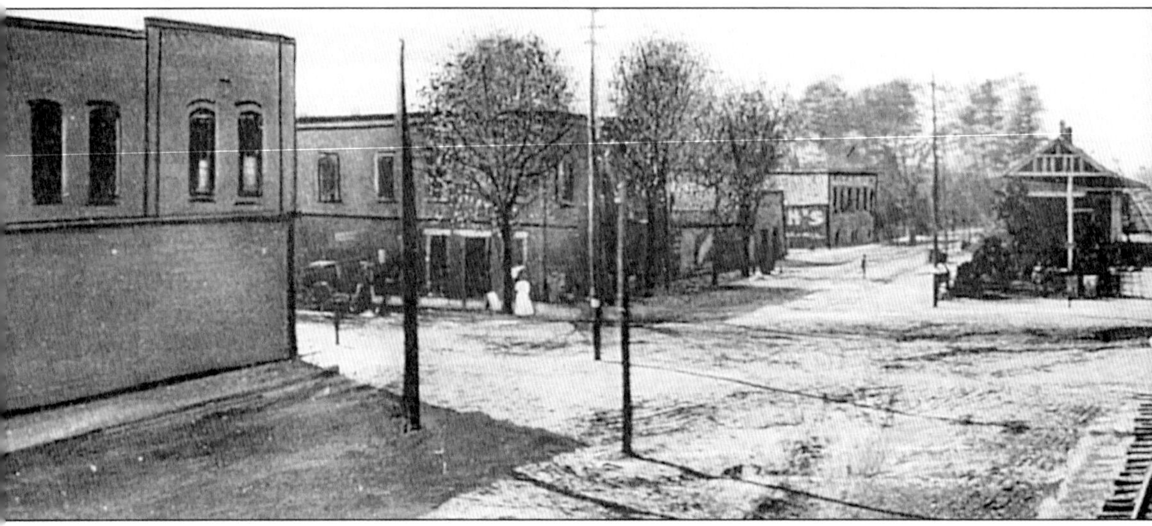

**Railroad Avenue Looking West, Bamberg, S.C.** (Hand-Colored Collotype, 3.5" x 11", [Trenkler Co., Leipzig, Germany]; A.M. Simon, #15 504, New York, NY, importer; 1912.) "The city of Bamberg," wrote local historian Evelyn King Brabham, "is a circle with a 3–4 mile radius from a center point at the site of the old Southern passenger station." A rare panoramic view, above, depicts this center point and documents the importance of the railroad to Bamberg County's largest town—with 2,000 people in 1910—which began as a little settlement

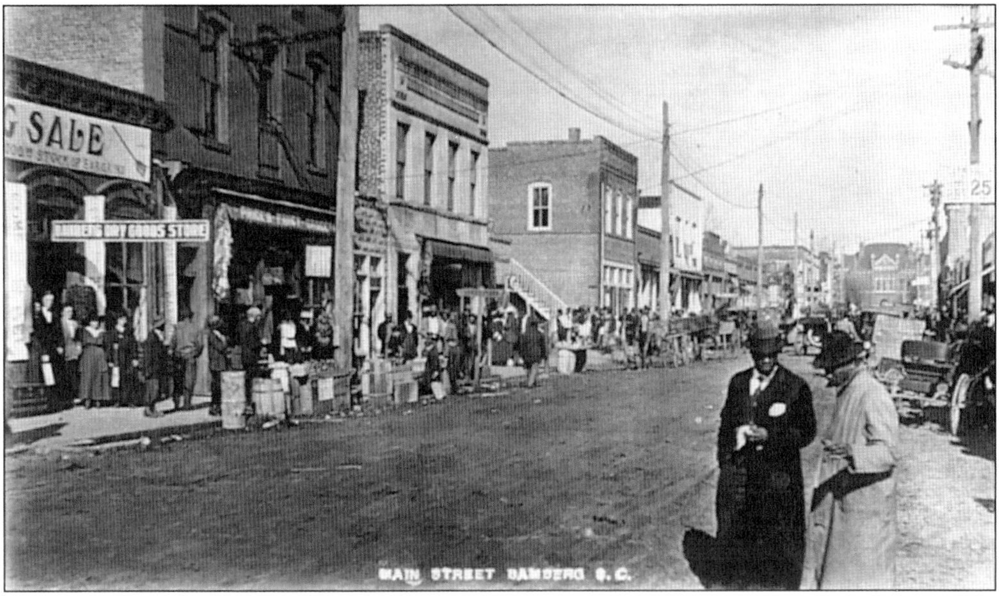


**MAIN STREET, BAMBERG, S.C.** (Photoprint, 3 1/2" x 5 1/2"; *c.* 1915.) The courthouse is still visible in the distance in this view of lower Main Street. The sign on the telephone pole at right indicates that the photograph was taken sometime near or during Carnival Week at Christmas time. The sign of the Bamberg Dry Goods Store is clearly legible at the left, and the grocery store next door has set up an informal produce market on barrels and crates in the street out front.

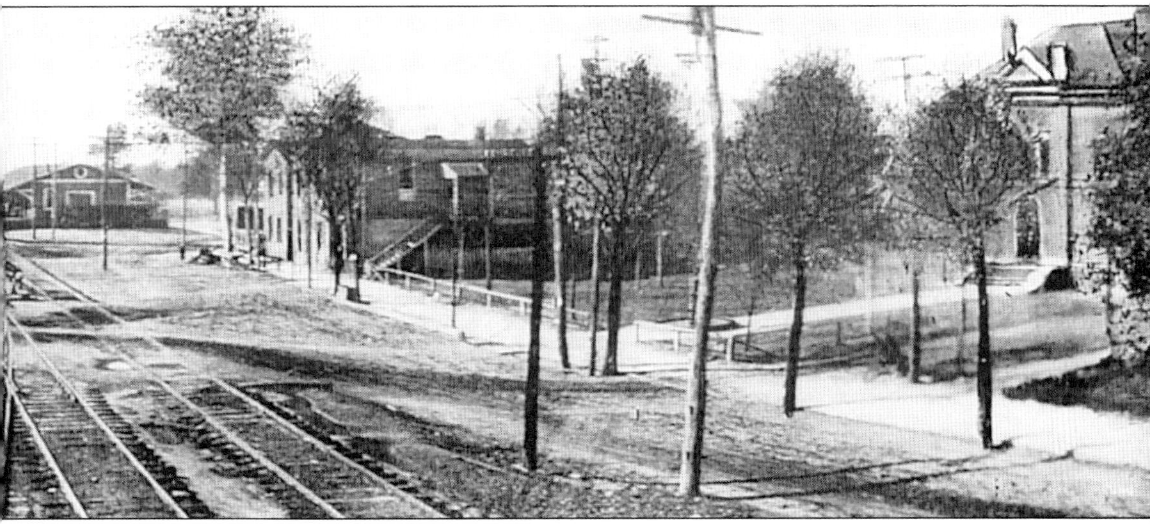

clustered around a water tank built to serve the 136-mile Charleston-to-Hamburg railway that was completed in 1833. The tracks seen here may constitute the "railroad bed" of the *Best Friend of Charleston*, the region's first commercial train. The Southern Railway depot stands to the left of the tracks. Railroad Avenue, the chief residential street and axis of the town, runs east to west on both sides of the tracks. The courthouse can be seen at the far right, its southern entrance facing the Main Street corridor.

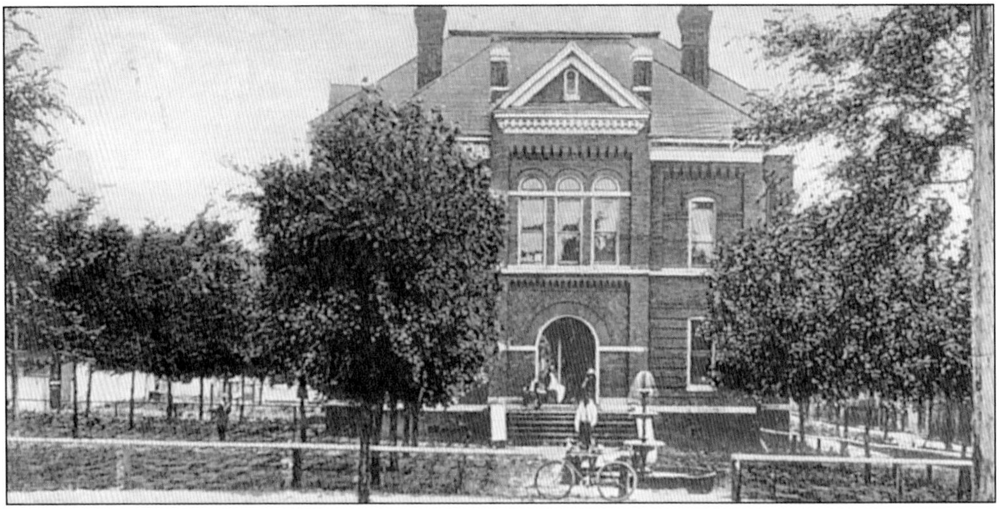

**Court House Square, Bamberg County, Bamberg, S.C.** (Hand-Colored Collotype, 3 1/2" x 5 4/10", Valentine and Sons Publishing Co., #401, 734, Dundee, Scotland; 1908.) In order to win the county seat, the Bamberg city fathers promised to build a courthouse—which they did, with the issuance of $10,000 in bonds and the use of state penitentiary labor. Evelyn King Brabham claimed that, along with a county jail, it was erected in 1897, soon after the legislature authorized the creation of the new county in the spring of that year. In 1950, the courthouse was moved to the east, where it now stands on U.S. 301, or Main Street, in its enlarged and modernized form.

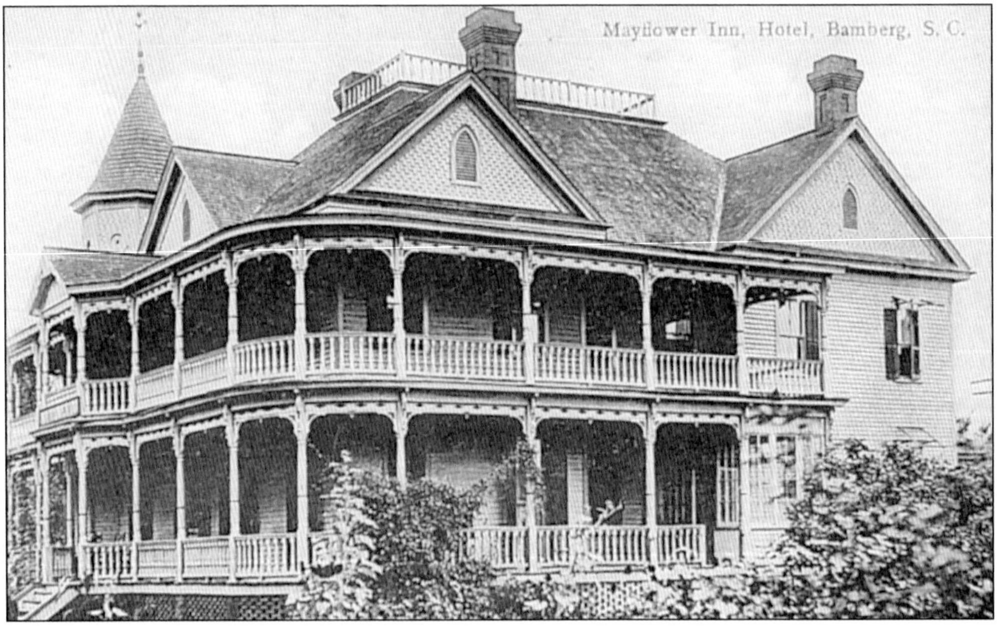


**Mayflower Inn, Hotel, Bamberg, S.C.** (Collotype, 3 1/2" x 5 1/2", Germany; 1908.) The Cope House became the Mayflower Inn when the Brooker family purchased it sometime between 1904 and 1909. Some claimed it as the best hotel in lower Carolina during the early years of the twentieth century. Located on the corner of North Railroad Avenue and Bridge Street as early as 1898, it served several generations of travelers. Later called the Bamberg Hotel, it was demolished in November 1958.

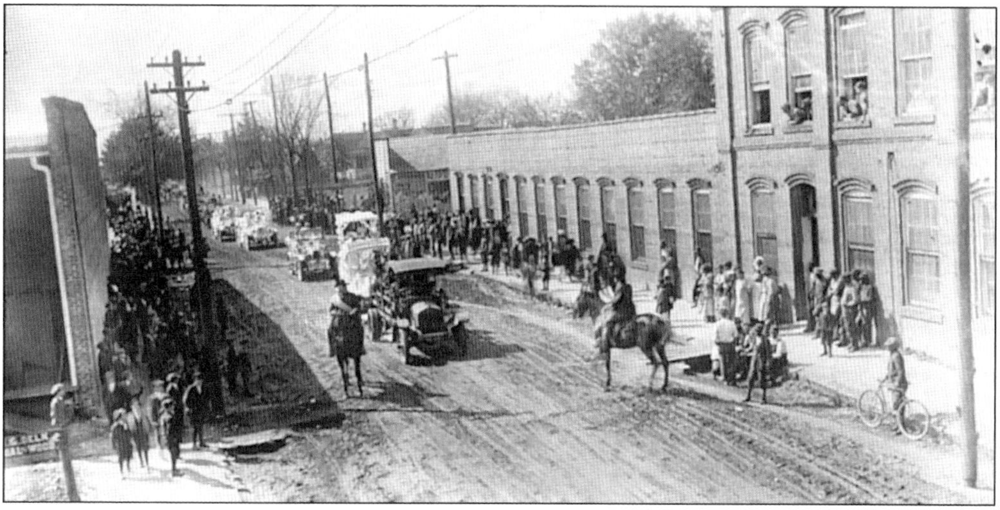

**[PARADE, BAMBERG, S.C.]** (Photoprint, 3 1/2" x 5 1/2", E.E. Burson, Denmark, SC, photographer; *c.* 1915.) Employees on the upper floors of the Bamberg Cotton Mill watch with other townspeople as the decorated vehicles and their mounted escorts in an unidentified parade, having crossed Church Street, make their way north on Main (now Highway 301) towards Elm. Denmark photographer E.E. Burson may have taken the picture during the Thanksgiving or Christmas season.

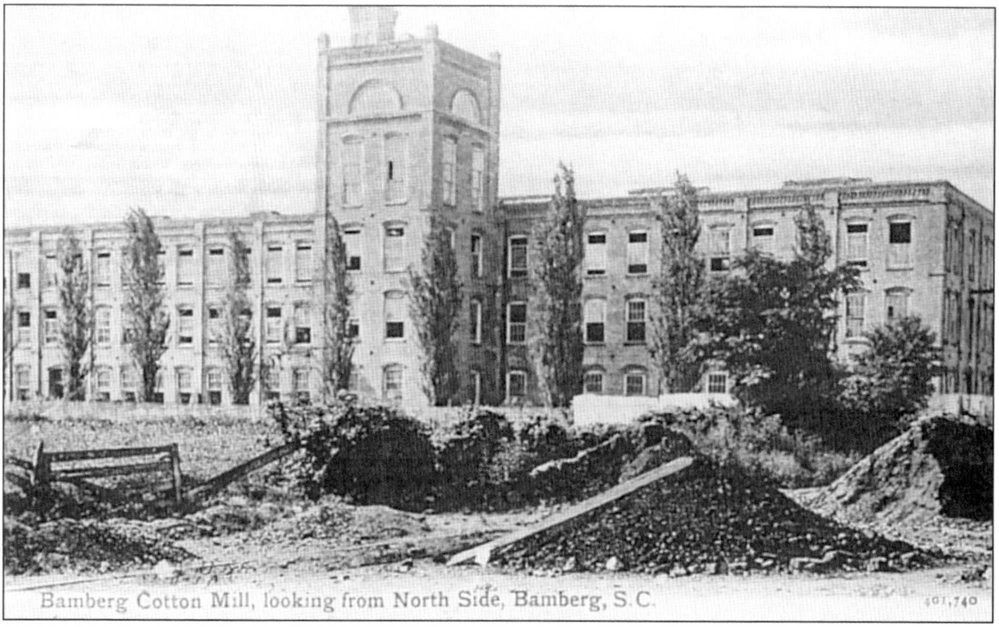


**BAMBERG COTTON MILL, LOOKING FROM NORTH SIDE, BAMBERG, S.C.** (Collotype, 3 1/2" x 5 1/2", Valentine and Sons Publishing Co., #401, 740, Dundee, Scotland; 1909.) Principal to Bamberg's well-being from 1892 to *c.* 1969, the Bamberg Cotton Mill, organized with local capital and built on the southwest corner of Main and Church Streets, initially produced yarn, but soon changed over to the manufacture of cotton cloth. In 1949, when the plant's newest owners proposed to close it down and sell off the machinery, local citizens rallied to save it and operated the Bamberg Textile Mills for some 20 more years. Demolition of the three-story brick structure finally occurred in 1997.

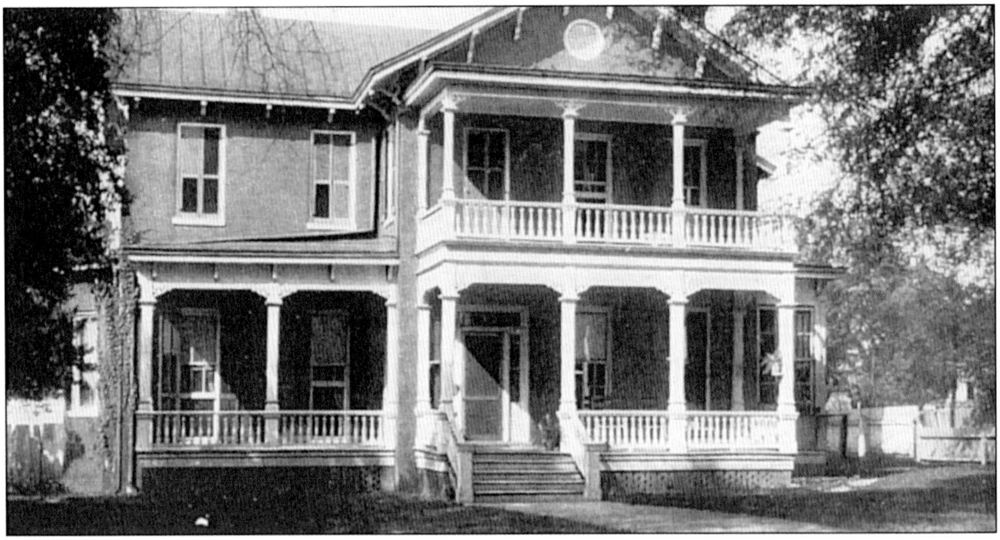

**Mrs. M.A. Bamberg's Residence, Bamberg, S.C.** (Halftone, 3 1/2" x 5 1/2", E.C. Kropp Co., Milwaukee, WI; 1916.) This early Victorian house, the oldest brick residence remaining in Bamberg, stands at the northwest corner of Railroad Avenue and North Carlisle Street. Built before 1880 by General Francis Marion Bamberg, for whom the county is named, it was a center of local and state politics from the 1870s to the turn of the century. Here, it is believed, the discussions and planning took place which led to the formation of the county in 1897.

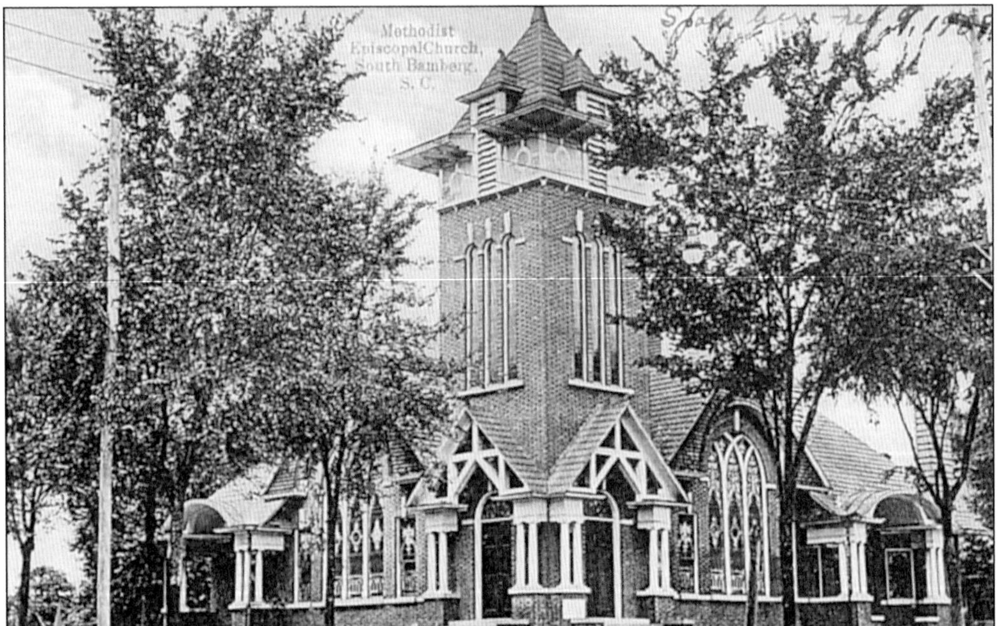


**Methodist Church, Bamberg, S.C.** (Collotype, 3 1/2" x 5 1/2", Valentine and Sons Publishing Co., #401, 735, Dundee, Scotland; *c.* 1908.) Trinity Methodist Episcopal Church South, now Trinity United Methodist Church, still stands on the south side of Railroad Avenue. The cornerstone of the architecturally eclectic sanctuary bears the date 1904. It was designed by the architectural firm of Edwards & Walter, with J.A Benson as contractor. The Reverend M.W. Hook was pastor at the time.

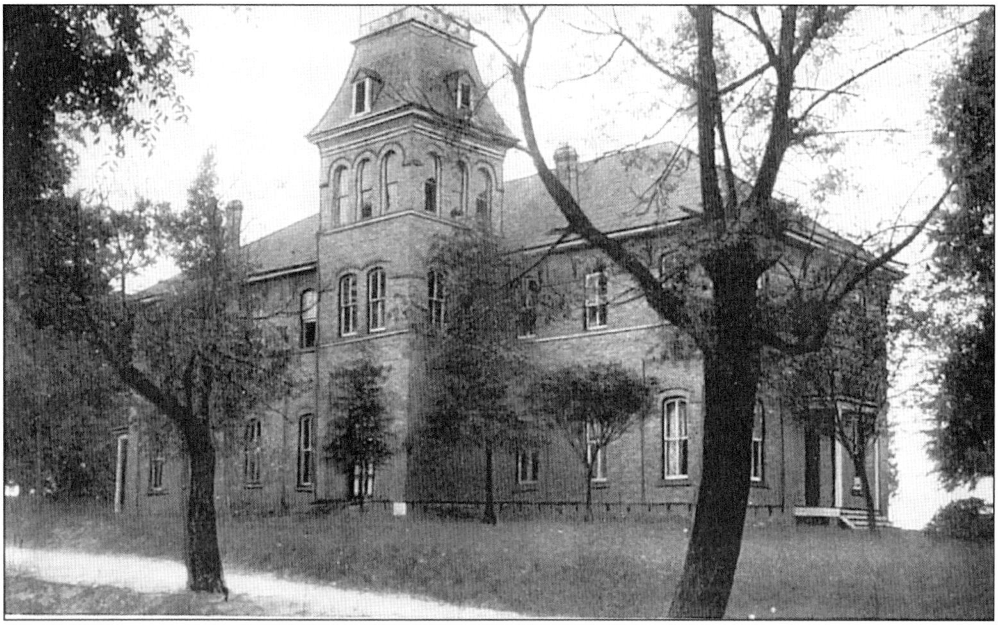

**Main Building, Carlisle School, Bamberg, S.C.** (Color Lithography, 3 1/2" x 5 1/2", [Gut & Steers Lithographic Co., New York, NY]; 1912.) Along with the Bamberg Cotton Mill, the Carlisle School, located in the southeast section of Bamberg, was the other of the two institutions whose existence would become basic to the life and economy of the town for many years. Begun in 1892 by South Carolina Methodists as a coeducational preparatory school for Wofford College, Carlisle Fitting School was named for James H. Carlisle, president of Wofford from 1875 to 1902. Shown here is the school's original building, whose cornerstone was laid September 7, 1892, with Masonic rites.

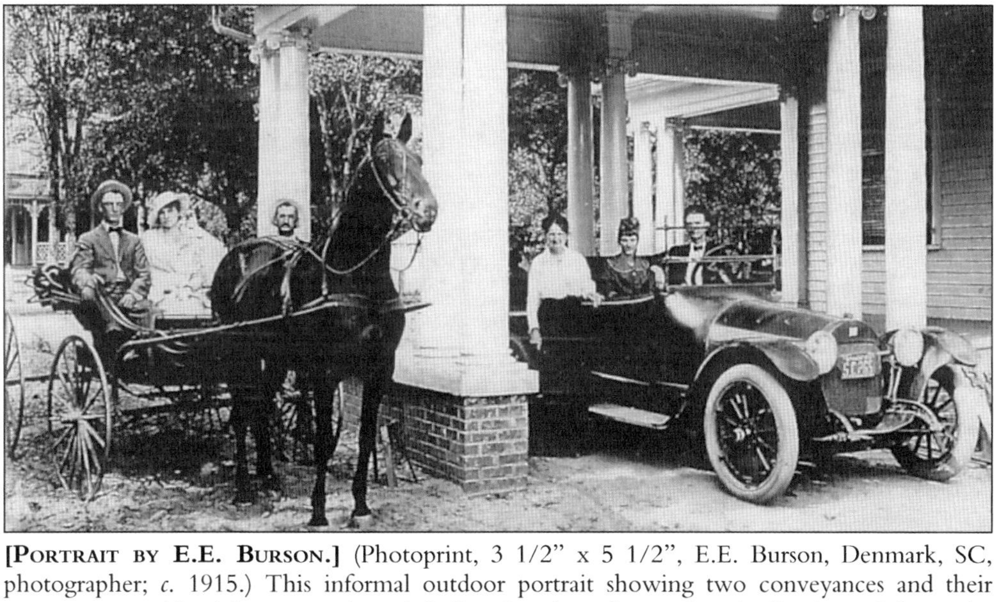

**[Portrait by E.E. Burson.]** (Photoprint, 3 1/2" x 5 1/2", E.E. Burson, Denmark, SC, photographer; *c.* 1915.) This informal outdoor portrait showing two conveyances and their owners at a residential porte cochere is believed to have been taken in Bamberg. It bears the embossed logo of photographer E.E. Burson, who operated a studio in neighboring Denmark from *c.* 1905 to 1920.

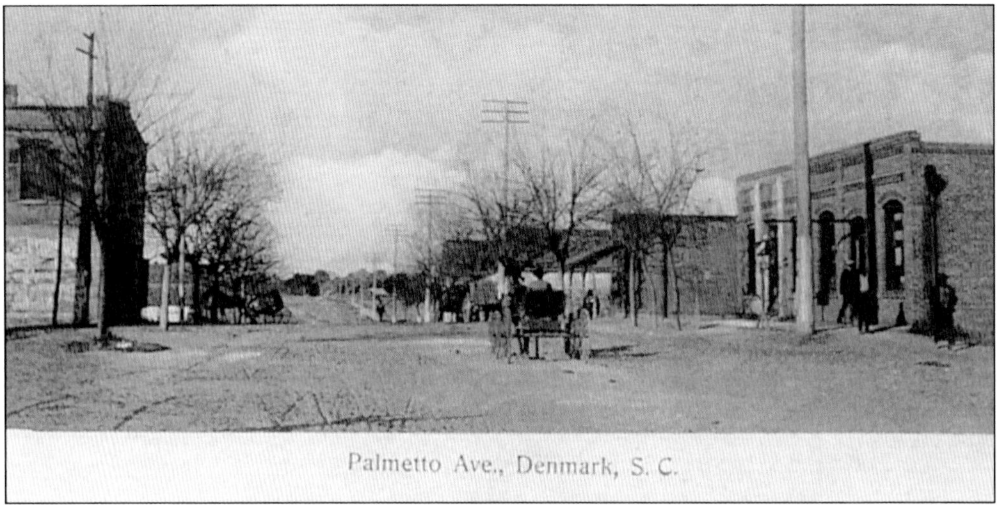


**Palmetto Avenue, Denmark, S.C.** (Hand-Colored Collotype, 3 1/2" x 5 1/2", unknown German printer; Paul E. Trouche, Charleston, SC, importer; 1909.) Looking south on Palmetto Avenue, Denmark's main street, this view, taken at least by 1908, shows at left the People's Bank building, later the Bank of Denmark, now the site of the McCain Agency. At right is the unit of buildings presently occupied by Jim Harrison's studio and store. The street was not paved prior to 1924.

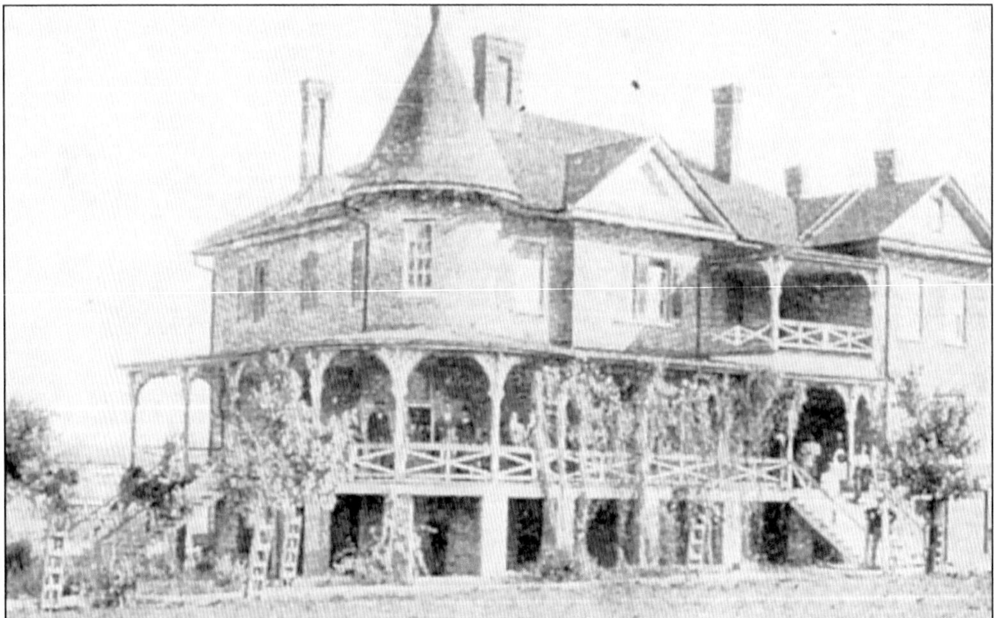

**Rice's Hotel, Denmark, S.C.** (Halftone, 3 1/2" x 5 1/4", 1906.) The red-brick hotel built in 1893—later called Rice's Hotel, and then the Denmark Hotel—stood on the west side of town across from the depot, serving passengers arriving on the Seaboard line. Today a Seaboard depot still stands on Highway 78. A Napa Auto Parts store and an Exxon station now occupy the site of the old hotel pictured here on a card used by Mr. and Mrs. L.C. Rice to convey New Year's greetings.

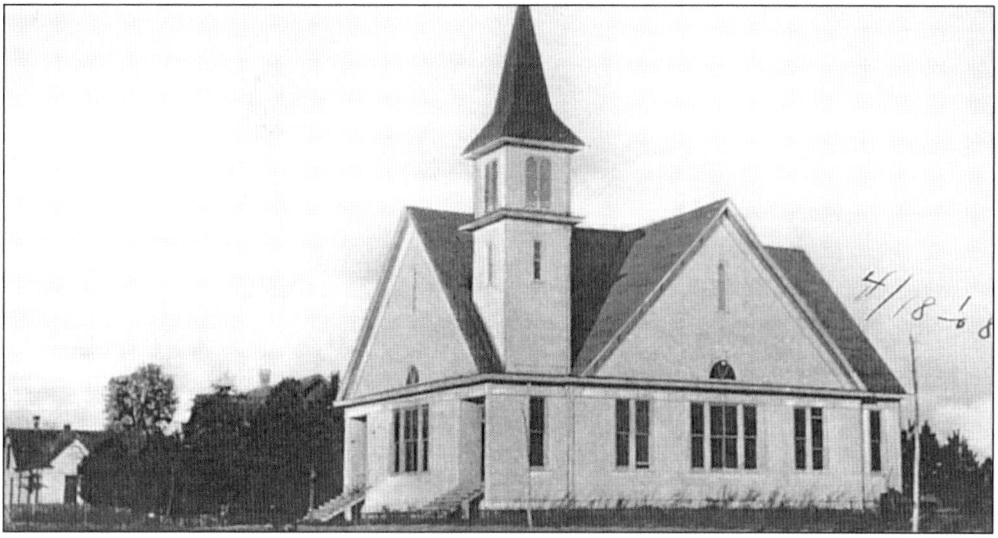

**First Baptist Church, Denmark, S.C.** (Hand-Colored Collotype, 3 1/2" x 5 1/2", unknown German printer; Paul E. Trouche, Charleston, SC, importer; 1908.) The first Baptist church of Denmark started out near Bamberg in 1844 as the Cedar Springs Baptist Church before removing to Graham's Turnout in 1849. The sanctuary pictured on this card, which was mailed in 1908, was the first one erected on the present property at the corner of South Beech and Timrod Streets in Denmark. With the donation of free labor and material and at a cost of approximately $25,000, the building of the Denmark Baptist Church was completed, debt-free, in 1904 during the ministry of the Reverend B.M. Foreman.

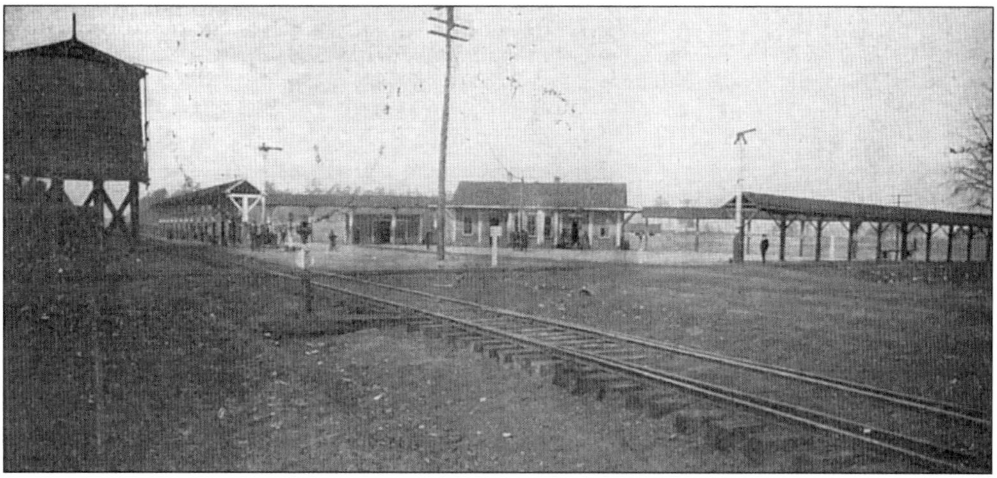

**Union Station, S.A.L. and Southern R.R., Depot, Denmark, S.C.** (Halftone, 3 3/8" x 5 3/8", [N.E. Paper and Stationery Co., #8012, Ayers, MA], *c.* 1910.) The railroad is at the center of the history of the town of Denmark, including the origin of its present name. Originally established in 1837 as Graham's Turnout, the town became incorporated as Grahams in 1870. But in 1890–91, with the crossing of two major railroad lines—the Southbound Railroad (which became the Seaboard Air Line) and the South Carolina Railroad—about a mile west of Grahams, the settlement shifted to this intersection. In 1891, the town was renamed for Captain Isadore Denmark of Savannah, an official of the Seaboard who had shown some special interest in the development of the area. With the completion of a stretch of the Manchester and Augusta Railroad near the town, it became a railroad junction of some importance.

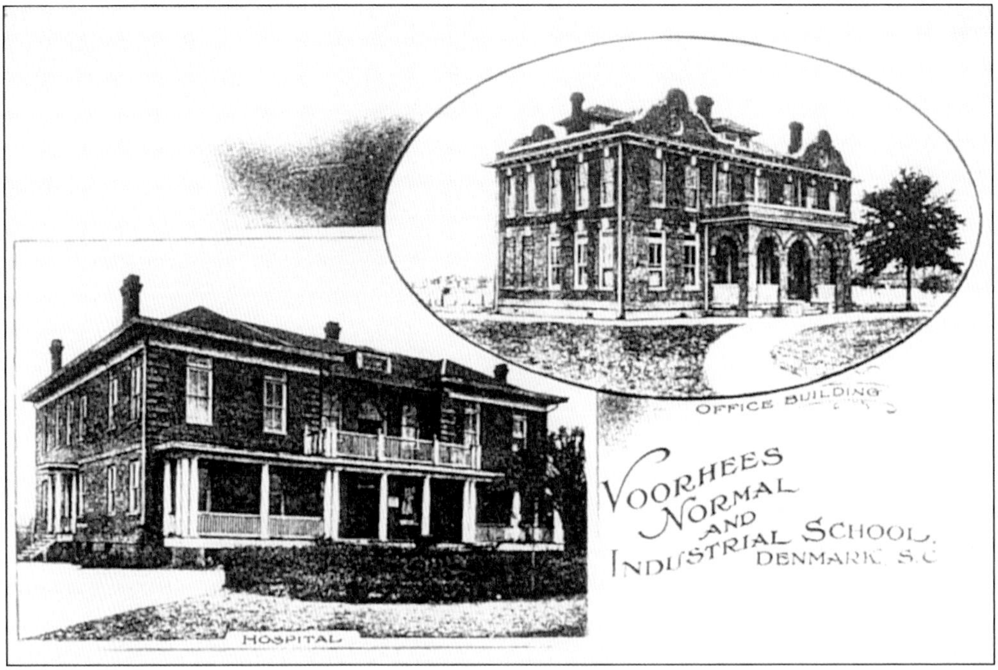


**Voorhees Normal & Industrial School, Hospital, Office Bldg., Denmark, S.C.** (Collotype, 3 1/2" x 5 1/2", Albertype Co., Brooklyn, NY; 1916.) Begun in 1897 by Tuskegee graduate Elizabeth E. Wright, Voorhees Normal and Industrial School (later called Voorhees Industrial School, now Voorhees College) has long been one of Denmark's, and Bamberg County's, defining institutions. The dual-image card above displays two of the campus's handsome permanent buildings: at left, the brick, 30-room Booker T. Washington Hospital, the gift of Ralph Voorhees of Clinton, New Jersey, which was completed in 1905; at right, the Administration Building, the gift of Mrs. Voorhees, which was finished in 1916. The old hospital, recently renovated, now houses the offices of the college president.

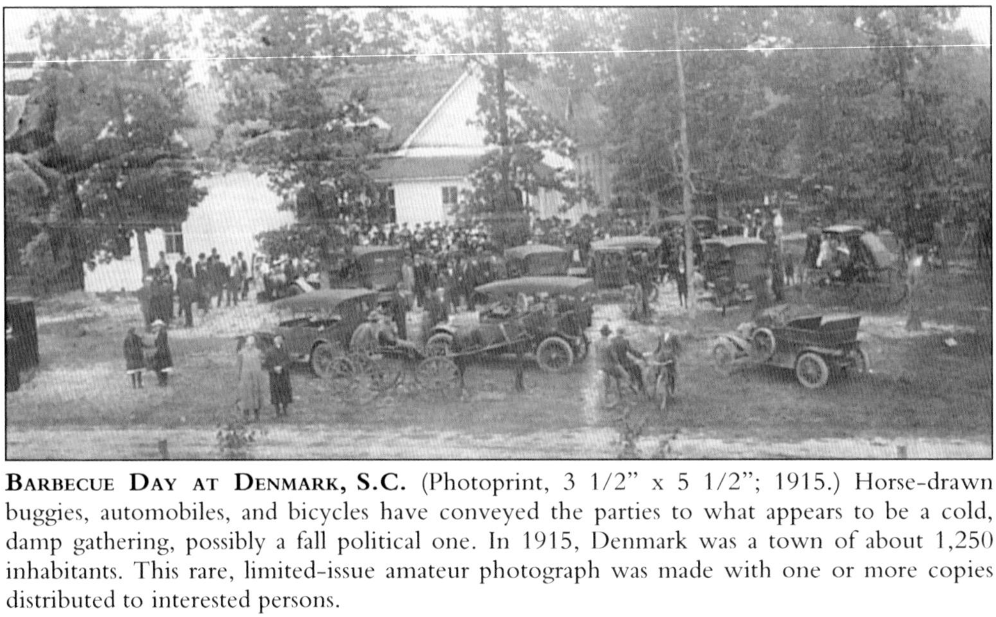

**Barbecue Day at Denmark, S.C.** (Photoprint, 3 1/2" x 5 1/2"; 1915.) Horse-drawn buggies, automobiles, and bicycles have conveyed the parties to what appears to be a cold, damp gathering, possibly a fall political one. In 1915, Denmark was a town of about 1,250 inhabitants. This rare, limited-issue amateur photograph was made with one or more copies distributed to interested persons.

# *Six*

# Allendale County

Allendale County is South Carolina's youngest, formed from portions of Hampton and Barnwell Counties in 1919—through the "concerted effort of loyal, wide awake citizens of Allendale, Fairfax and their immediate communities," wrote Thomas E. Crane in *Opportunities in Edisto-Savannah* (1927). The county was called Allendale after its central town, which had grown up as a trading center along the Port Royal-Augusta railroad in the mid-1860s and had been chartered in 1873, its name derived from that of the family owning much of the property on which the town was built.

Comprised of some 435 square miles situated between the Savannah and Big Salkehatchie Rivers, Allendale has always been an agrarian county characterized by field and forest, which have shaped both its economic and leisure pursuits. Thomas Crane in the mid-1920s lists among the county's attractions its mild climate, rich soil, lengthy growing season, variety of trees, abundant wildlife, pure water, good roads, progressive towns, excellent schools, a church-going people, and "breezes that blow from the ocean upon a land where spring is eternal sunshine."

Because it is the youngest county, all but one of the cards in this chapter were made before it was created.

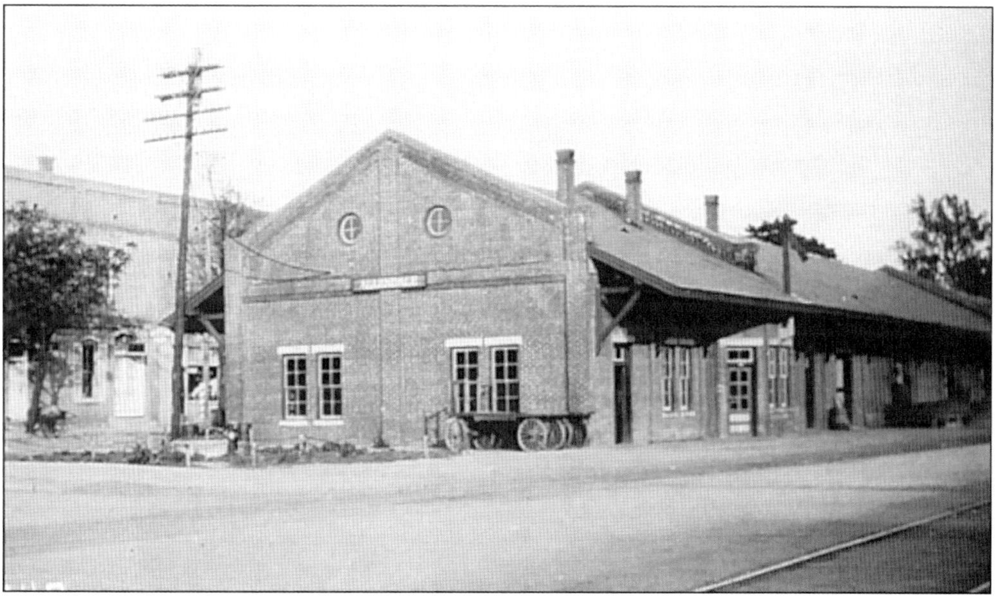

**Charleston & Western Carolina Station, Allendale, S.C.** (Photoprint, 3 3/8" x 5 3/8", #147; 1929.) Incorporated in 1890, Allendale depended upon the railroad for much of its life as a commercial center. Its later Union Station, which was located on the east side of the railroad tracks across from the Gilldare Hotel seen here at left, eventually served both the Charleston & Western Carolina and the Southern lines. J.T. Talbert retired as Allendale's last railway agent in 1968. J.V. Spigener, a local cotton planter, is remembered as having had an office in the station before it was demolished.

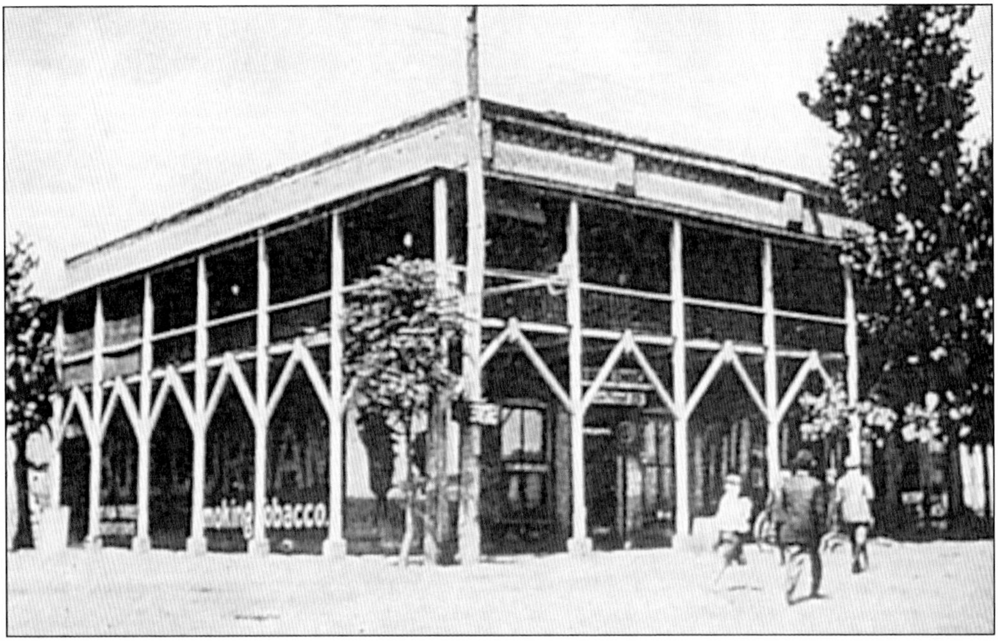


**Cleveland Hotel, Allendale, S.C.** (Collotype, 3 1/2" x 5 1/2", Albertype Co., Brooklyn, NY; 1915.) The rooms of the old Cleveland Hotel, on the west side of the railroad tracks at the corner of Main and Railroad, occupied the second floor above a general merchandise store. It was in operation until shortly after World War II and still stands, without the unusual two-sided arcade, in a much-diminished condition.

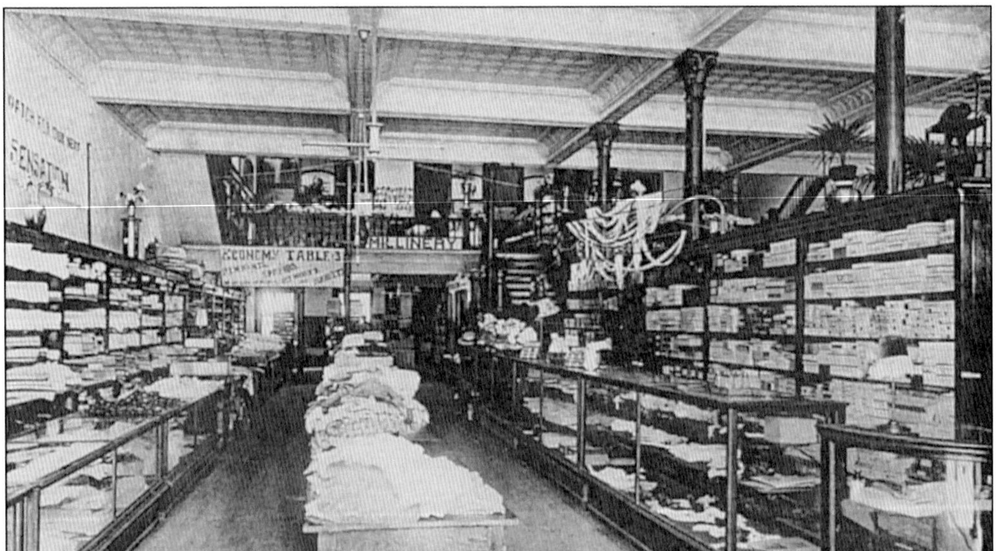


**Interior, Wolff's Department Store, Allendale, S.C.** (Collotype, 3 1/2" x 5 1/2", Albertype Co., Brooklyn, NY; *c.* 1913.) On the reverse of this view of Wolff's Department Store is an invitation to "attend our millinery and dress goods display" to be held from March 17–19, 1913. Bits of the blue-and-white tile mosaic which once spelled out its name on the sidewalk in front of the store were still visible in 1998 outside the deserted building, on the northwest corner of Main and Bay across from the Carolina Commercial Bank.

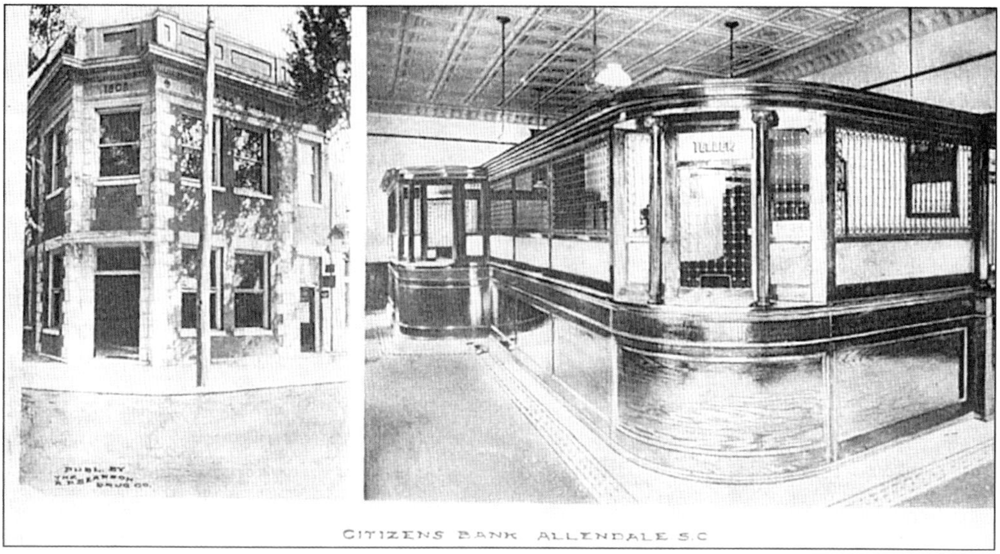


**CITIZENS BANK, ALLENDALE, S.C.** (Collotype, 3 1/2" x 5 1/2", Albertype Co., Brooklyn, NY; *c.* 1910.) The Citizens Bank, exhibited in this unusual dual-view card published by Searson's Drug Company, was built at the corner of Bay and Main in 1909. The Carolina Commercial Bank now occupies the building, which looks much the same now as it does here. The large Searson's series, like Luther's in Beaufort, included other businesses, schools, churches, homes, and residential street scenes for an extensive documentation of the community.

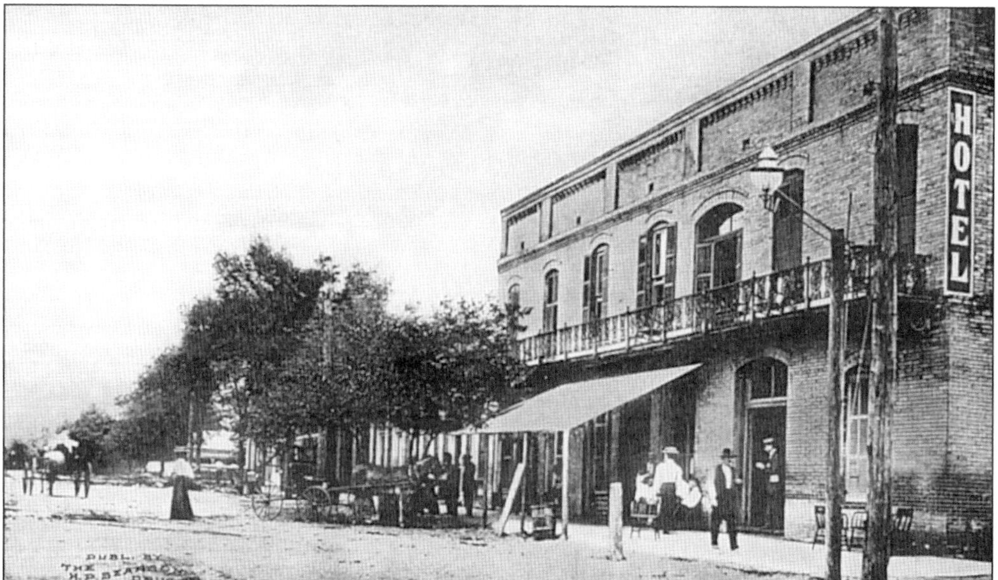


**PORTION OF MAIN STREET, ALLENDALE, S.C.** (Collotype, 3 1/2" x 5 1/2", Albertype Co., Brooklyn, NY; *c.* 1915.) The Gilldare Hotel, seen here at right, is the principal focus of this view of a portion of the south side of Allendale's Main Street. In existence at least as early as 1907, it later became known as the New Warren and stayed in business through the mid-1950s. It can still be seen, with a much modified brick front, on the southeast corner of Main and Railroad. In 1910, the business establishments running east down the block to the bank on the corner included stores for general merchandise, candy, clothing, and shoes.

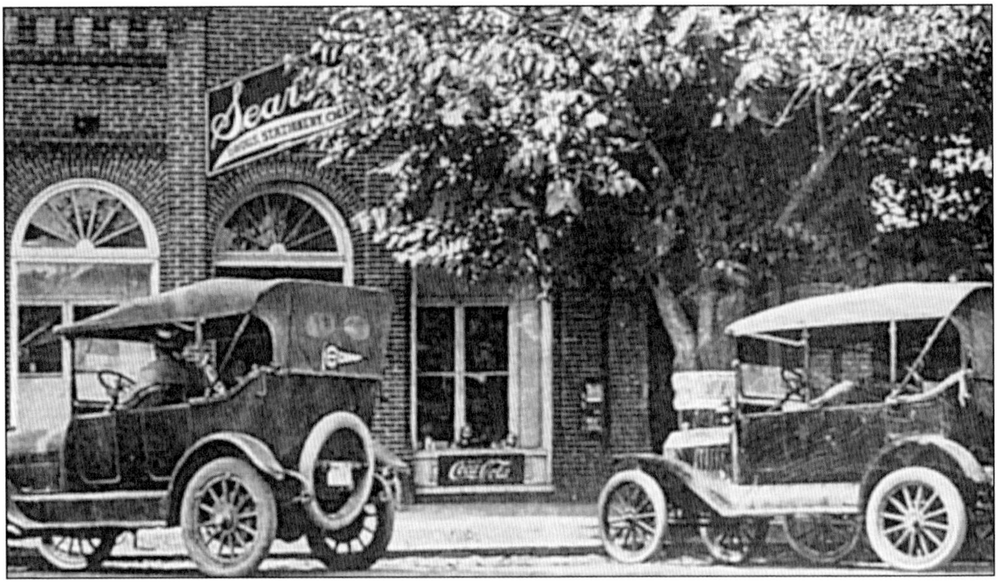


**SEARSON'S DRUG STORE #1 AND POST OFFICE, ALLENDALE, S.C.** (Collotype, 3 1/2" x 5 1/2", Albertype Co., Brooklyn, NY; 1915.) The building here that once housed Searson's Drug Store still stands in the middle of the western side of Railroad Avenue, without some of its decorative brickwork and minus the tree in front of the post office at right. The much beloved Robinson Plato Searson (1842–1916), the University of Chicago-educated pharmacist who owned the store, also functioned as Allendale's postmaster for about 40 years and was at the time of his death the oldest one in South Carolina, having been appointed in 1885.

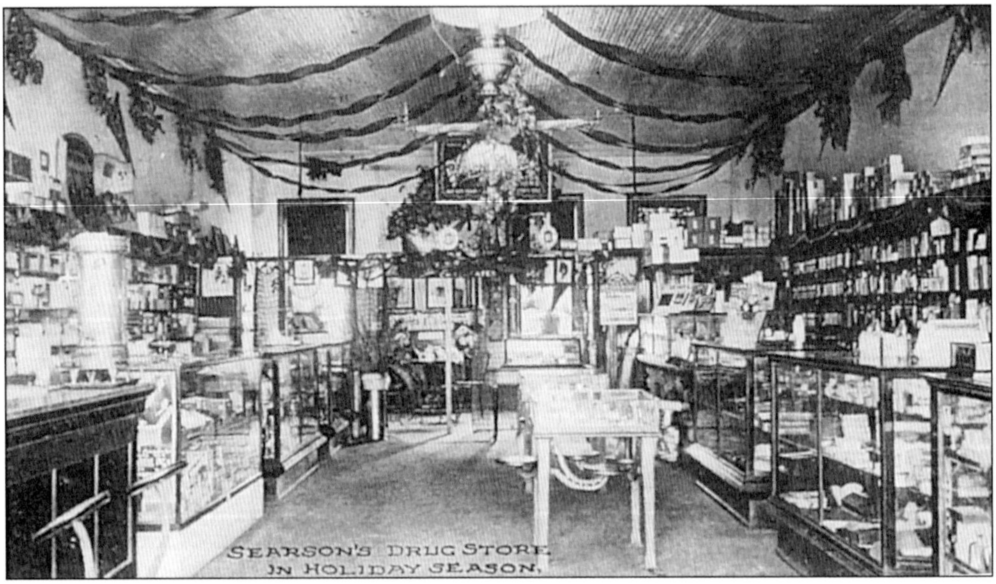


**SEARSON'S DRUG STORE IN HOLIDAY SEASON, ALLENDALE, S.C.** (Collotype, 3 1/2" x 5 1/2", Albertype Co., Brooklyn, NY; 1915.) Many of the postcards of Allendale's sites and scenes were published by the R.P. Searson Drug Company and certainly would have been sold in the store. Dr. Searson, a native of Coosawhatchie, had worked and studied business in Charleston, served in the Civil War, and run a plantation in Georgia before returning to South Carolina, where in 1878 he opened his drugstore and became a pioneer in the building of Allendale.

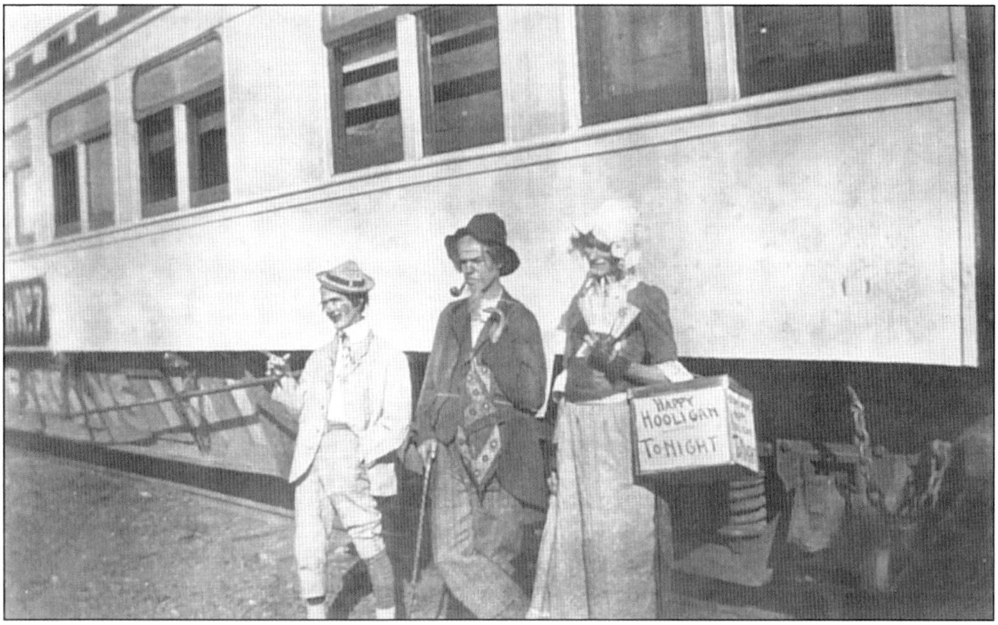


**[Happy Hooligan Tonight, Allendale, S.C.]** (Photoprint, 3 4/10" x 5 1/2"; *c.* 1911.) A note penned across the verso of this very rare card reads as follows: "Taken in Allendale, S.C. Rae—Charlie and Hap." Here three theatrical troupers, in costume to advertise their evening performance in "Happy Hooligan," pause to have their picture taken next to the train which would have conveyed them on their whistle-stop tour across the region. Allendale, with a 1910 population of 1,200, was probably a frequent stop for traveling shows.

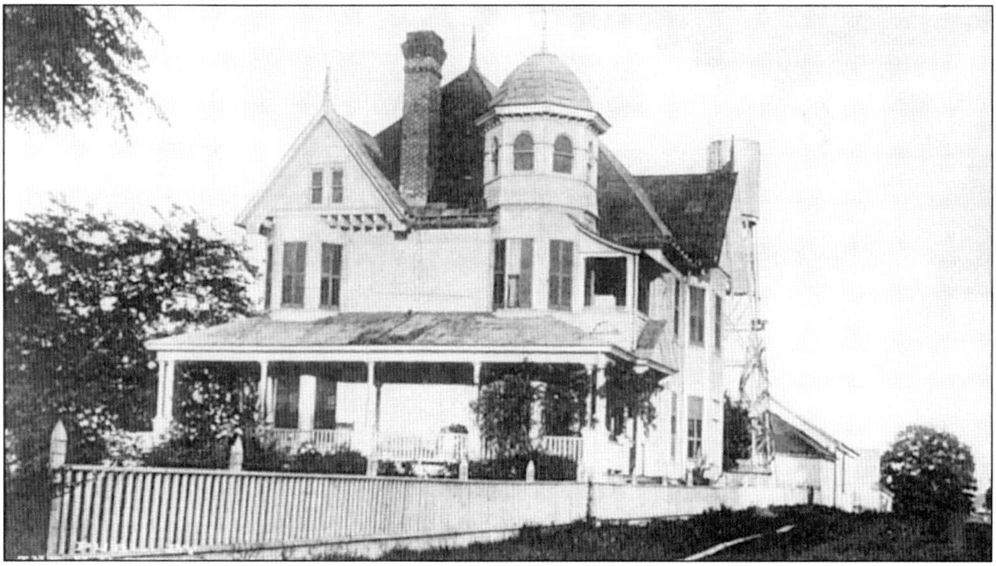

**Residence, Flatte Street, Allendale, S.C.** (Collotype, 3 1/2" x 5 1/2", Albertype Co., Brooklyn, NY; *c.* 1912.) Built by James L. Oswald about 1889, this Queen Anne Victorian-style residence is the only known surviving example in America of a house adapted from Design No. 25 in the marketing catalogue of George F. Barber and Company, the mail-order architectural firm which operated in Knoxville *c.* 1888–1908. The house, now renovated inside and out, has been in the possession of Mr. and Mrs. Henry S. Laffitte for more than 20 years.

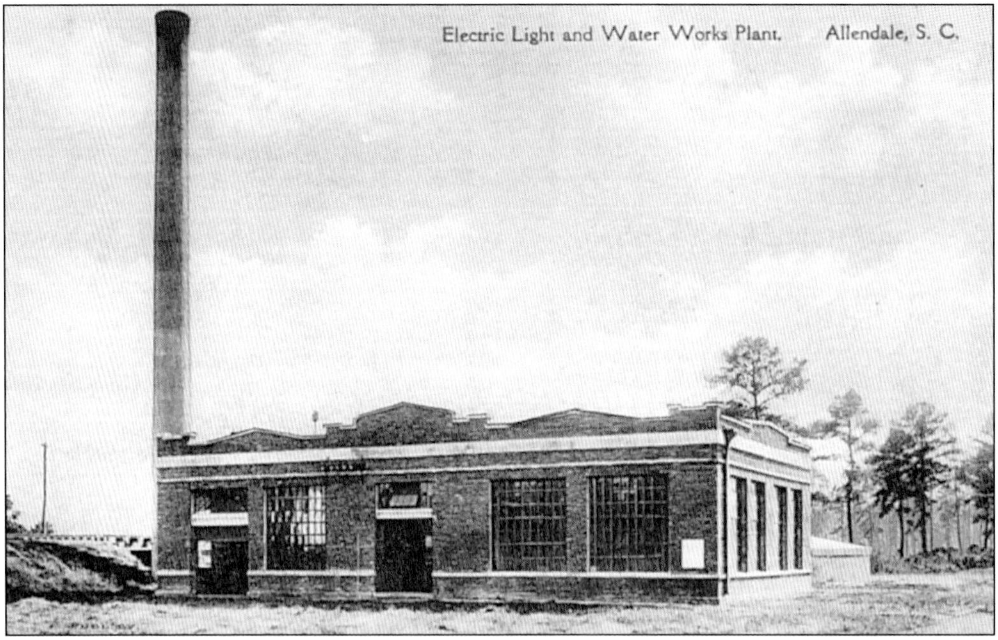


**Electric Light and Water Works Plant, Allendale, S.C.** (Collotype, 3 1/2" x 5 1/2", Albertype Co., Brooklyn, NY; *c.* 1915.) This municipal utilities plant, erected in Allendale in 1915, had two generators (one 100-kw, one 48-kw) operating day and night to produce the town's electricity. Two coal-fueled 100-hp boilers pumped its water from a flowing well into a 150,000-gallon reservoir and through 3,000 feet of pipe to an elevated 100,000-gallon tank. By 1922, Allendale's average daily consumption was 70,000 gallons. The building, with its identifying stone slab at right still intact, continues to be used by the town and can be seen on Barton Road between Gum and Walker Streets.

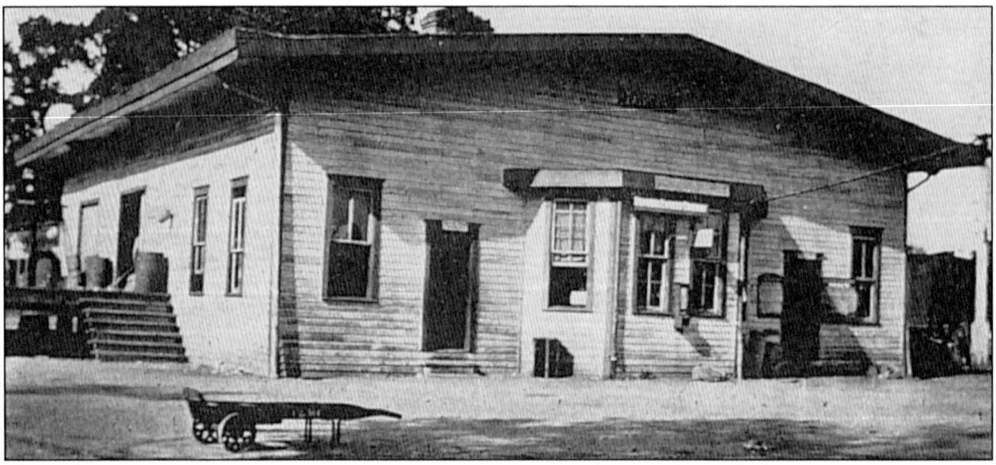

**Passenger Station & Freight Depot, Fairfax, S.C.** (Halftone, 3 4/10" x 5 4/10", [Ess an Ess Photo Co., New York, NY]; *c.* 1910.) Incorporated in 1896, Fairfax, like many other small towns in South Carolina, owed its existence and growth to the development of the railroad. By 1910, it had grown to 725 inhabitants. This frame station—used by the Charleston & Western Carolina (east and west route) and the Seaboard Air Lines (north and south route)—was later replaced by a brick one. The mail-order card was published by Isaac Knopf, who owned and operated a drugstore as well as a general mercantile store in Fairfax.

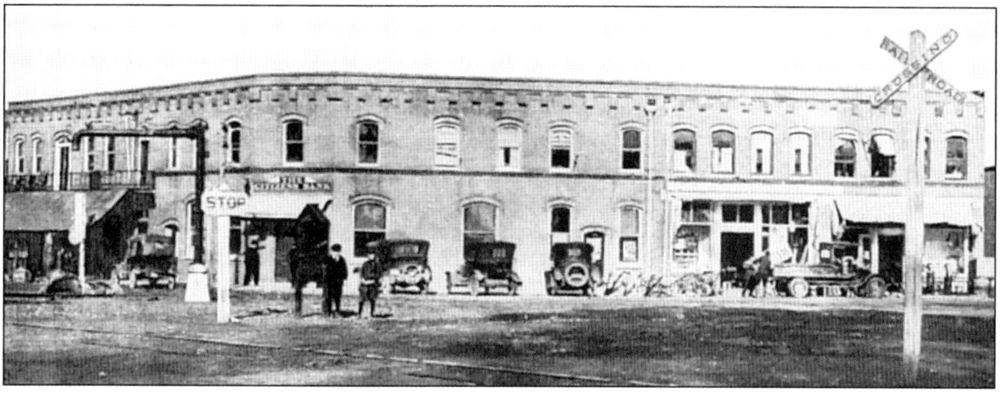


**The Citizens Bank Block, Fairfax, S.C.** (Halftone and Blue Sky, 3 4/10" x 5 1/2", E.C. Kropp Co., Milwaukee, WI; *c.* 1914.) One can still stand at the railroad crossing in downtown Fairfax and view the bank block, shown here. Just behind the "stop" sign to the left is the corner entrance to the Citizens Bank, subsequently the Fairfax Bank and Trust Company and, since 1981, the Allendale County Bank—whose new facade was added in 1989. Fairfax Furniture and Hardware Company occupied the end units to the right in this large two-story brick complex, which dominates the town's commercial center.

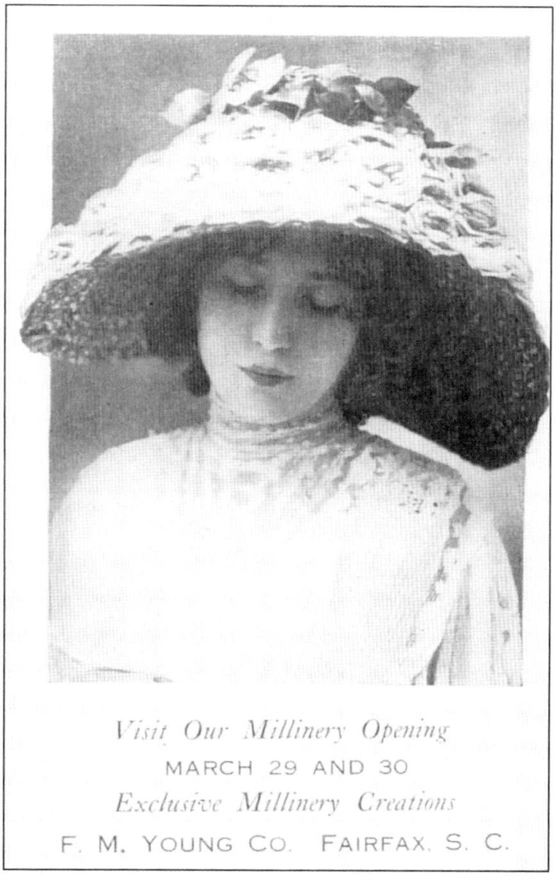


**Visit Our Millinery Opening, F.M. Young Co., Fairfax, S.C.** (Halftone, 5 4/10" x 3 1/2", Millinery Trade Review, New York, NY; 1911.) Used as a stock advertising piece, the generic "souvenir postcard" was simply overprinted with the local merchant's message and mailed out in bulk to prospective customers. This one announces a millinery opening at the F.M. Young Company in Fairfax in 1911. Since hats were an integral part of women's dress during this period, separate millinery shops or hat departments in larger stores were an essential part of the small-town commercial scene.

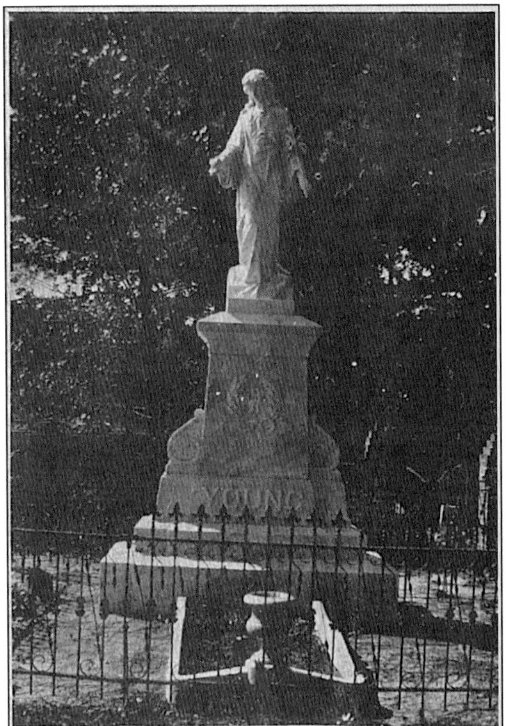

MONUMENT, FAIRFAX, S. C.—To Memory of Mrs. Virginia D. Young, Great Temperance Leader and Exponent of Womans Rights.

**Monument, Fairfax, S.C.** (Halftone, 5 3/10" x 3 4/10", [Ess an Ess Photo Co., Inc., New York, NY], 1910.) Located in Fairfax Cemetery, this sculptured figure was erected in memory of Georgetown native Virginia Durant Covington Young (1842–1906), pioneer worker on behalf of temperance and women's suffrage. These words have been engraved on the south side of the monument: "Standing for truth and human rights, she heralded the new day out of the night. She climbed the heights, and held aloft the torch of liberty for her sex."

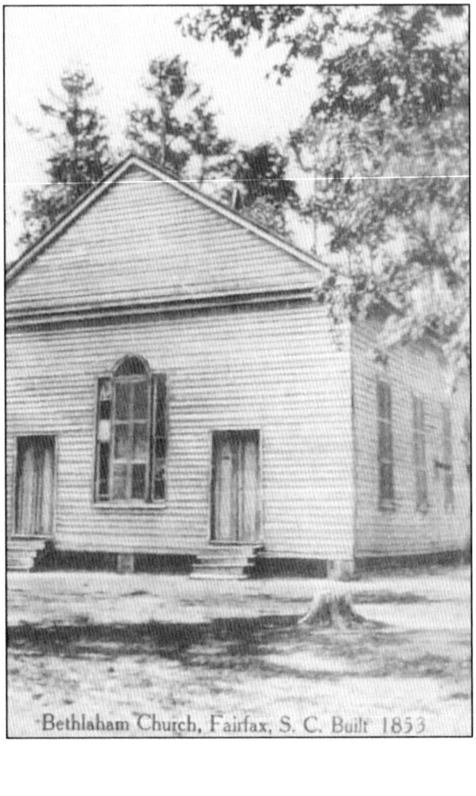
Bethlaham Church, Fairfax, S. C. Built 1853

**Bethlaham [sic] Church, Fairfax, S.C.** (Collotype, 5 3/8" x 3 3/8", [McGown-Silsbee Litho. Co., New York, NY]; *c.* 1912.) Built with hand-hewn timbers and wooden pegs, the first house of worship of this Baptist church was erected in 1853 for a congregation which had been organized with ten members the previous year by the Reverend W.G.M. Williams. This sanctuary was replaced by another one in 1913, and by a third in the early 1960s, by which time the church was known as the First Baptist Church of Fairfax.

# *Seven*

# Barnwell County

Barnwell County, which had been a part of old Orangeburg District (and later, briefly, bore the name Winton County), was named for the Barnwell family of Beaufort District, and probably specifically for the brothers John and Robert Barnwell, distinguished early leaders from the district (see Joyce S. O'Bannon's "Names in Barnwell County," in *Names in South Carolina*, Winter 1968). In 1798, the General Assembly designated the territory between the South Edisto and Savannah Rivers as Barnwell District, which encompassed the present counties of Barnwell and Bamberg, part of Aiken, and most of Allendale. It became Barnwell County in 1868. Covering an area of 522 square miles, it is among the smaller counties of the state. In 1925, it had an estimated population of 23,251.

Like its six sister counties, Barnwell has been characterized by a rural economy and small-town way of life, largely dependent upon the railroad for its wider communication links during this period. And like the others at the time, it was engaged in conscious attempts to diversify its agricultural production, develop its roads and schools, maintain the old or build new homes and churches, and generally promote, as Horace J. Crouch put it in *Opportunities in Edisto-Savannah Territory*, "a Southern air of culture, refinement, and hospitality."

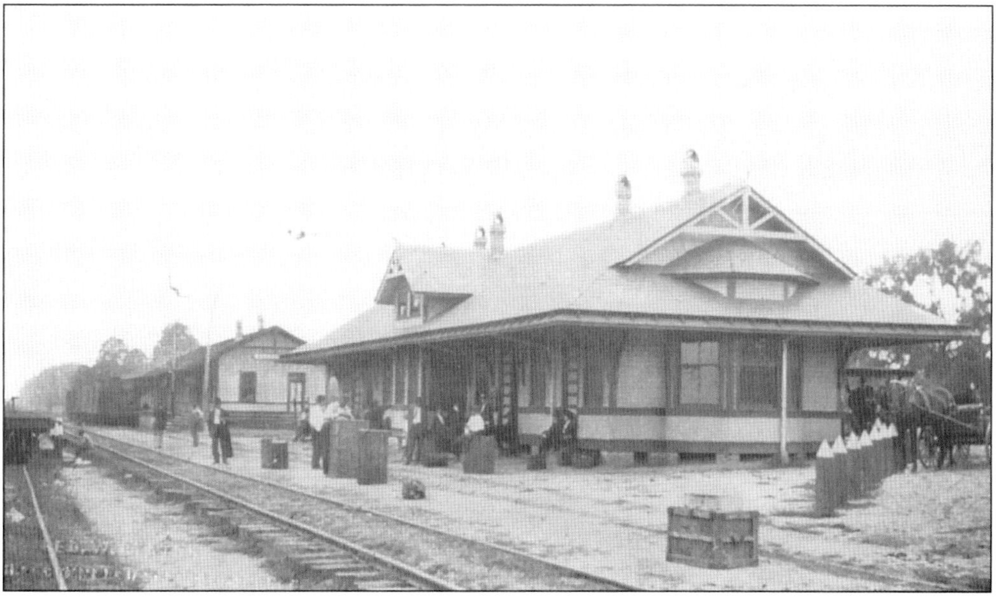

**ACL Depot, Barnwell, S.C.** (Halftone, 3 1/2" x 5 1/2", [C.U. Williams, #18410, Bloomington, IL]; *c.* 1914.) The Atlantic Coast Line depot is believed to have been built in 1900, when the railroad came to Barnwell. It was rebuilt in 1952 and demolished 30 years later. This station served Barnwell's east-west rail line, while the Southern depot served its north-south. The cotton platforms are visible here beyond the depot itself in this view looking northwest. The depot's foundation can still be seen just south of Baxley's Pawn Shop on the west side of Patterson Street, about seven blocks from downtown Barnwell.

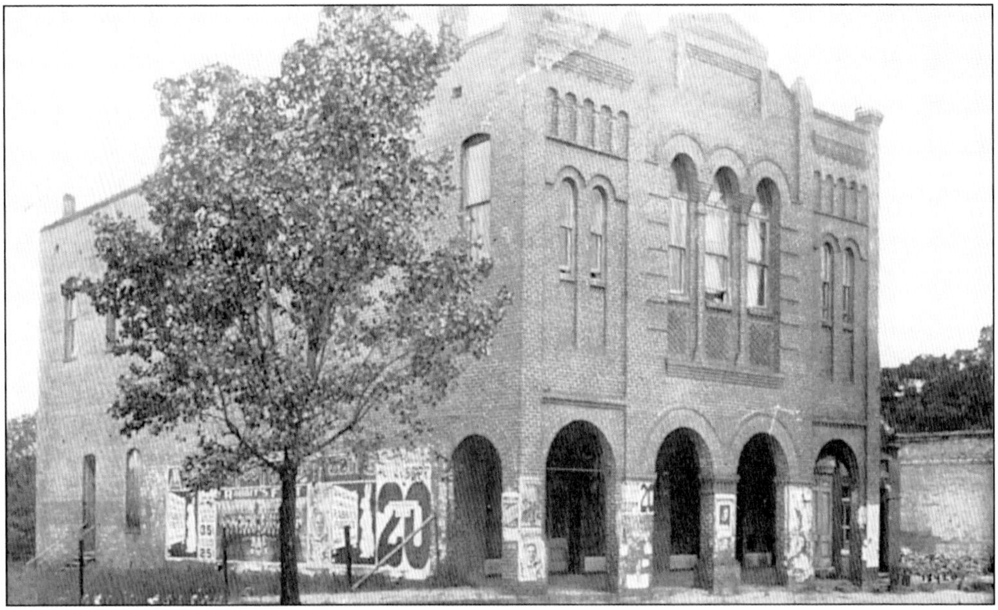

**Opera House, Barnwell, S.C.** (Halftone, 3 1/2" x 5 1/2", [C.U. Williams, #18420, Bloomington, IL]; *c.* 1914.) With an arcade and windows in the Romanesque style, this much more ornate and articulated brick two-story Opera House, which once stood near the corner of Main and Jackson, replaced an 1889 Town Hall and Opera House, which burned on June 2, 1892. It served as the site of Barnwell's public entertainment, local benefits, and public school commencements. The liquor dispensary and bottling works were housed on its ground floor. Destroyed by fire on October 3, 1915, it was never rebuilt.

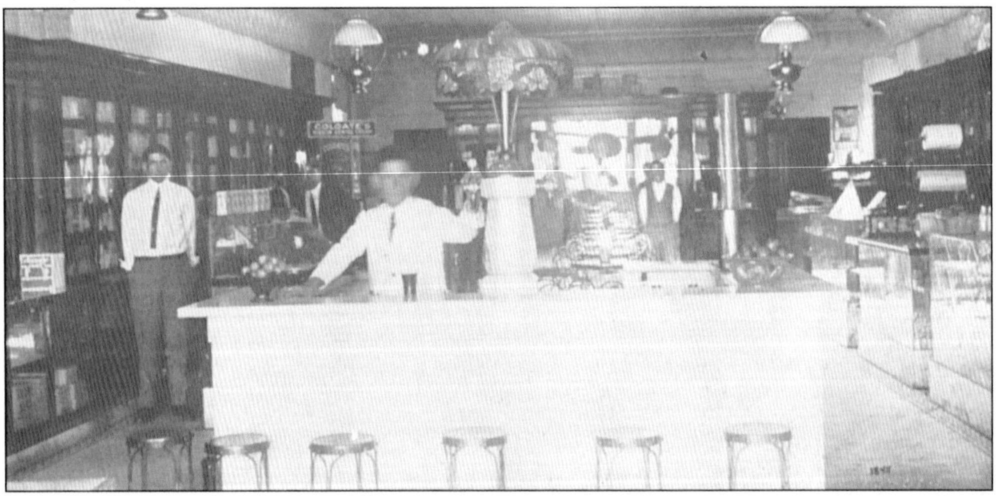

**Interior View of Burckhalter's Drug Store, Barnwell, S.C.** (Halftone, 3 1/2" x 5 1/2", [C.U. Williams, #18411, Bloomington, IL]; *c.* 1914.) Mention of Burckhalter's Drug Store can be found in the *Barnwell People* as early as October 15, 1908, and in May 28, 1925, the store is listed in a paid advertisement as one of four drug-dispensing businesses in Barnwell registering a complaint about having to collect taxes on certain commodities. Burckhalter's Drug Store, like Searson's in Allendale and Luther's in Beaufort, sponsored a large series of view-cards on Barnwell. Burckhalter's cards were made by the mail-order C.U. Williams Company and carried the codes #18409 to #18422.

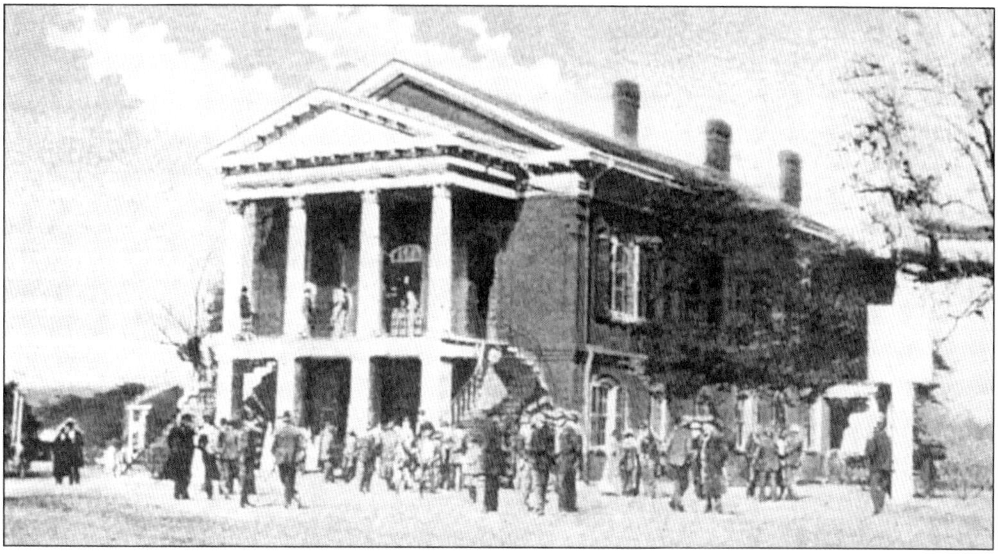

**The Court House, Barnwell.** (Color Lithography, 3 4/10" x 5 4/10", [Souvenir Post Card Mfg. Co., Rockford, IL]; 1910.) The present courthouse, corner of Pechmann Lane and Main Street, is the third one to be erected on the 5-acre plot donated by Benjamin Odom in 1799. Built in 1878–1879, supposedly with brick hauled from Blackville by mule team, it replaced the courthouse burned by Sherman in 1865. At right stands the vertical sundial presented to the town in 1858 by local planter, benefactor, and philanthropist Joseph D. Allen. The only surviving one of its kind in America, it is shown here prior to 1918, when concrete curbing was added to protect it against traffic hazards.

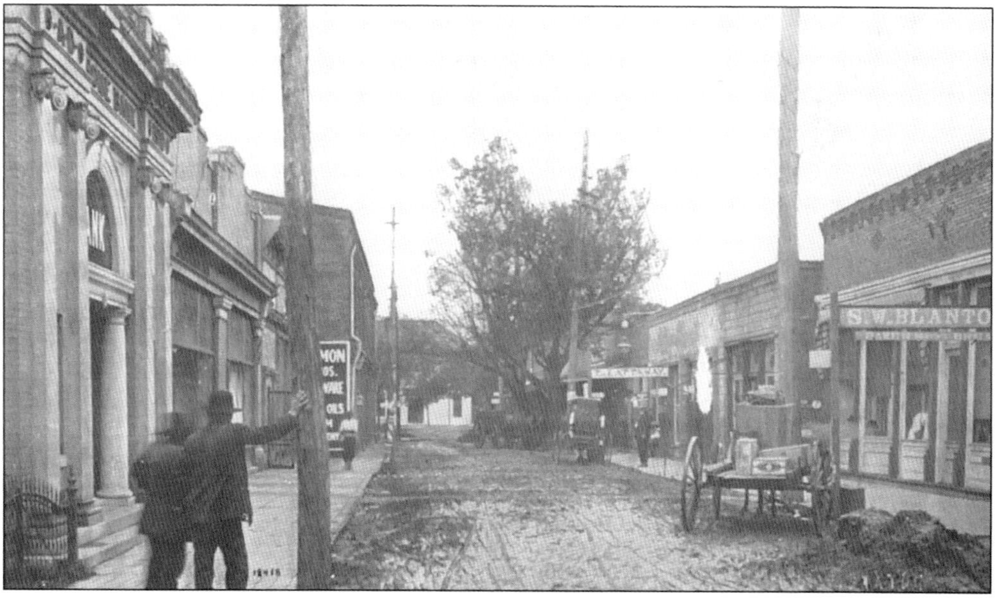


**Main Street, Barnwell, S.C.** (Halftone, 3 1/2" x 5 1/2", [C.U. Williams, #18418, Bloomington, IL]; *c.* 1914.) At left in this view of Main Street is the Home Bank building (1910), which in the late 1990s was acquired, renovated, and opened as the Bank of Barnwell County. The unit of stores beyond Blanton's Bakery seen here at right on the north side of the street has disappeared and the space has been turned into a parking lot.

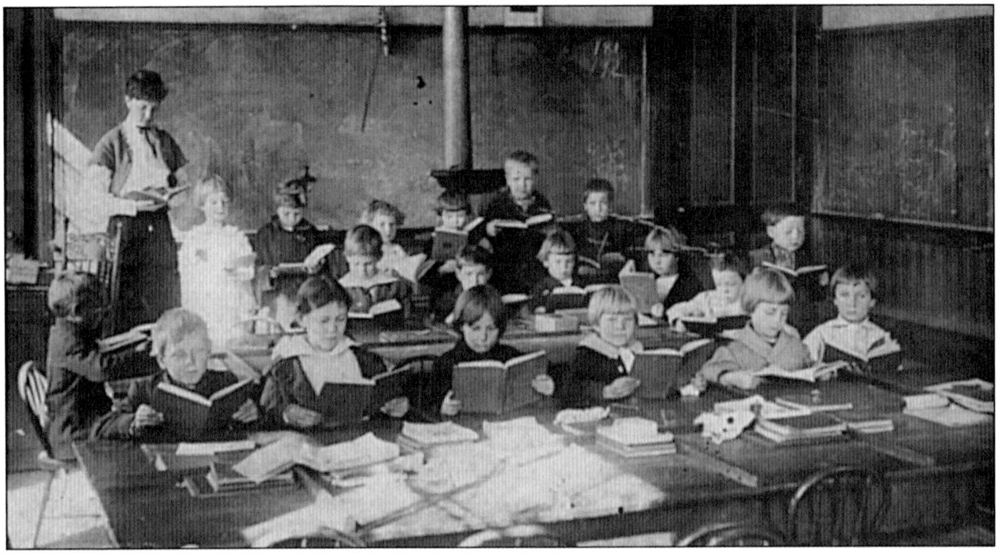

**First Grade, Barnwell Public School.** (Photoprint, 3 4/10" x 5 4/10"; *c.* 1910.) This rare picture of Barnwell elementary students in their classroom may well be one of the few surviving views of the interior of one of the town's old public school buildings, with its coal-burning stove seen at the rear. "A few years ago," Superintendent Horace J. Crouch wrote in *Opportunities in Edisto-Savannah Territory*, "the county had the distinction of expending more per white pupil for educational purposes than any other county in South Carolina."

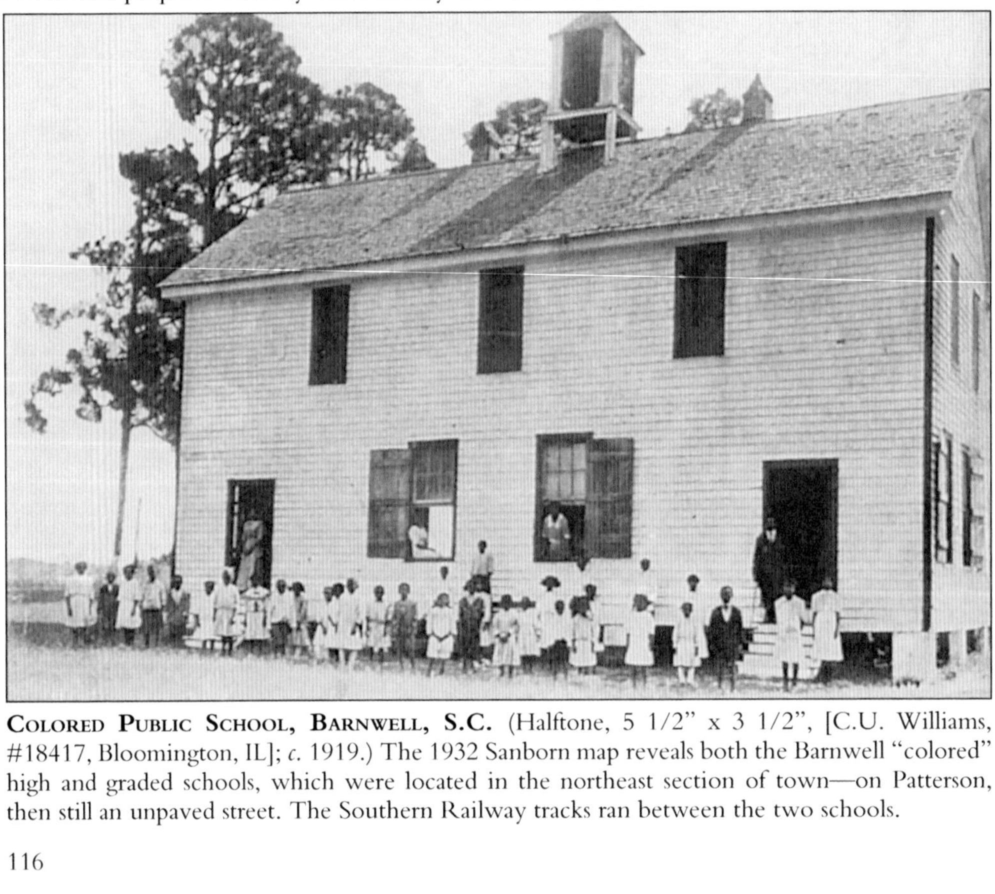

**Colored Public School, Barnwell, S.C.** (Halftone, 5 1/2" x 3 1/2", [C.U. Williams, #18417, Bloomington, IL]; *c.* 1919.) The 1932 Sanborn map reveals both the Barnwell "colored" high and graded schools, which were located in the northeast section of town—on Patterson, then still an unpaved street. The Southern Railway tracks ran between the two schools.

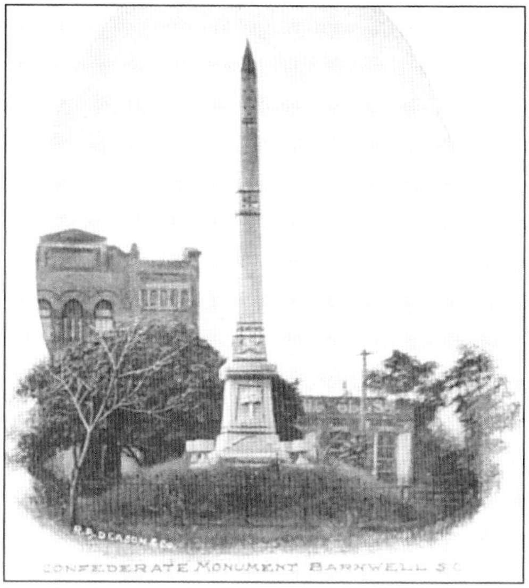


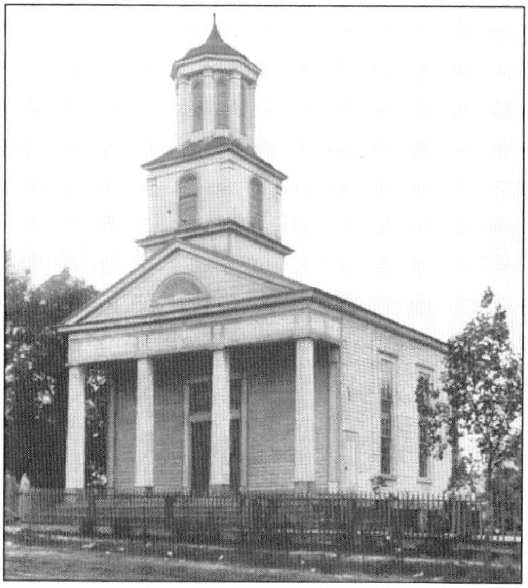

*Left:* **Confederate Monument, Barnwell, S.C.** (Collotype, 5 1/2" x 3 1/2", Albertype Co., Brooklyn, NY; *c.* 1907.) The Confederate Monument in Calhoun Park looks west toward the imposing opera house. The gray marble and granite obelisk designed by the Artope and Whitt Marble Yard of Macon was erected by the Barnwell Ladies' Memorial Society at a cost of $800. The cornerstone was laid on August 22, 1900, with Masonic rites.

*Right:* **Baptist Church, Barnwell, S.C.** (Halftone, 3 1/2" x 5 1/2", [C.U. Williams, #18419, Bloomington, IL]; *c.* 1914.) This *c.* 1850 sanctuary, which stood at the top of old Red Hill at the corner of Jackson Street and Dunbarton Boulevard, served Barnwell Baptists until its replacement by a new one on the same site in 1926. The Red Hill Burying Ground is still maintained.

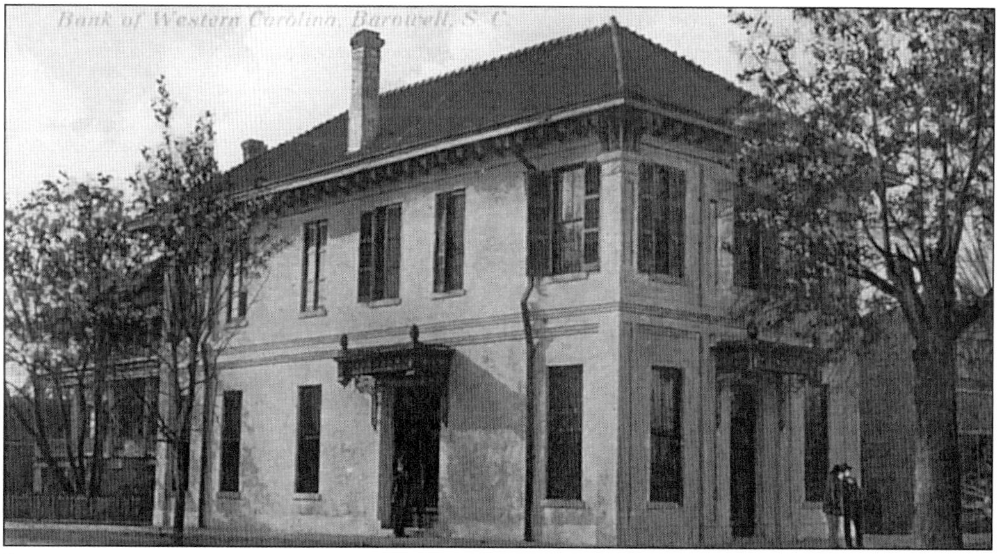


**Bank of Western Carolina, Barnwell, S.C.** (Color Lithography, 3 1/2" x 5 4/10", [Curt Teich, Chicago, IL]; Commercial Colortype Co., #30567, Chicago, distributor, *c.* 1912.) This building continues to function as a bank (First Citizens). Handsomely restored and somewhat changed, it is recognizable on the corner of Main and Jefferson directly across from the courthouse.

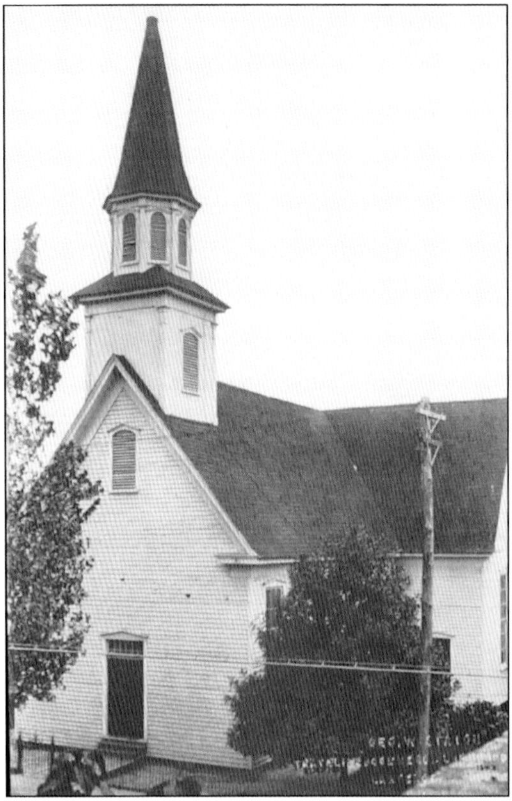

**Methodist Church, Barnwell, S.C.** (Halftone, 3 1/2" x 5 1/2", [C.U. Williams, #18413, Bloomington, IL]; *c.* 1914.) Still located on its original site on the south side of Main Street near the old Home Bank, the Methodist Church underwent major renovations in the late 1920s, when an education building was added at the rear and the spire and bell tower seen here were removed. While the original floor plan was retained in the 1928 remodeling, the exterior appearance was substantially changed by the addition of a brick facade with two turrets.

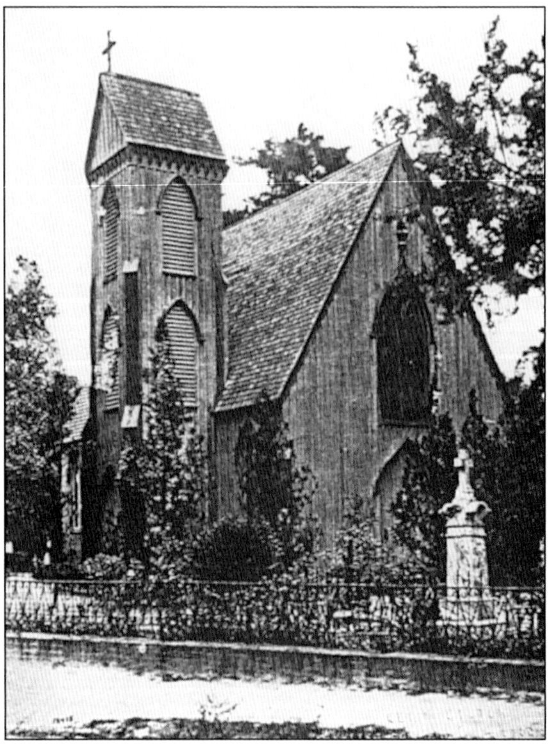

**Episcopal Church, Barnwell, S.C.** (Halftone, 3 1/2" x 5 1/2", [C.U. Williams, #18415, Bloomington, IL]; *c.* 1914.) The Episcopal Church of the Holy Apostles, 1706 Hagood Avenue, was built and consecrated in 1857 for a congregation which had been organized in 1848 with 38 white and 10 African-American members. Constructed of cypress in the neo-Gothic style, it lost its original steeple to an 1886 hurricane. It is listed on the National Register of Historic Places.

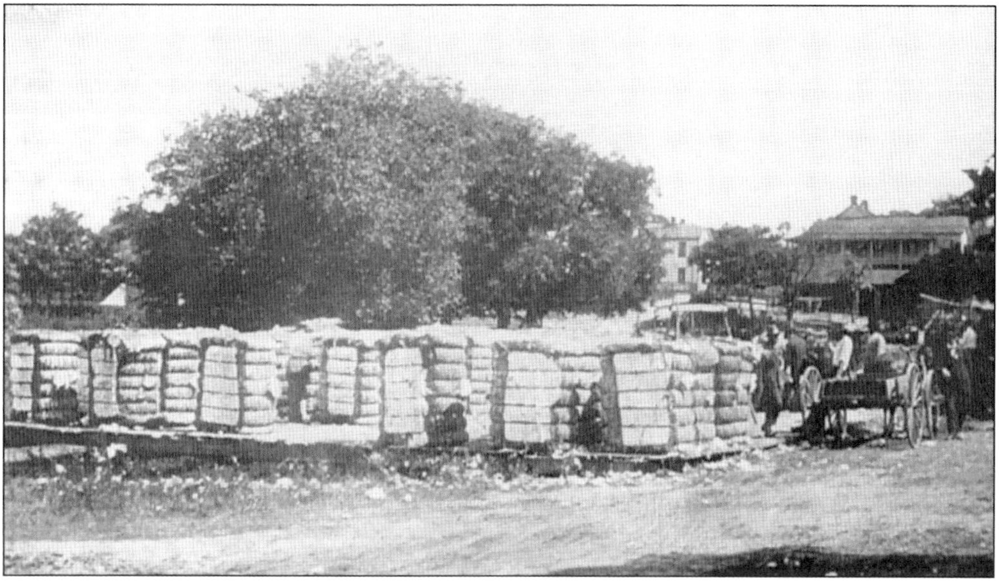

**Cotton Platform, Barnwell, S.C.** (Halftone, 3 1/2" x 5 1/2", [C.U. Williams, #18416, Bloomington, IL]; 1919.) Barnwell was almost entirely an agricultural county, and according to Horace J. Crouch, it was remarkable that "the productions are far in excess of the amount of effort put forth." In 1926, the Department of Commerce reported that 29,244 bales of cotton were ginned in the county. The 1900 Sanborn map of Barnwell indicates a cotton platform on a site on the north side of Main Street west of Jackson.

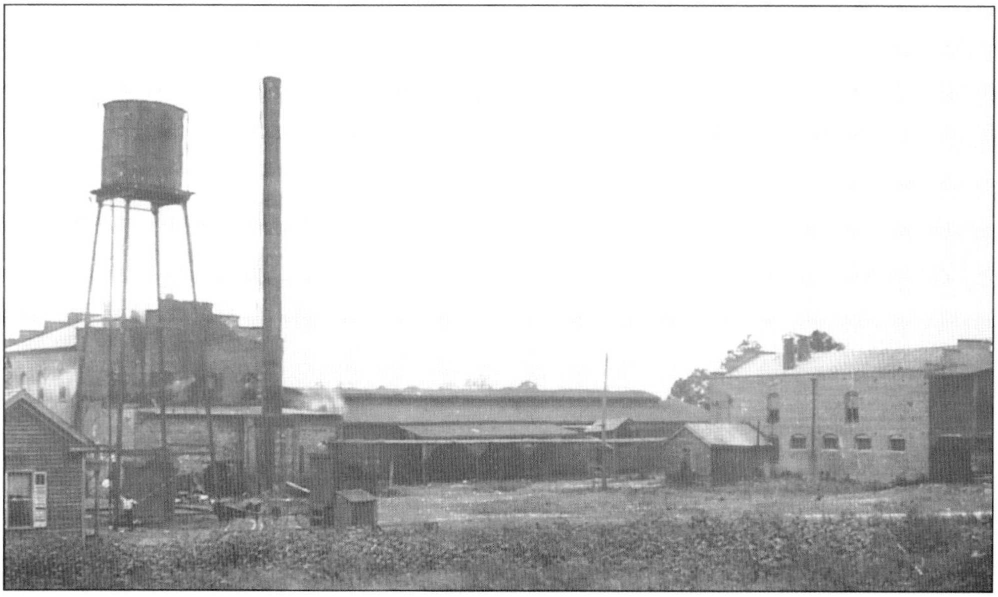

**Oil Mill, Barnwell, S.C.** (Halftone, 3 1/2" x 5 1/2", [C.U. Williams, #18422, Bloomington, IL]; *c.* 1914.) Sanborn maps of Barnwell issued between 1900 and 1922 reveal a Southern Cotton Oil Company located on the east side of the railroad tracks about half a mile northeast of the courthouse. In this westward-looking view can be seen the 60-foot water tank (capacity: 12,000 gallons); behind it, at left, a two-story building housing the press room and linters; the long, low cotton seed house; and, at right, the engine room attached to a cotton house.

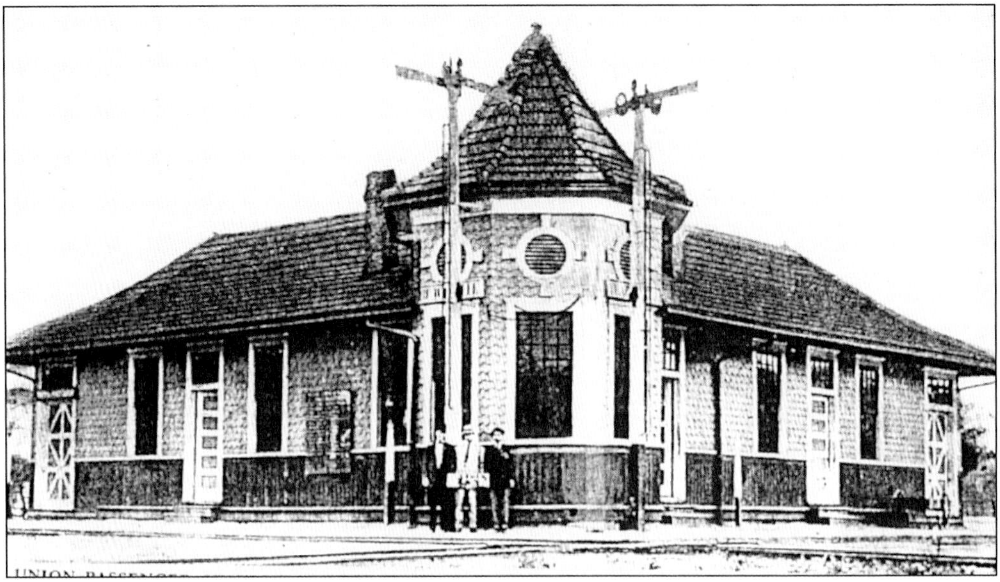

**Union Passenger Station, Blackville, S.C.** (Halftone, 3 1/2" x 5 1/2", [Curt Teich Co., Chicago, IL]; [Gilbert Postcard Co., #6823, Chicago, IL]; 1918.) Shown here in its original location at the town's railroad intersection, the Victorian-style Union Passenger Station was moved in the 1980s to the grounds of the old Blackville High School, corner of Solomon Blatt Boulevard and Pascallas Street, where it now serves as the community library.

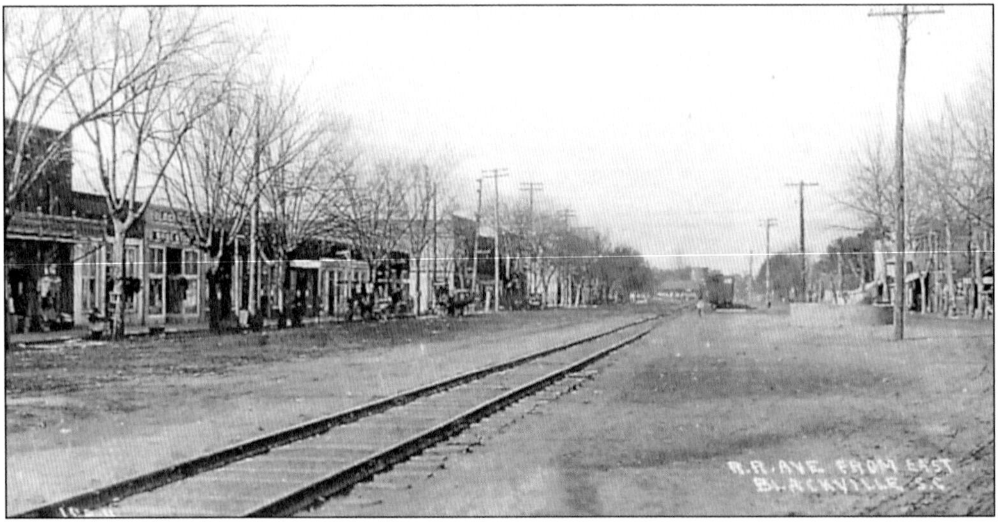


**R.R. Ave. from the East, Blackville, S.C.** (Photoprint, 3 1/2" x 5 1/2"; #178-11; 1915.) Blackville was a Charleston-Hamburg Railroad town, becoming an overnight stop for the first commercial steam locomotive in America when the line was completed in 1833. By 1910, its inhabitants numbered 1,400. According to Joyce S. O'Bannon (see *Names in South Carolina*, Winter 1968), it was named for Alexander Black, the Charleston businessman who petitioned the legislature for the charter and organized the million-dollar railroad project. Union Station can be seen in the far distance in this *c.* 1915 view of Railroad Avenue (now Main Street) looking west. This image may have been taken by an itinerant photographer who traveled the region by rail or wagon, taking code-numbered pictures and selling them to merchants and residents who wanted views of their towns and businesses.

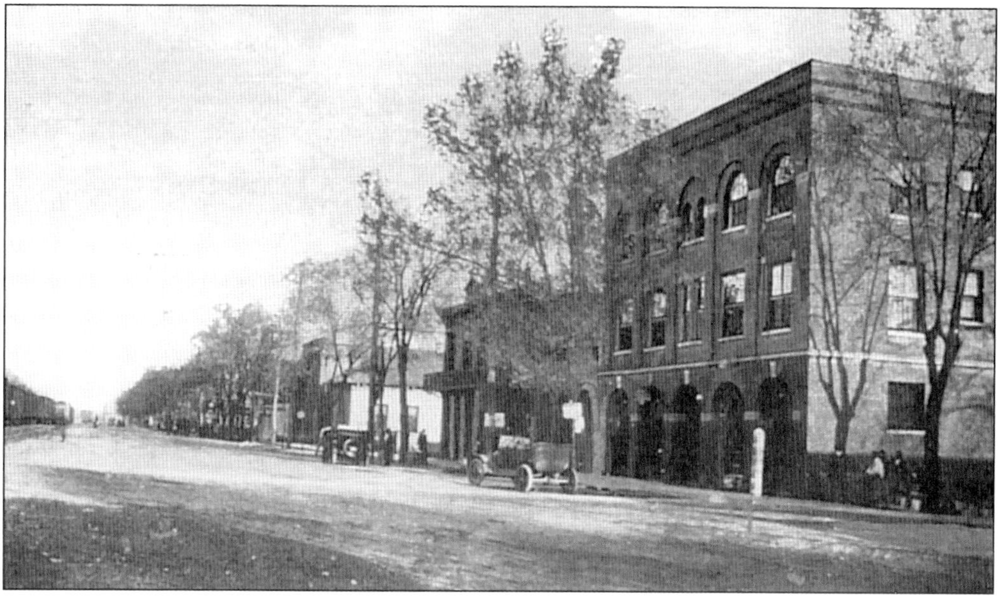

**Railroad Avenue, Looking East, Blackville, S.C.** (Color Lithograph, 3 1/2" x 5 1/2", [Curt Teich Co., Chicago, IL]; [Gilbert Post Card Co., #6822, Chicago, IL]; *c.* 1918.) Seen here at right is the old three-story, 25-room brick Shamrock Hotel, corner of Main (Railroad) and Walker along the railroad on the west end of town. Built in 1910 by local Irish-American businessman John Mitchell Farrell, it operated through the 1950s, maintaining a dining room and providing space for a drugstore (Epps Pharmacy) and bus station. In the late 1990s, efforts have been mounted to salvage the virtually collapsed landmark. A strip park now runs where the railroad tracks used to be.

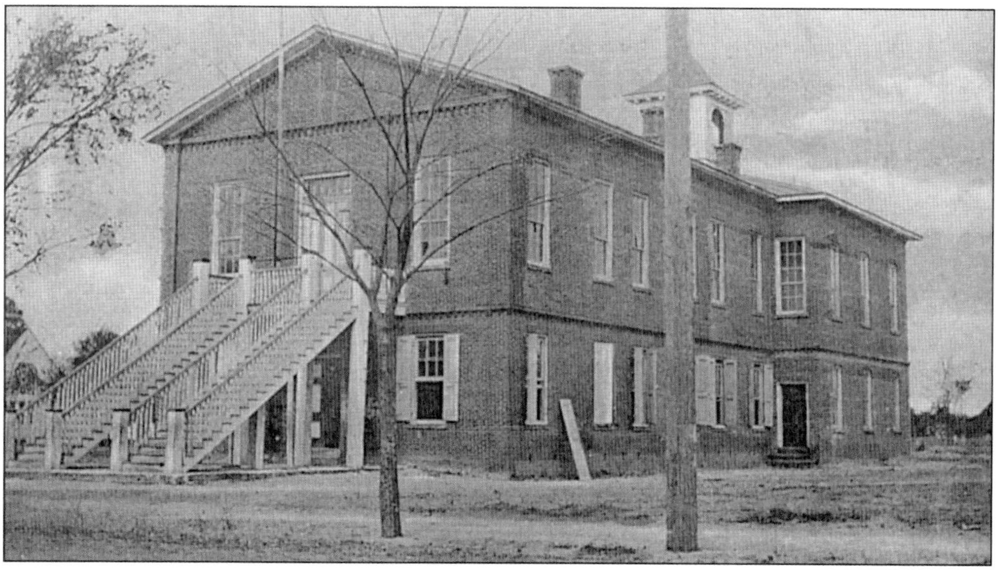

**Graded School, Blackville, S.C.** (Hand-Colored Collotype, 3 1/2" x 5 1/2", unknown German printer; Paul E. Trouche, Charleston, SC, importer; 1908.) When Blackville functioned as the Barnwell County seat between 1869 and 1874, this building served as the courthouse. It later became the "Graded School."

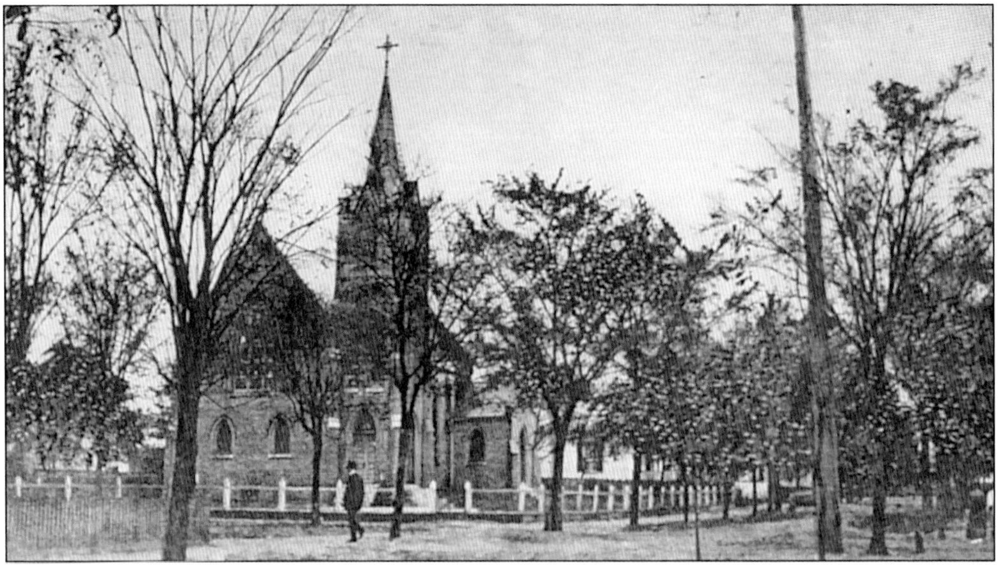

**Catholic Church, Blackville, S.C.** (Hand-Colored Collotype, 3 1/2" x 5 4/10", unknown German printer; Paul E. Trouche, Charleston, SC, importer; *c.* 1908.) Affectionately called "the Cathedral," the brick, Gothic-style Sacred Heart Catholic Church, corner of Lartigue and Dexter Streets (Highway 78), was built in 1898, replacing a frame sanctuary which burned in 1887. No regular services are held in the church, the fence is gone, and the cross is missing from atop the steeple, which was struck by lightning in the 1990s.

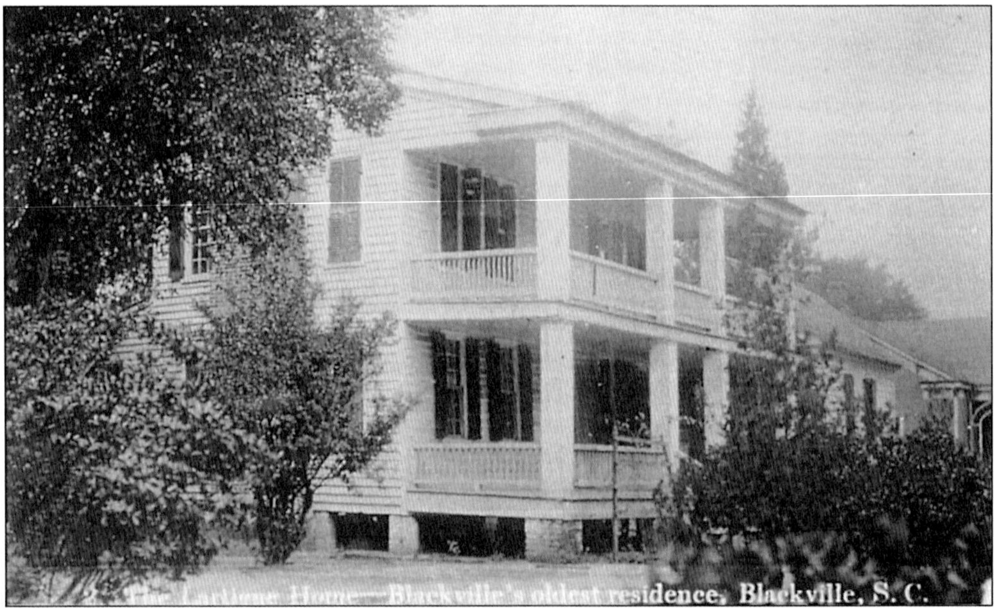


**Lartigue Home, Blackville, S.C.** (Photoprint, 3 1/2" x 5 1/2"; 1912.) Built about 1831, the Lartigue House at 304 South Boundary Street is thought to be Blackville's oldest surviving structure. During the Civil War, it is believed to have served as quarters for some of Sherman's officers. A few years ago, Solomon Blatt Boulevard was cut through the south side of town, replacing the house seen to the right.

**Zelda Springs, Blackville, S.C.** (Halftone, 5 1/2" x 3 1/2", Auburn Greeting Card Co., Auburn, IN, *c.* 1928.) Everyone has heard of Healing Springs and the legendary and practical powers of its waters, located in the northeastern section of Barnwell County, just off Highway 3 a few miles north of Blackville. But few remember Zelda Springs, shown here, a flowing spring on the same Windy Hill Creek line as its famous sister and obviously at some time during this period also promoted as a place to visit.

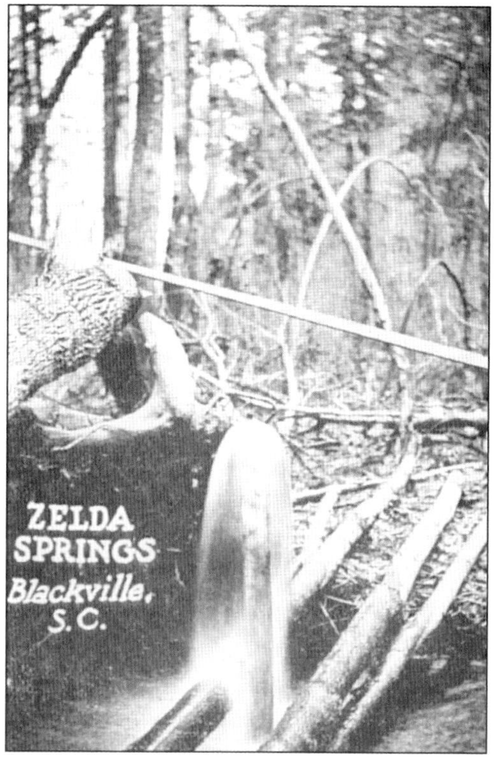


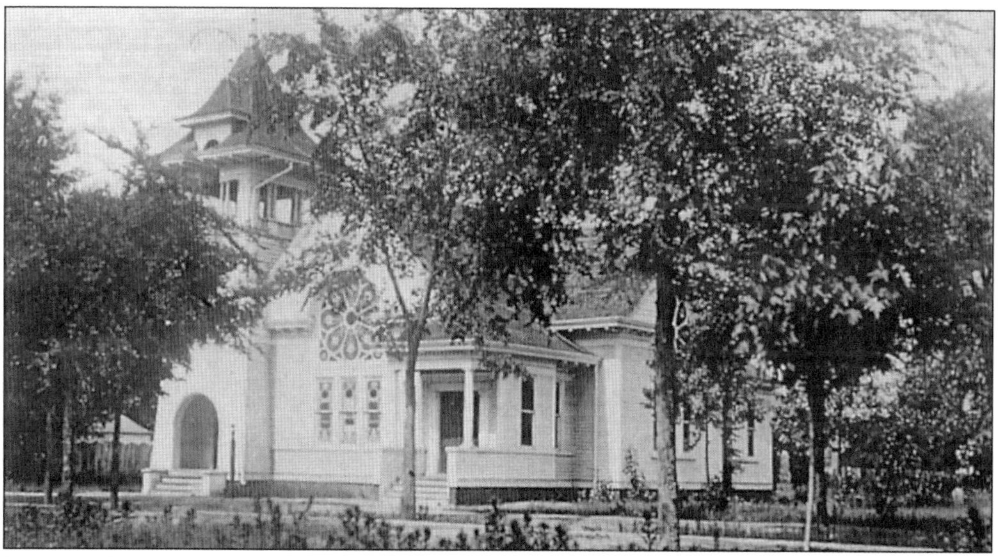

**Baptist Church, Blackville, S.C.** (Hand-Colored Collotype, 3 1/2" x 5 4/10", unknown German printer; Paul E. Trouche, Charleston, SC, importer; 1909.) The second sanctuary to be built by Blackville Baptists on the original lot given to the church in 1846, this one was dedicated on November 20, 1898, and served the needs of the congregation until it was replaced by a new one in 1921. The old church, according to reports, was moved "back on the same square" and fitted up "most comfortably" as "a very neat Parsonage." The Blackville Baptist Church officially became the First Baptist Church on October 12, 1952.

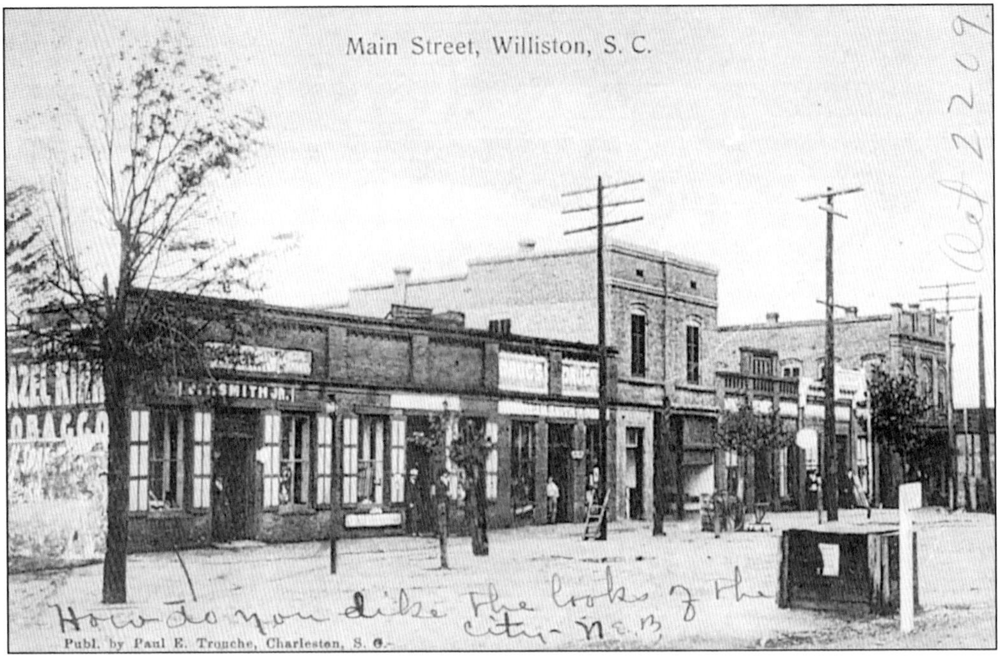


**MAIN STREET, WILLISTON, S.C.** (Hand-Colored Collotype, 3 3/8" x 5 3/8", unknown German printer; Paul E. Trouche, Charleston, SC, importer; 1909.) "How do you like the looks of the city?" asks the correspondent on this card, dated October 22, 1909, which features a view of the Main Street of Williston, looking west and taken from near the railroad tracks in the middle of town. Like Barnwell and Blackville, Williston developed to enjoy the benefits of municipal water and light systems by the mid-1920s, and made further claim to being the largest asparagus center in the world. In 1910, it had a population of 700.

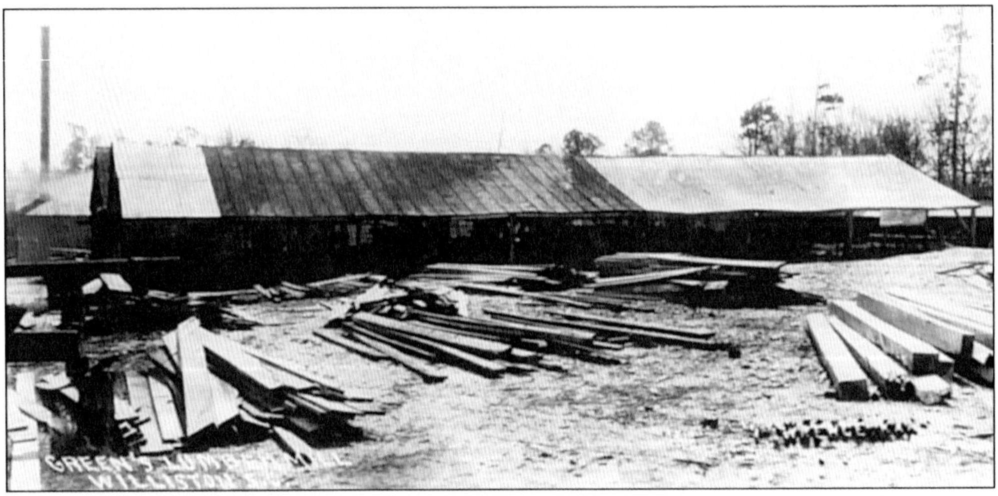

**GREEN'S LUMBER MILL, WILLISTON, S.C.** (Photoprint, 3 1/2" x 5 1/2"; *c.* 1915.) The presence of a lumber mill in Williston during this period is not surprising because of the town's location close to upland forests abounding in pine, hickory, and oak. Green's manufactured the crates used in shipping asparagus to market.

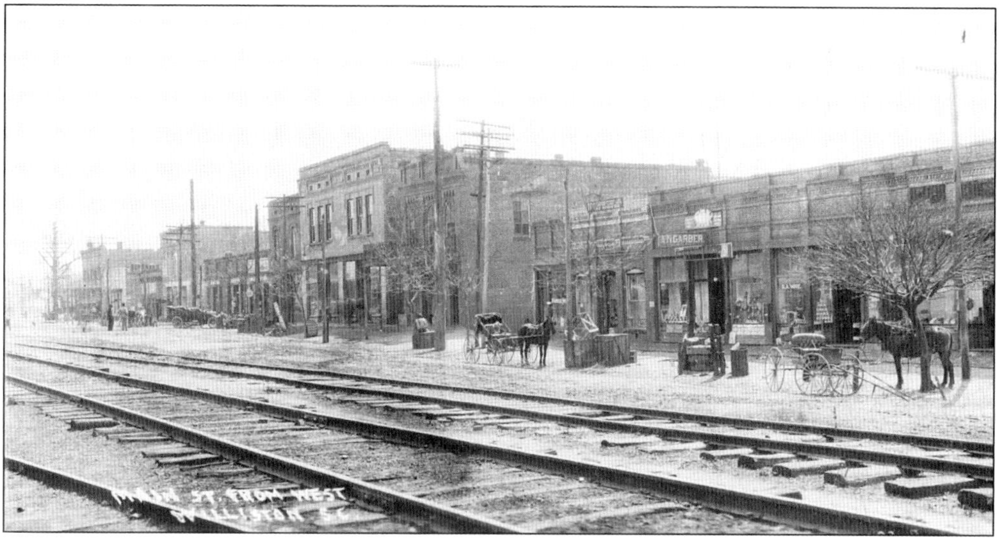


**MAIN STREET FROM WEST, WILLISTON, S.C.** (Photoprint, 3 1/2" x 5 1/2"; #183, *c.* 1915.) The commercial part of town seems to have grown up largely south of the railroad tracts, which were removed in 1995. The few period buildings which survive along a much-changed Main Street bear the dates 1913, 1915, 1919, and 1920. This view shows the end of town near the corner of Main and Bennett Streets. The low expanse of units to the right appears to be the site currently occupied by the Towne View Apartments. This item possibly represents another photocard taken by a traveling professional photographer.

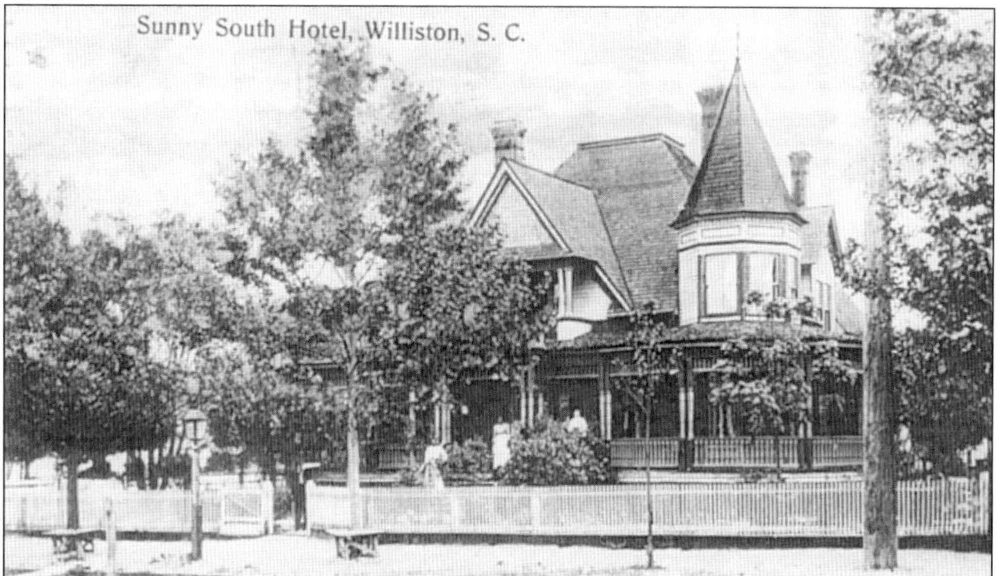


**SUNNY SOUTH HOTEL, WILLISTON, S.C.** (Hand-Colored Collotype, 3 3/8" x 5 3/8", unknown German printer; Paul E. Trouche, Charleston, SC, importer; 1908.) Probably a residence adapted from private to commercial use, as were many such establishments in the small-town world of South Carolina, the Sunny South Hotel would have largely served the business personnel arriving in Williston by train. All the county's towns, wrote Horace J. Crouch, have "magnificent homes, pretty shady streets, modern churches and schools, and a Southern air of culture, refinement, and hospitality unexcelled."

# APPENDIX:
## DATA ON POSTCARDS PUBLISHERS

[The hyphenated SC-related dates below signify the estimated earliest year of the appearance of a publisher's cards in the region.]

**ALBERTYPE CO.**, Brooklyn, NY [1897][SC-1906]: producer of high-quality collotype postcards. Stenciled, hand-colored, watercolor tints were used when color was requested. Albertype produced pioneer, private mailing cards, etc.; prices: 250 @ $3.75; 500 @ $5.50; 1,000 @ $8.

**AMERICAN NEWS CO.**, New York, NY [SC-1905]: imported German postcards and distributed gift and premium catalogs to newspaper companies across the nation.

**AUBURN POST CARD CO.**, Auburn, IN [SC-1911]: printed mail-order halftone views: 500 @ $4 in the eastern half of the United States.

**COMMERCIAL COLORTYPE CO.**, Chicago, IL [SC-1907]: nationally distributed color lithography and halftone processes printed by Curt Teich; halftone: 1,000 @ $3.75; 2,000 @ $3.

**ESS AN ESS PHOTO CO.**, New York, NY [SC-1910]: small mail-order halftone company.

**FACTORY TO CONSUMERS CO.**, Knoxville, TN [SC-1906]: small regional mail-order company [See page 8].

**GILBERT POST CARD CO.**, Chicago, IL [SC-1911]: small mail-order distributor of color lithography and halftone processes.

**GUT & STEERS LITHOGRAPHIC CO.**, New York, NY [SC-1910]: printed color lithography issues.

**ILLUSTRATED POST CARD CO.**, New York, NY [SC-1906]: imported view cards and set up its own printing factory for color lithography and halftone processes; distributed on the East Coast.

**KNACKSTEDT AND NÄTHER CO.**, Hamburg, Germany [pre-1898] [SC-1905]: [See page 9].

**KRAUSS MANUFACTURING CO.**, New York, NY [SC-1910]: mail-order producer of halftone cards: 500 @ $6.

**E.C. KROPP CO.**, Milwaukee, WI [1898] [SC-1911]: importer and postcard printer; hand-colored halftone cards: 500 @ $5.25.

**THE MCGOWN-SILSBY LITHOGRAPHIC CO.**, New York, NY [SC-1911]: began printing its postcards after the Payne-Aldrich 1909 tariff act taxed the import common view-card trade.

**NEW ENGLAND PAPER & STATIONERY CO.**, Ayer, MA [SC-1908]: small printer of halftone cards in the eastern United States.

**RICH PHOTO-PROCESS CO.**, New York, NY [SC-1906]: small mail-order company of halftone cards: 250 @ $5.50.

**ROTOGRAPH CO.**, New York, NY [SC-1905]: importer of German view-cards. [See page 9].

**ALFRED SCHULZE**, Berlin, Germany [SC-1906]: collotype: 1,000 @ $8; and color lithographic cards imported by the American New Company from 1905 until the 1909 tariff closed the trade.

**ADOLPH SELIGE PUBLISHING CO.**, St. Louis, MO [1900][SC-1906]: distributor of imported and domestic postcards throughout the South and West.

**SIGNAL PRINTING CO.**, Crowley, LA [SC-1906]: small printer that distributed halftone cards in the South.

**SOUVENIR POST CARD MFG. CO.**, Rockford, IL [SC-1909]: small regional producer of mail-order color lithographic cards: 1,000 @ $5.50.

**STENGEL AND CO.**, Dresden, Germany [pre-1898] [SC-1907]: collotypes and chromo-collotype lithography cards, assumed some of Charleston's Paul E. Trouche Company's view-card contracts.

**TANNER SOUVENIR CO.**, New York, NY [SC-1906]: distributed domestic black-and-white halftone and import collotype postcards, which were listed in its souvenir mail-order catalogs.

**The Curt Teich Co.**, Chicago, IL [SC-1909]: one of the most prominent national postcard companies after the 1909 tariff; five-color lithographic card: 3,000 @ $6.50 per 1, 000.
**Tichnor Brothers, Inc.** Boston, MA [SC-1912]: printed color lithography issues in the eastern United States.
**Trenkler & Co.**, Leipzig, Germany [pre-1898][SC-1906]: made collotypes and chromo-halftone lithography; a five-color lithograph: 5,000 @ $40; 10,000 @ $65.
**Paul F. Trouche Co.**, Charleston, SC [SC-1907]: wholesale/retail stationery and postcard supplier with jobbers traveling to all South Carolina regions and serving small-town merchants.
**United View Co.**, Newark, DE [SC-1911]: small mail-order printer of halftone cards.
**Valentine & Sons**, Dundee, Scotland [pre-1898][SC-1908]: printer of collotype; and color lithographic U.S. view-cards: 1,000 @ $10. The 1909 tariff caused it to merge its United States view-card trade with other domestic companies and stop view-card exports to this country.
**C.U. Williams**, Bloomington, IL; [pre-1908]: small mail-order printer of halftone cards.

# Index


African Americans: 19, 22–23, 26–27, 36–38, 59, 116
Agriculture: 36, 52, 70, 94
Allendale: 105–110
Allendale County: 105–112
Army: 53
Arsenal: 20, 28
Bamberg [town]: 96–101
Bamberg County: 95–104
Banks: 16, 78, 81, 84, 91, 107, 111, 115, 117
Baptist church: 28–29, 38, 58, 60, 62, 74, 92, 103, 117, 123
Barnwell County: 113–125
Beaufort [city]: cover, 11–35
Beaufort County: cover, 11–56
Blackville: 120–123
Bluffton: 54–55
Bottling Companies: 19
Boats: 11–13, 15, 20, 32–33, 35, 39–41, 51, 54–55
Bridges: 35, 93
Brunson: 74–78
Business blocks: 72–73, 111
Camp St. Mary: 56
Carlisle School: 101
Catholic churches: 24, 56, 122
Churches: 20, 24, 28–29, 38, 40, 52, 55–56, 60, 90, 92, 100, 103, 104, 112, 117, 118
Civil War period: cover, 7, 17, 20, 23, 26–27, 29–31, 38, 52, 54–55, 58, 60, 115
Colleton County: 87–94
Combahee: 94
Commercial Businesses: 15, 18–20, 36, 42, 57, 61, 67, 70, 72–73, 75–76, 78, 80–81, 83–84, 91, 97, 106–108, 111, 114–115, 117, 121
Commercial Buildings: 15–16, 18, 36, 42, 57, 61, 67, 70, 72–73, 75–76, 78, 81, 83–84, 89, 91, 96–97, 99, 102, 106–108, 111, 114–115, 117,
Commercial Buildings (continued): 121, 124–125
Confederate: 54, 117
Cotton: 14, 15, 119
County Courthouses: 20, 60, 80, 88, 98, 115, 121
Crane, T.E.: 105
Crouch, H.J.: 113, 116, 124–125
Dabbs, E.M.: 35, 37–38
Denmark: 101–104
Department Stores: 61, 62
Depots: 15, 17, 41, 62, 74, 86, 87, 95–97, 103, 113, 120
Docks: 13, 14, 15, 51
Drugstores: 18, 42, 72, 108, 114
Ehrhardt: 95
Electric Light & Water Works Plant: 110
Episcopal Church: 30, 87, 118
Estill: 72–74
Fairfax: 110–112
Fire station, fires: 32–33, 86
Fort Fremont: 39
Frogmore: 35–36
Garnett: 69–71
Generic cards: 111
Gillisonville: 64–65
Gin [cotton]: 15
Good Hope Camp: 59
Grays: 66
Hampton: 79–85
Hampton County: 69–86
Harbor: 12–13, 14,
Hardeeville: 57–58
Harper, M.M.: 69, 70, 75, 76, 86
Horse or animal transportation: 14, 21, 28, 63, 66, 68, 73, 80, 101
Hospitals: 45–46, 91
Hotels: 20, 77, 79, 91, 98, 102, 106–107, 121, 125
Hunting clubs: 53, 59, 67, 71

Infirmaries: 91
Interiors: 18, 20, 30, 49, 106–108
Jails: 90
Jasper County: 57–68
Jefferies, R.M.: 57, 62
Jewish synagogue: 29
Knight, A.W.: 100, 105
Luther's Drug Store: Cover, 14–16, 18, 21, 24–26, 28–30, 34, 39
Maritime: 13, 39–41, 55
Marine Base: 43–51, 53
Mather School: 22
Methodist churches: 55, 62, 90
Military: 20, 28, 39, 43–51, 53, 81
Mills: 16, 99, 119
Montessori class: 25
Monuments: 112, 117
Naval Base: 43–46
Newspapers: 83
Novelty cards: 50, 52, 88, 111
Opera houses: 114
Oyster Canning Factory: 40, 55
Parris [Paris] Island: 43–51
Penn School: 36–38
Perry, G.F.: 57, 61,
Photographers:
  Burson, E.E.: 99, 101
  Cleland, R.L.: 65–66, 84–86
  Foltz Studio: 56, 66
  Harvey's Studio: 65
  Miner, Leigh Richmond: 37
  Wilson, M.E.: 20, 26
Pioneer card: 4
Plantations: 52, 53
Portraits: 19, 25, 42, 46, 50, 53, 61–66, 68, 76–85, 89, 92, 94, 101, 109, 116
Port Royal: 40–47
Postcard history: 4, 6, 9, 18
Postcard companies:
  Albertype Co.: cover, 14–16, 18, 20–21, 24–25, 27, 30–31, 34, 43–44, 52, 59, 93, 104, 106–110, 117
  American News Co.: 12, 17, 27, 29–30, 33, 87, 89–90
  Asheville Post Card Co.: 39, 72–74, 93
  Auburn Post Card Mfg. Co.: 88, 90, 123
  Colortype Co.: 4
  Commercial Colortype Co.: 117
  Ess and Ess Photo Co., Inc.: 110, 112
  Factory to Consumers Co.: 6, 28
  Gilbert Postcard Co.: 120–121
  Gut & Steers Lithographic Co.: 101
  Illustrated Post Card Co.: 35–36, 38
  Krauss Mfg. Co.: 60–62, 64
  Kropp Co., E.C.: 96, 100, 111
  McGown-Silsbee Litho. Co.: 112
  Millinery Trade Review: 111
  N.E. Paper and Stationery Co.: 103
  Rich Photo-Process Co.: 80–81, 84
  Röder, C.G.: 88
  Rotograph Co.: 9, 12–13, 15, 18, 26, 29, 31–32, 44–45, 52
  Schulze Co., Alfred: 87
  Selige Pub. Co., Adolph: 20
  Signal Printing Co.: 94
  Simon Co., A.M.: 18, 39, 44–45, 52, 96–97
  Souvenir Post Card Mfg. Co.: 115
  Stengel & Co.: 34
  Tanner Souvenir Co.: 26, 28, 32
  Teich Co., Curt: 13, 17, 22–23, 63, 72–74, 91, 117, 120–121
  Tichnor Brothers, Inc.: 91
  Paul F. Trouche Co.: 40–42, 102–103, 121–125
  United View Co.: 14
  Valentine Co.: 98–100
  Williams, C.U.: 57–58, 113–119
  Woehler Co., H.L.: 34
Private mailing cards [1898–1902]: 23
Railroad lines:
  Atlantic Coast Line: 62, 87, 103, 110, 113
  Charleston & Western Carolina: 15, 17, 41, 74, 79, 86, 105,
  Southern Rail Way: 96–97, 103,
Railroad stations: 15, 17, 41, 62, 95–97, 103, 105, 110, 120
Residences: cover, 17, 24–25, 28, 30–34, 53, 62, 69, 70, 122
Revolutionary era: 17, 60
Ridgeland: 59–64
Robertville: 67–68
Schools: 22–23, 25–27, 36–38, 58, 62–63, 65, 73, 75–76, 82, 101, 104, 116, 121
Seafood industries: 39–40, 55
Ships, commercial: 11–12, 39
Ships, military: 46, 51
Shrimping: 39
Spanish-American War: 18, 39
Sports: 24, 59, 67, 71,
St. Helena Island: 35–39
Steamer landing: 14, 51
Stores: 36, 42, 57, 61, 67, 70
Street scenes, commercial: 16, 18, 72, 89, 91, 96–97, 102, 107, 115, 120–121, 124–125
Street scenes, main: 16, 18, 72, 75, 86, 88–89, 96–97, 102, 107, 115, 120–121, 124–125
Street scenes, residential: 21, 26
Synagogue: 29
Theatre: 49
Transportation: 11–15, 17, 19, 39, 41, 51, 68
Varnville: 85–86
Voorhees School: 104
Walterboro: 87–92
Waterfront: 12–13, 32–33
Williston: 124–125
World War I: 28, 43, 47, 49, 51
Yemassee: 53